MW00356534

THE POETICS OF PLANTS IN SPANISH AMERICAN LITERATURE

ILLUMINATIONS CULTURAL FORMATIONS OF THE AMERICAS

John Beverley and Sara Castro-Klarén, *Editors*

THE POETICS OF PLANTS

IN SPANISH AMERICAN

LITERATURE

LESLEY WYLIE

UNIVERSITY OF PITTSBURGH PRESS

Published by the University of Pittsburgh Press, Pittsburgh, Pa., 15260

Copyright © 2020, University of Pittsburgh Press

Manufactured in the United States of America

Printed on acid-free paper

10 9 8 7 6 5 4 3 2 1

Cataloging-in-Publication data is available from the Library of Congress

ISBN 13: 978-0-8229-4625-0
ISBN 10: 0-8229-4625-4

Cover art: Kapok or silk cotton tree (*Ceiba petandra*) growing by a village in Surinam. Colored lithograph by P. Lauters, ca. 1839, after P. J. Benoit. Courtesy of the Wellcome Collection, London.

Cover design: Alex Wolfe

FOR FLORA AND CONSTANCE

CONTENTS

ACKNOWLEDGMENTS

This book has benefited enormously from the observations, suggestions, and encouragement of many people. I am particularly grateful to Mark D. Anderson, Rabah Aissaoui, Daniel Balderston, Alberto Baraya, Steven Boldy, Francisco-J. Hernández Adrián, Fiona J. Mackintosh, Jorge Marcone, Felipe Martínez-Pinzón, Rory O'Bryen, Sheldon Penn, Helen Rawlings, Charlotte Rogers, Margarita Serje, Alison Sinclair, Amanda M. Smith, Marina Spunta, Ana Varela Tafur, Javier Uriarte, Erna von der Walde, and Bruce Dean Willis. Peter Hulme, as always, has been more than generous in his support. I would also like to thank Juan Carlos Galeano for sending me English translations of a number of his poems and Andrew Laird for last-minute assistance with references. For editorial help and suggestions that have greatly improved the book, I sincerely thank my editor Josh Shanholtzer, Amy Sherman, and the two anonymous reviewers for the University of Pittsburgh Press. I am very grateful to Alex Wolfe for designing the cover. Pippa Letsky has been an attentive and patient copy editor.

I am very grateful to the Leverhulme Trust for awarding me a Research Fellowship (2017–2019), which enabled me to complete this book, and to the School of Arts at the University of Leicester for a period of sabbatical leave in 2017. Thanks to the Leverhulme Trust, I was able to carry out research in collections in Chile and in Cuba. I am immensely grateful to staff at the following archives and libraries for their assistance: Fundación Alejo Carpentier, Havana, Cuba (especially to Graziella Pogolotti Jacobson, and to Yuri Rodríguez González and Armando Juan Raggi

Rodríguez for their attentiveness and good humor); Fundación Pablo Neruda, Santiago, Chile (especially to Darío Oses for his hospitality and immense knowledge); Archivo Central Andrés Bello, Universidad de Chile, Santiago (especially to Loreto Millar Valle and to Alessandro Chiaretti, who showed me the beautiful "Álbum pintoresco herbario"); Fitzwilliam Museum, University of Cambridge (especially to Lucinda Green and Emma Darbyshire).

Much of this book started out as talks presented at conferences and seminars, and I am grateful to the organizers and participants for their enthusiastic engagement with the project, especially during the 2017 Norman MacColl Symposium at the University of Cambridge; the 2017 Latin American Cultural Colloquium at the University of Edinburgh; and to my coorganizer and copanelists in the session "Plants Studies: New Approaches to Latin American Cultural Studies" at the Latin American Studies Association Congress in 2018. In some cases, sections of this book have been published elsewhere in an earlier form. My discussions of Andrés Bello in chapter 1 and of *La vorágine* and the work of Juan Carlos Galeano in chapter 4 draw on my published chapter "Anthropomorphism and Arboricide: The Life and Death of Trees in the American Tropics," in *Ecological Crisis and Cultural Representation in Latin America: Ecocritical Perspectives on Art, Film, and Literature*, edited by Mark Anderson and Zélia M. Bora (Lanham: Lexington Books, 2016). Likewise, an earlier version of the section on *María* in chapter 2 appeared as "Floriography, Sexuality and the Horticulture of Hair in Jorge Isaacs' *María*," *Bulletin of Spanish Studies*, 95, nos. 9–10, *"The Lyf So Short, the Craft So Long to Lerne": Studies in Modern Hispanic Literature, History and Culture in Memory of James Whiston*, edited by C. Alex Longhurst, Ann L. Mackenzie, and Ceri Byrne, with an introduction by Ann L. Mackenzie and Ciaran Cosgrove (2018): 147–58 (copyright the Editors of the *Bulletin of Spanish Studies*).

Finally, I would like to thank my family (especially my mother, Dorothy) for their unstinting support throughout all stages of the project.

I am indebted to my husband, Ross Wilson, without whose tireless and good-humored help this book would never have been finished. This book is dedicated to my two beautiful daughters, Flora (whose name now has new meaning for me) and Constance.

NOTE ON TRANSLATIONS

Throughout the book, English translations follow Spanish quotations, either in the text or in the relevant note. Where possible I have used published translations. When a translation into English does not have a page reference, the translation is my own. In the case of poetry, my translations aim to convey the sense rather than the meter or rhyme of the original. I provide an English translation of the title of each literary work when they are first referred to (unless the translation coincides exactly with the original). If a published translation is available, the English title is given in italics or quotation marks; if not, the title appears in roman type and without quotation marks.

LIST OF ABBREVIATIONS

CA   Galeano, Juan Carlos. *Cuentos amazónicos*. Iquitos: Tierra Nueva, 2007.

CC   Carpentier, Alejo. "The City of Columns." In *Baroque New Worlds: Representation, Transculturation, Counterconquest*, edited by Lois Parkinson Zamora and Monika Kaup, 244–58. Durham: Duke University Press, 2010.

Cdlc   Carpentier, Alejo. "La ciudad de las columnas." In *Obras completas: Ensayos*, 13:61–73. Mexico: Siglo XXI, 1990.

CG   Neruda, Pablo. *Canto general*. In *Obras completas*, vol. 1, edited by Hernán Loyola, 415–837. Barcelona: Galaxia Gutenberg, 1999.

CGS   Neruda, Pablo. *Canto general*. Translated by Jack Schmitt. Introduction by Roberto González Echevarría. Berkeley: University of California Press, 1991.

DR   Schweblin, Samanta. *Distancia de rescate*. Barcelona: Penguin Random House, 2015.

EC   Carpentier, Alejo. *Explosion in a Cathedral*. Translated by John Sturrock. Minneapolis: University of Minnesota Press, 2001.

FA   Galeano, Juan Carlos. *Folktales of the Amazon*. Translated by Rebecca Morgan and Kenneth Watson. Westport, CT: Libraries Unlimited, 2009.

FD   Schweblin, Samanta. *Fever Dream*. Translated by Megan McDowell. London: Oneworld, 2017.

LS   Carpentier, Alejo. *The Lost Steps.* Translated by Harriet de Onís. New York: Noonday Press, 1989.

OC   Neruda, Pablo. *Obras completas*, Vols. 1–5. Edited by Hernán Loyola. Barcelona: Galaxia Gutenberg, 1999-2002.

OCP   Bello, Andrés. *Obras completas*, Vol. 1, *Poesías*. Prologue by Fernando Paz Castillo. Caracas: Ediciones Ministerio de Educación, 1952.

PP   Carpentier, Alejo. *Los pasos perdidos*. Madrid: Alianza, 1999.

RM   Landívar, Rafael. "*Rusticatio Mexicana*, the Latin Text and an English Prose Translation by Graydon W. Regenos." In Andrew Laird, *The Epic of America: An Introduction to Rafael Landívar and the* Rusticatio Mexicana, 119–258. London: Duckworth, 2006.

SL   Carpentier, Alejo. *El siglo de las luces.* Madrid, Alianza, 2003.

SW   Bello, Andrés. *The Selected Writings of Andrés Bello.* Translated by F. M. López-Morillas. Edited by I. Jaksić. Oxford: Oxford University Press, 1997.

THE POETICS OF PLANTS IN SPANISH AMERICAN LITERATURE

INTRODUCTION

THE POETICS OF PLANTS IN SPANISH AMERICAN LITERATURE

In his essay "Literatura de fundación" (A literature of foundations) Octavio Paz chooses a striking botanical metaphor to illustrate the differences between Spanish and Spanish American literature: "La rama creció tanto que ya es tan grande como el tronco. En realidad, es otro árbol. Un árbol distinto, con hojas más verdes y jugos más amargos. Entre sus brazos anidan pájaros desconocidos en España" (The branch grew so much that it is already as big as the trunk. In reality, it is another tree. A different tree, with greener leaves and more bitter sap. Birds unknown in Spain nest among its branches).[1] Recourse to the language of plants in order to grapple with questions of cultural identity and expression is recurrent in Spanish American literature, where the pervasiveness of botanical imagery indicates the defining role of the natural world and an enduring concern about the relationship between people and plants. Spanish American writers from the late colonial period to the present have appealed to plants—to images of roots, trunks, and branches as well as questions of vegetal life and ethics—as a means of exploring aesthetics and identity. My aim in this book is to show how plants have been fundamental to counterhegemonic identities across Latin American culture from the colonial period onward, exploring how vegetal discourses underpin local expressions of postcolonialism (Andrés Bello), feminism (Gertrudis Gómez de Avellaneda, Ana Mendieta), communism (Pablo Neruda), and posthumanism (Juan Carlos Galeano). Knowledge of the cultural histories of flora in Latin America, particularly of sacred trees such as the *Ceiba petandra*, reveals the deep connections between people and plants in Spanish American culture and facilitates counterdiscursive readings of canonical works, where plants articulate submerged histories, often at variance with those expressed by the central narrative. In this way, plant-centered readings of Spanish American culture reveal connections across seemingly disparate texts and traditions—colonial poetry, the plantation novel, the New World baroque, and feminist avant-garde art.

In this book I explore how plant imaginaries have allowed writers from across Spanish America not only to express ecological concerns but also to register their dissension with Western conceptions of nature—particularly exploitative modes of production that have underpinned capitalism in the New World from the tropical plantation to the agro-industrial expansion of soy in Argentina today. Although not always explicit, the redefinition of the relationship between humans and plants in Latin American literature is predicated largely on indigenous American modes of perception, in which the identities of humans and nonhumans are fluid and plants are considered sentient beings that we should respect and nurture. As Kate Soper notes, the entrenched Western "metaphysical" view of nature has been one in which the categories of the human and the nonhuman are held in opposition to one another. In contrast, the texts and authors considered here consistently stress the continuities and interdependencies between people and the natural world.[2] From the earliest days of independence, the view of nature expressed by Spanish

American writers has often dovetailed with indigenous American beliefs and, especially through their engagement with plants, prefigured much contemporary ecological thinking. In his recent *Capitalism in the Web of Life*, Jason W. Moore holds up the nature/society binary as one of the great ills in Western culture, "implicated in the colossal violence, inequality, and oppression of the modern world" and "a fundamental condition of capital accumulation." Over the past thirty years or so, as part of the spatial turn in the humanities, critics have consistently undermined the stability of this divide. Donna Haraway's work, for instance, traces the multiple interactions between people, technology, animals, and living organisms, and Anna Lowenhaupt Tsing has recently explored "interspecies entanglements" via a study of the matsutake mushroom. As Bruno Latour states clearly in *We Have Never Been Modern*: "*the very notion of culture is an artifact created by bracketing Nature off.* Cultures—different or universal—do not exist, any more than Nature does. There are only natures-cultures."[3]

Establishing the important role of plants in human society (a so-called plant turn) has been central to the redefinition of this nature/culture divide. The development of critical plant studies over the past decade has given rise to a number of important interventions in the question of how vegetal life relates to humans and of its influence in philosophy and literature.[4] In his accounts of vegetal metaphysics and plant ethics, Michael Marder has emerged as one of the most original and significant thinkers about the relationship between people and plants. Far from passive, nonmoving, and noncommunicative entities, or simply as material for human use (for instance, as food or firewood), plants, according to Marder, are complex interactive beings who demand our attention and consideration. Marder's work, especially his concept of "plant-thinking," has been intrinsic to my understanding of how the view of plants expressed by many Spanish American writers is at variance with Western conceptions of nature.[5] Throughout the book I also draw on philosophical accounts of plant life by Matthew Hall, Luce Irigaray, and Emanuele Coccia to trace how Latin American writers draw on plant imaginaries in order to foster ecological responsibility and awareness. In *Plants as Persons*, Hall notes the dearth of cultural and philosophical treatments of plants, despite the fact that "most places on earth which contain life are visibly *plantscapes*." Through an extended analysis of the relationships between people and plants across different cultures, including in the Americas, Hall's study helps "to locate the most appropriate human behavior toward plants" in a moment of global environmental crisis.[6] Irigaray and Coccia both offer extended considerations of the relationship between plants and people, including the way in which plants and humans share air. Coccia's view of humans as immersed in a world of infinite "encounter and mixture," with plants at its center, is consonant with the phytocentric tendencies of much Spanish American literature.[7]

Key to my understanding of the transcendent role vegetation has played across Latin America are the pioneering anthropological studies of Philippe Descola and Eduardo Viveiros de Castro, especially the concepts of "perspectivism" and "multinaturalism," which efface the differences between humans and nonhumans and stress a mutuality of culture and the possibility of metamorphosis into and out of other states.[8] With specific relation to plants, Eduardo Kohn's formulation of an anthropology "beyond the human" in *How Forests Think*—the idea that "seeing, representing, and perhaps knowing, even thinking, are not exclusively human affairs"—provides an important anthropological analogue to the literary expositions of human/nonhuman encounters explored in this book.[9] Likewise, the political ecological approach to people-plant relationships taken in Theresa L. Miller's recent ethnography, *Plant Kin*, is a reminder of the depth and complexity of multispecies alliances in Latin America and of how such alliances might mediate ecological crisis.[10] Although the focus of Miller's book is the Canela people who live on the Brazilian Cerrado and are therefore outside the geographical purview of this study, the relationships that she sets out between humans and plants closely resemble those across many indigenous communities in South and Central America. Marisol de la Cadena presents a similar worldview in *Earth Beings* as well as in her account of indigenous "Cosmopolitics" (the appeal to nonhuman entities by indigenous movements), which she regards as having a central role to play in the reconfiguration of human/nonhuman relationships in politics and beyond.[11] The figure of people as intimately connected to plants in Spanish American culture—of their interdependencies, interactions, and even anatomical commonalities—not only draws out the indigenous foundations of Latin American culture but is oriented toward present and future ecologies of survival and interdependence. Plants are imbued with a political edge in Spanish American culture and have been fundamental to the formulation of countercultural forms and expression.

The reevaluation of the perception of plants in philosophy and anthropology has been complemented by recent advances in plant science, which have shown that the long-established view of plants as unresponsive and unfeeling is incorrect. As Richard Karban has demonstrated, in addition to being able to sense a wide range of stimuli including light, chemicals, touch, and temperature, plants can communicate not only with other plants but with animals and microbes.[12] Although it is well known that flowers interact with other species via smell (the scents of damask roses, or "Stargazer" lilies, or the stinking titan arum, popularly known as the "corpse flower"), the fact that plants have a "language" or can communicate by sound has only recently been discovered by scientists working in the field of bioacoustics.[13] These findings provide an important context for my understanding of many of the observations about the human qualities of vegetal life in Spanish American literature, which abounds in instances of plants talking, moving, and breathing. Anthropomorphism has been a staple of Western conceptions of nature and is often regarded as anthropocentric, but I suggest that the transformations of people into plants and plants into people in Spanish American culture should be understood not as a repetition of a Western trope but, rather, in light of indigenous animisms and also, potentially, of now scientifically proved views of plants as intelligent, communicative, and thoughtful beings.[14]

Although the corpus of works considered in this book dates from the late eighteenth century, it is important to note that plants have played a significant role in the culture and society of Central and South America and the Caribbean since pre-Columbian times. Flora figures prominently in pre-Columbian cosmologies and myths, and people's knowledge of and important relationships to plants in the precolonial period are confirmed by a wealth of detailed botanical illustrations from across Central and South America, from Colombian ceramics to Maya codices.[15] Flower imagery dominates Nahuatl poetry, bound up in a complex constellation of meanings extending from human sacrifice to war.[16] As Robert Westerfelhaus notes, in the Aztecs' religious code, flowers were regarded as "symbolic vehicles capable of conveying profound spiritual truths."[17] Bernardino de Sahagún, a Spanish friar and the so-called first anthropologist of New Spain, recorded in some detail the rituals surrounding flowers among the Aztecs, including how, during the ninth month of the solar calendar, the festival Tlaxochimaco or the "Offering of Flowers" involved the collection of every kind of flower in bloom.[18] These flowers were later strung together and used to decorate the god Huitzilopochtli.[19] One of the most significant flowers from the Aztec tradition was the marigold (*Tagetes*), known as the *cempoalxochitl* and used for more than two thousand years for ritual, medicinal, and ornamental purposes.[20] The marigold formed an important part of Aztec rituals for the dead—explaining its popular name, *Flor de muerto*—and the flower continues to be used today during the festivities surrounding *El día de los muertos*.[21] Symbolic crops such as tobacco or amaranth also figure prominently in pre-Columbian and indigenous rituals.[22] John E. Staller has shown that maize, in particular, "was central to the mythological origins, ethnic identification, and very existence of the Mesoamerican people." In indigenous metaphysical thought, as Eleanor Wake notes, "the flesh of maize and the flesh of man were as one." Maize is one of a number of plants identified by Miller as continuing to play a central role among contemporary indigenous people, who believe that maize plant-people can communicate with shamans as well as with other plants.[23]

Throughout this book I am attentive to pre-Columbian beliefs about plants, while at the same time remaining mindful of how the meanings attached to flora have shifted over time from the pre-Columbian to the colonial and postcolonial eras. Although, for instance, the Maya regarded the ceiba as the "World tree," which, as Davíd Carrasco notes, was believed to "embody the most essential powers of fertility, stability, and the renewal of life on earth," for Afro-Cubans it became a substitute for the sacred iroko, a long-lived tropical tree native to West Africa.[24] For postrevolutionary Cuban Americans in exile in the United States, the ceiba was later adopted as a potent symbol of home. I trace the close relationship between people and plants in Spanish American culture not only to pre-Columbian beliefs about native flora but also to the heterogeneous histories of human-plant engagements that also emerged after the Conquest. Plants played a transcendent role in the negotiations between the Old and the New Worlds, with the early modern conquistadores often foregrounding American flora as a central point of difference as well as a potential source of wealth.[25] In the now classic account of the agrarian changes wrought by colonialism in the Americas, *The Columbian Exchange*, Alfred W. Crosby establishes the ecological as well as the cultural consequences of the Conquest, through which nonnative crops such as sugar and coffee—grown by African slaves—supplanted native plants and trees.[26] Nonindigenous plants were ultimately absorbed into local imaginaries, and native flora took on new meanings in the colonial era. Carlos Fuentes, for instance, adopts one of the preeminent trees of the Old World and Spain as a symbol of *mestizaje* in his 1993 collection of short stories *El naranjo (The Orange Tree)*.[27] And conversely, during the Amazonian rubber boom, new plant-centered mythologies evolved in tandem with historical events, as native and nonnative tappers told stories of how the "mother of rubber," a figure with bleeding arms and legs, would appear to workers if they were too severe in their treatment of the *Hevea brasiliensis*.[28]

In the book I am attentive to indigenous and local beliefs about plants, as well as to shifting plant imaginaries within colonial and capitalist contexts. I am also mindful of the different histories of plants from region to region. The biogeographic area that is the focus of this book—the so-called Neotropical realm, which includes Central and South America and the Caribbean—contains many of the world's most important zones of biodiversity, including the Valdivian temperate forests in the Southern Cone and the vast Amazon rainforest, home to at least forty thousand species of plants alone.[29] Across Spanish America, flora varies markedly according to climate and habitat, and each country has a specific history in relation to plants. Whilst acknowledging differences in plants across the region, as well as in ecologies and agricultural practices, in this book I will show that Spanish American cultural engagements with plants often transcend local particularities and engage in national and continental debates about identity and aesthetics.

I also draw on and situate the book within the field of Spanish American ecocriticism. In her illuminating study, *Políticas de la destrucción/ poéticas de la preservación* (2013), Gisela Heffes includes a detailed history of the development of the discipline of ecocriticism, particularly in the context of Latin American studies.[30] Among the landmarks of Latin American ecocriticism she includes Beatriz Rivera-Barnes and Jerry Hoeg's *Reading and Writing the Latin American Landscape* (2009), Adrian Taylor Kane's edited collection, *The Natural World in Latin American Literatures* (2010), and Laura Barbas-Rhoden's *Ecological Imaginations in Latin American Fiction* (2011).[31] These works have all informed my understanding of the ecological dimensions of Spanish American literature, as have more recent publications such as Scott M. DeVries's *A History of Ecology and Environmentalism in Spanish American Literature* (2013) and Mark Anderson and Zélia M. Bora's edited collection, *Ecological Crisis and Cultural Representation in Latin America* (2016).[32] Some of these works include considerations of plant life. DeVries discusses the trope of the forest in the *novela de la selva* (jungle novel) as well as agriculture and timber extraction. Rivera-Barnes considers deforestation and the presence of indigenous crops in the work of Neruda. More recently, in his essay in Kane's volume, Raymond L. Williams notes that Morelli in Julio Cortázar's *Rayuela* proposes a mystical view of "vegetable life" as "an alternative to post-Enlightenment Western constructs of nature."[33]

While remaining mindful of existing ecocritical work on Latin America, I deepen the discussion of the significance of plants in Spanish American culture. As well as drawing on critical works attentive to the role of vegetation in Spanish American literature, I refer to a number of plant-centered critical works from different cultural perspectives.[34] The importance of plants to Western literature has received some attention, particularly over the past two decades.[35] As Molly Mahood has shown in *The Poet as Botanist*, plants were significant for a number of British writers, including John Clare and William Wordsworth. This was not just a case of these poets using flora metaphorically or anthropomorphically; for Mahood, these were writers "who also had some claim to be called botanists" (as I suggest of Neruda in chapter 5).[36] Beverly Seaton's study of European floriography is fundamental to my understanding of flower symbolism in chapter 2, as is Debra Rosenthal's concept of "floral counterdiscourse" in US abolitionist literature; Natania Meeker and Antónia Szabari's formulation of the ecological dimensions of "plant horror" in US cinema clarifies my understanding of the trope in *La vorágine* (*The Vortex*) in chapter 4; and reflections on plants by figures such as Georges Bataille, Elaine Scarry, and Michael Taussig have all helped me to understand key moments in Spanish American cultural engagements with vegetal life.[37]

More recently, scholars have become interested in discourse that, in the words of Monica Gagliano, John C. Ryan, and Patrícia Vieira, is "attuned to the lives of plants—one that resists the figuration of the vegetal for human constructs."[38] This focus dominates in, for instance, the essays included in Gagliano, Ryan, and Vieira's edited volume, *The Language of Plants*, Randy Laist's collection *Plants and Literature*, and in Prudence Gibson's *The Plant Contract*, all of which seek to explore how traditional philosophical views of plants as inferior to humans are contested in literary and visual culture as well as in science.[39] This is an approach that I also adopt in this book, where the concern is with how representations of human-plant interactions in Spanish American culture have contributed to the destabilizing of dominant (Western) binaries such as nature/culture, or human/nonhuman, and have been an important means of expressing ecological consciousness.

As Gagliano, Ryan, and Vieira note in the opening line of their recent collection: "Plants are perhaps the most fundamental form of life, providing sustenance, and thus enabling the existence of all animals, including us humans."[40] It is my contention that, in the case of Latin America, they are also fundamental to culture. I draw upon recent philosophical, anthropological, and aesthetic considerations of plants as well as advances in plant science to illuminate, for the first time, the centrality of plant life to Spanish American culture. Throughout, I show that plants permeate literature and visual art, from the persistent use of flora as metaphors to extended examples of "vegetal-thinking," which dissolves the differences between humans and plants and offers radical, phytocentric understandings of contemporary culture and politics. Plants are pivotal not only to the imaginaries of particular authors, centrally Alejo Carpentier and Pablo Neruda, but also to genres such as the plantation romance and forms such as the New World baroque. Multispecies interactions have long been a part of Latin American cultural expression and central to how Spanish American writers have formulated their relationships to nature and modernity across the region. Botanically attentive texts in Latin America are often twinned with literary renovation or innovation, as is the case with Bello's postcolonial rewriting of the classical georgic using the *silva*—a strophe that in both name and form is suggestive of the tropical jungle that, on the surface, the poem aims to contain. The works included in this book are wide-ranging, from canonical texts such as Neruda's foundational *Canto general* to the obscure eighteenth-century Latin poem the *Rusticatio Mexicana*, written in Bologna by the exiled Guatemalan Jesuit Rafael Landívar. I repeatedly show how the treatment of plants in Spanish American culture is distinctive from that in other traditions—from tropical reappropriations of the agrarian literature of ancient Greece and Rome to Creole rewritings of nineteenth-century European floriography and Carpentier's reworking of the baroque.

Although the idea that trees or flowers are sentient, communicative beings has only recently begun to be explored by contemporary philosophers and scientists, this is a theme that has long been established in Spanish American literature. This view of plants has its origins in pre-Columbian cosmologies and persists in the animistic thinking of many indigenous groups today, particularly in the Amazon. One of my main claims in this work is that animistic thinking about plants is not restricted to indigenous cosmologies but figures prominently in Creole configurations of nature from the late colonial period onward. In the *Rusticatio Mexicana* (the subject of chapter 1), the poet's apprehension about harmful agricultural practices is revealed through an extended anatomical metaphor that renders plants as maimed or bleeding bodies. Some 150 years later, during the Amazonian rubber boom, the highly celebrated Colombian novelist and poet José Eustasio Rivera revives this image of bleeding plants in his descriptions of the "white blood" of the rubber trees (see chapter 4). In the case of Jorge Isaacs's *María* (see chapter 2), the aliveness of plants is emphasized through their complex associations with the female protagonist's hair, which I relate to the Aristotelian concept of the "Vegetative soul." As I show, far from conforming to Aristotle's belief in a clear division between people and plants or animals, the presentation of María's hair serves to illustrate the continuities between humans and nonhumans and advances the novel's protoecological and feminist subtexts. I argue that the persistent anthropomorphism of plants and the merging of human and vegetal bodies in Spanish American culture is evidence of a deep dissatisfaction with Western conceptions of nature and of a sympathy with indigenous and ecological patterns of thought.

I do not attempt a comprehensive treatment of botanical texts. Flora has figured prominently in Spanish American literature over the past 250 years and such a treatment would amount to little more than a catalogue of poems or novels about plants: W. H. Hudson's "El Ombú," María Luisa Bombal's "El árbol" ("The Tree"), Dulce María Loynaz's *Jardín* (*Garden*), Rubén Darío's "Caupolicán," and Carlos Pellicer's "Poema en tiempo vegetal" (Poem in vegetal time).[41] In this book I privilege extended consideration of botanically attentive literary traditions, such as the plantation romance, or of authors who have engaged in sustained "vegetal-thinking"—a term I apply in chapter 5 to Neruda's exploration of roots and seeds as a model for social and political transformation— rather than individual works that include reflections on plants.

The book consists of five chapters. In chapters 1 to 3 the focus is largely on Spanish American revisions to European forms or genres through recourse to botanical language or themes. Chapter 1 is an examination of how two texts from the late colonial and early postcolonial periods— Landívar's *Rusticatio Mexicana* and Bello's foundational "La agricultura de la zona tórrida" ("Ode to Tropical Agriculture")—rework classical georgics to reflect local practices and beliefs about plants that concludes with a comparison to a recent ecohorror from Argentina, Samanta Schweblin's *Distancia de rescate* (*Fever Dream*). Chapter 2 is an exploration of the prominence of floriography in two plantation romances, Avellaneda's *Sab* and Isaacs's *María*. It traces how botanical imagery provided the means for both political and literary contestation in the novels, including through the novelists' attraction to "flowery" language that was arguably a precursor to the New World baroque. In Chapter 3 I extend the findings of the previous chapter by setting out in detail the centrality of plants to Carpentier's conception of the New World baroque. As well as revealing the crucial importance of plants to the work of one of Latin America's most significant authors, I offer a thoroughgoing revisionary interpretation of the New World baroque as an aesthetic movement propelled by the forms and logic of plants.

The focus in the final two chapters of this book is on a central theme in Spanish American cultural engagements with plants—the correspondences between plant and human life. This view originates in pre-Columbian cosmologies but persists in Creole representations of nature from the late colonial period on. I focus, in particular, on how twentieth- and twenty-first-century writers and (in chapter 4) visual artists pose ontological questions about the separation between plants and people, often imagining the way in which people might turn into plants and vice versa. In chapter 4 I bring the well-known Colombian novel *La vorágine* into dialogue with a number of rarely discussed works—including poetry, folktales, and a documentary film by the Amazonian writer and filmmaker Juan Carlos Galeano and the "Tree of Life" series by the Cuban American artist Ana Mendieta—to elucidate the important figure of the human-plant hybrid in Latin American culture. In chapter 5 I build on some of the philosophical questions raised in chapter 4— the concept of "plant-thinking" and ideas about vegetal intelligence and subjectivity—in my examination of the representation of plants in the writings of Neruda, particularly his *Canto general*. The afterword is a reflection on the connections between "plant-thinking" and political and ecological awareness, including through reference to Silvina Ocampo and Aldo Sessa's collection of poems and photographs, *Árboles de Buenos Aires* (Trees of Buenos Aires).

Throughout the book, I offer a sustained consideration of the presence of plants in Spanish American cultural expression over the past 250 years and across a range of places and historical moments—colonial Guatemala, Communist Cuba, the Amazon rainforest in the 1920s and today. I demonstrate that, despite cultural and geographical differences, botanical discourse and thinking in Spanish American texts is remarkably coherent and key to the articulation of cultural imaginaries and aesthetic forms. As I suggest in the afterword, "plant-thinking" among Spanish American writers has also been very prescient, antici-pating much contemporary ecological thought. As early as the writings of Landívar and Bello, Spanish Americans were expressing concern about the environmental costs of plantation farming—concerns that only intensified for Isaacs, Avellaneda, Rivera, Neruda, Ocampo, and, more recently, Galeano and Schweblin, during the various extractive and agricultural booms to hit the extended region. I show how botanical dis-course not only dominates cultural debates about identity and aesthetics in Spanish America but also, from the start, has been inseparable from ecological thinking, demanding a reconfiguration of human relationships with the vegetal and a recognition of the transcendent place of plants in the literature, culture, and environment of the region.

CHAPTER 1

"¡SALVE, FECUNDA ZONA!"

Sugar, Soy, and the Limits of the
Spanish American Georgic

griculture, defined in the *Oxford English Dictionary* as "the theory or practice of cultivating the soil to produce crops," has played not only an important economic role in Spanish America but a defining cultural role as well. According to Londa Schiebinger and Claudia Swan, from the earliest days of the Conquest, European travelers to the Americas sought "profitable plants" for national and personal gain. In his study of the "Columbian Exchange," Crosby notes that one of the roles undertaken by the early modern colonialists was that of "agriculturalists." On his second voyage to the New World, Columbus, for instance, brought seeds and cuttings for a range of Old World plants, including wheat, grapes, and sugarcane, as well as fruit stones to establish orchards, while flora native to the Americas was collected for cultivation in Europe and beyond.[1] Although pre-Columbian cultures had developed a range of successful agricultural techniques, including Andean terrace cultivation by the Incas and the Aztec *chinampas* (floating gardens), the arrival of Europeans caused a transition in native ecologies. The swidden agriculture used in forested tropical regions for thousands of years, for instance, intensified with the supply of new metal tools from Europe and the demands of a growing population to feed. By the seventeenth century, large rural haciendas were being established, and commercial agriculture was on the rise. The introduction of large plantations, sustained by slave labor from Africa and necessitating widespread deforestation, shaped the demographic makeup of the Americas and transformed long-established local horticultural practices. Plants such as tobacco and sugar, as Fernando Ortiz sets out, also generated new cultural identities through a process of "transculturation."[2]

In the late colonial and early postcolonial eras, expansionist rhetoric continued to crystallize around the idea of agricultural endeavor, with Creole politicians and poets allied in their view of farming—specifically large-scale plantations of profitable crops—as key to the future of Latin America. In the nineteenth century scientific tracts were published on the growing of important plants, such as Luis de la Rosa's *Memoria sobre el cultivo del maíz en México* (Memoir of the cultivation of maize in Mexico; 1846), alongside literary celebrations of husbandry, including Manuel Alonso's coffee-inspired *El Gíbaro: Cuadro de costumbres de la isla de Puerto Rico* (Gibaro: Customs from the island of Puerto Rico; 1849).[3] Even in the middle of the twentieth century Pablo Neruda continued to laud farmers and to speak of South America's "tierra de agricultura" ["earth of agriculture"] in his epic *Canto general*.[4]

Although classical writers such as Virgil were important models for an emergent agricultural literature in Latin America, the subject matter and semantic field of eighteenth- and nineteenth-century Spanish American authors were determinedly local. Gregorio Gutiérrez González's 1886 poem (the title of which is an echo of De la Rosa's agricultural handbook), *Memoria sobre el cultivo del maíz en Antioquia* (Memoir of the cultivation of maize in Antioquia) anticipates the tradition of the *novela de la tierra* (telluric novel) in its recourse to regional expressions and local color.

And even the most Virgilian of authors, Rafael Landívar, who published his didactic poem *Rusticatio Mexicana* in 1781 (heavily influenced by the *Georgics* and written in Latin hexameter verse), is firmly focused on the landscapes of Central America.

A further breach with the classical tradition is betrayed by the Spanish American writers' circumspection about the kinds of agricultural practices that result in deforestation or habitat destruction. This circumspection is often expressed through the rhetorical figure of pathos. The evocation of the countryside in classical poems such as Virgil's *Georgics* differs from Latin American writers' depiction of the intensive agriculture of the tropical plantation. Unlike the classical tradition, Creole poems about farming are often tinged with regret for the loss of "pristine" nature, as well as concern about the negative impact of plantation culture on the indigenous people, flora, and fauna. In this chapter I will explore the representation of agriculture in two foundational Spanish American poems: Landívar's *Rusticatio Mexicana* and Andrés Bello's "La agricultura de la zona tórrida," considering, in particular, how Spanish American writers have, from the late colonial period onward, shown an interest in and sympathy toward vegetal life, particularly plants native to the Americas. I will conclude with a reflection on a recent short novel from Argentina, Samanta Schweblin's *Distancia de rescate*, in which the antiagricultural impulses already present in Landívar and Bello reach a new intensity.

THE *RUSTICATIO MEXICANA* AND "LA AGRICULTURA DE LA ZONA TÓRRIDA"

Rafael Landívar, born in Guatemala in 1731, has been described as "one of the most outstanding poets from the Americas to write in Latin."[5] A Jesuit humanist, he was expelled by Carlos III of Spain in 1767 and spent the remainder of his life in Bologna. Although an obscure figure today, Landívar was known and admired by many of his contemporaries, including Alexander von Humboldt, who refers to the poet's account of the eruption of the Jorullo volcano in 1759 in what is now central Mexico.[6] The fifteen books of the second expanded edition of the *Rusticatio Mexicana* (1782) provide what Antony Higgins has called a "totalizing picture" of the nature of "Mexico," a geographical denomination that, as Landívar explains in the poem's preface, was used by Europeans in the colonial period to refer to the whole of New Spain, including his homeland, Guatemala.[7] The poem includes sections on different geographical features, minerals, and in particular, agricultural products of the region.

Although there is no single section dedicated to plants, botanical references span the work as Guillermo Putzeys Álvarez has argued. The fertility of the tropical landscape is foregrounded throughout. The poem refers to more than twenty-five species of trees and flowers, a wide range of fruits and cereals, and botanical spaces such as the field, meadow, garden, and forest.[8] Like Bello's "La agricultura de la zona tórrida," the focus of much of Landívar's work is the growing, harvesting, and processing of crops such as sugarcane and indigo, as well as botanical by-products like cochineal, a dye drawn from an insect that feeds exclusively on cacti.

In his illuminating book on the *Rusticatio Mexicana*, Higgins argues that the poem advances from a crisis of representation—whereby neoclassical poetics are challenged by the unrepresentability of tropical nature, particularly sublime features such as cataracts and volcanos—to a "rationalization of colonial space" that stresses Creole knowledge about, and ability to exert control over, the natural environment.[9] Throughout the poem, there is not only an attempt, as Higgins insists, to establish "*criollo* mastery" over the flora and fauna of Central America but also, as John Browning affirms, to discredit the widespread European belief in the unhealthiness of tropical America, producing a more "detailed, accurate, scientific picture" that would contribute to an awakening of the region's agricultural potential.[10] These readings of the poem convincingly show how Landívar channeled Virgilian poetics into commercial and, indeed, political ends. Yet, Landívar's *Rusticatio Mexicana* is, nevertheless, profoundly ambiguous about the agricultural methods it sets out to extol. Even those sections from Book 4 onward that methodically describe the steps for successful crop production and processing often flounder in their attempt to provide a rational, dispassionate account of plants. Rather, the poem draws on the trope of vegetal superabundance as a persistent threat to farming in the Americas, as well as the motif of pathos to arouse sympathy in the reader for the botanical and animal life that is sacrificed in the name of agricultural progress.

A similar dynamic can be observed in the poetry of Andrés Bello. Born in Caracas in 1781 (the year Landívar's poem was first published), Bello was, alongside Simón Bolívar, one of the key figures of the Latin American independence movement.[11] By the time Bello came to write his celebrated *silva* "La agricultura de la zona tórrida," however, the revolution was largely concluded, and in the poem Bello is concerned with establishing a model for peace and prosperity in Latin America, as well as, according to Pedro Henríquez Ureña, literary independence.[12] "La agricultura de la zona tórrida" (1826) was conceived by Bello as one part of a longer foundational poem on the theme of America, but this project was never completed.[13]

Like Landívar, Bello had received a classical education. He was fluent in Latin and was strongly influenced by the works of Virgil, including the *Georgics*, which inspired an early poem, "Oda a la vacuna" (Ode to the vaccine). Unlike the epic cadences of the 1823 "Alocución a la poesía" ("Allocution to Poetry"), "La agricultura de la zona tórrida" is written in the georgic mode, a form that, as Mary A. Favret notes, celebrates the "practical and everyday work of cultivation" over the glories of war.[14] Throughout the *Georgics*, Virgil draws on the topos of the *Beatus ille* to advocate the simple pleasures of the farming life, which not only yields abundant harvests but also a happy domestic existence: "O farmers, happy beyond measure, could they but know their blessings!" As Anthony Low explains, Virgil regarded farming as "a cultural and a civilizing activity," a basis for establishing a government and for ensuring peace and prosperity.[15] Bello followed the *Georgics* in his view of agriculture as the foundation of a new political and social order in Spanish America and a source of personal happiness: "honrad el campo, honrad la simple vida / del labrador, y su frugal llaneza" ("Honor the fields, honor the simple life, and the farmer's frugal simplicity").[16] In his first poetic manuscript, written around 1811, Bello adopted the metaphor of the farmer as legislator, scoping out the land to determine which plants were most likely to flourish there:

> Tú que pides al suelo . . .
>
> sustancias que a los hombres nutran,
>
> antes que todo observa del terreno
>
> el clima y temple: . . .
>
> y cuál sea
>
> de antiguos labradores la costumbre,
>
> y qué nativas plantas alimente.[17]

Here and elsewhere, agriculture and its raw material—namely, plants— form the metaphorical substratum of Bello's poetry. Nevertheless, despite his frequent recourse to a Virgilian framework and imaginary, he is ambivalent in his treatment of agriculture. Indeed, as DeVries notes, Bello often expresses "despair about endangered species of plants and animals with abstractions and idealizations of the natural world that evoke its intrinsic value."[18] As in Landívar's *Rusticatio Mexicana*, although seemingly advocating the control and exploitation of tropical flora, Bello's "La agricultura de la zona tórrida" is inflected with nostalgia for an earlier age where an untended and abundant nature supplied all of man's needs.

   The appeal to the classical topos of the Golden Age, which derives from Hesiod's *Works and Days*, is an important reference point for Landívar's and Bello's antiagrarian poetics. In the early books of the *Rusticatio Mexicana*, Landívar presents the New World in the first stage of humanity, located in a perennial spring, when a bountiful nature provided for all without the requirement of work: "This city had first been established by the Indians at the foot of an impenetrable mountain, in a beautiful country thickly wooded and covered with flowers of the field, though wild, yet ever fragrant and painting the green ridges of the mountain with bright colors. Moreover, the fertile soil in their gardens, even without aid of the hard plowshare, yielded an abundance of ripe fruits."[19] Although the idyll enjoyed by the indigenous people in the above description is cut short by the arrival of the Spanish, the nature of the first books of the *Rusticatio Mexicana* is consistently fertile, containing "ever verdant fields," "joyous crops and a lovely turf, interspersed with thick-leafed trees," and "meadows with various kinds of flowers, mixing marigolds with violets, and lilies with nard, which in their individual places beautify the mountain with their blossoms" (*RM*, 124, 125, 144).[20] This is a nature not fashioned merely for agricultural ends but that has a decorative and aesthetic function as well. There are multiple references to lovely or sweet-smelling gardens. Flowers abound, often described according to color rather than species, and remind us of the importance of plants to the Aztecs. According to Patrizia Granziera, the first Spanish colonists were amazed by the size and magnificence of the gardens of the Aztec elite, which contained a profusion of "ornamental, aromatic, and medicinal plants," valued above all for their beauty and fragrance.[21] Landívar refers to one of the most significant flowers for the Aztecs—the marigold (appearing in the poem under its Latin name, *calthus*)—which was intrinsic to rituals of the dead. In his description of the Valley of Oaxaca in Book 4 of the *Rusticatio Mexicana*, Landívar focuses on the beauty of the native vegetation as well as its munificence: "The fields are ever brightly arrayed with flowers, and the fruit trees are clothed in verdant foliage, one generously bending under the weight of ripened fruit, another holding back its tender fruit for you" (*RM*, 149). The image of the laden tree can be seen to correspond with the colonial imaginary of Mexico as a land of plenty, with its crops there for the taking. It also is a throwback to a preagricultural Golden Age when, according to Hesiod, "the grain-giving soil bore its fruits of its own accord in unstinted plenty."[22]

Plants are rarely individualized in the *Rusticatio Mexicana* but form part of larger areas like forests or gardens.[23] Likewise, botanical spaces such as gardens, meadows, or fields are almost always referred to in the plural.[24] This tendency, alongside the inclusion of adjectives such as "grassy" and "fertile" (*RM*, 125, 133), foregrounds the fecundity of plant life, which is always presented as multiple and diffuse. Similarly, the poem contains some twenty-five references to greenness—more than any other color—in descriptions of the "green laurel" ["viridi puppim"], "green vegetation" ["viridis . . . herba"], or a "green tree" (*RM*, 129, 205, 213) ["virescenti . . . arbore" (1.242, 10.263, 11.253)]—all compounding the sense of a lush tropical landscape.[25] Throughout the *Rusticatio Mexicana* Landívar presents tropical flora as a potential source of great wealth for his country, but wealth that will require the move from a Golden Age to one of agriculture and industry.

Like Landívar, Bello wrote his poem in exile, not surrounded by the tropical nature it describes but in London where he was employed by a number of the newly established South American republics.[26] Nevertheless, his physical distance from the subject matter of his poem does nothing to dull the exuberance of the recollected nature of the *silva*. The poem opens with a celebration of the American landscape—"¡Salve, fecunda zona[!]" (*OCP*, 65)—which, as almost every critic to have written on the work has observed, closely imitates the much cited line from the second book of Virgil's *Georgics*: "salve, magna parens frugum" ["Hail, . . . mighty mother of crops"].[27] In Bello's first stanza, this "fecunda zona" is depicted as abounding in both New World and Old World plants: sugarcane, maize, cocoa beans, and (epitome of tropical superabundance) the banana.[28] As in the *Rusticatio Mexicana*, the classical motif of the Golden Age is invoked to convey the beneficence of tropical nature, which does not require human toil:

Tú tejes al verano su guirnalda
de granadas espigas; tú la uva
das a la hirviente cuba; . . .

    Tú das la caña hermosa,
de do la miel se acendra,
por quien desdeña el mundo los panales; . . .
bulle carmín viviente en tus nopales. (*OCP*, 65)[29]

Here, like Landívar, Bello draws upon classical models and form to produce a very American scene. In the *silva*, the Ancient Greek and Roman taste for wine and sapphires is met with agave syrup and indigo; the "ambrosía" ["ambrosia"] of the tropics is the pineapple, and the cotton plant supplies the "rosas de oro" (*OCP*, 66) ["golden roses" (*SW*, 30)] of the Old World. Maize, personified as a "jefe altanero" (*OCP*, 66) ["proud chief" (*SW*, 30)], is the most important plant of the tropics, just as it had been for the ancient Maya who had a maize deity represented as a man, embodying ideas of botanical and human fertility—beliefs reflected in Miguel Ángel Asturias's novel *Hombres de maíz* (*Men of Maize*; 1949).[30]

Throughout this opening stanza Bello appeals to the reader's senses through references to the colors, tastes, and smells of the tropics. As in Landívar's poem, tropical nature is shown to be as beautiful as it is productive, with native flowering vines such as the passionflower, which was widely disseminated in Europe from the seventeenth century onward, as well as food crops.[31] Drawing on a broad palette of colors, Bello compares the fruits of the tropics to precious stones and metals such as sapphires and gold (*OCP*, 65–66), although as in the *Rusticatio Mexicana*, the dominant color is green, a symbol of fertility and profusion. The opening section of the *silva* stresses the uncontainable vigor of tropical plant life not only through epithets such as "fresca" ["fresh"] and "nectáreos" (*OCP*, 66) ["sweet" (*SW*, 30)], an adjective that alludes to the drink of the gods in Greco-Roman mythology, but repeated images of bubbling or

spilling, such as "la hirviente cuba" ["the bubbling pail"] and "la espu-
mante jícara" (*OCP*, 65) ["the foaming . . . cup" (*SW*, 29)].

As in Landívar, the imagery of the first fifty or so lines of Bello's poem
is firmly rooted in the Golden Age, where the banana tree sags under
the weight of its harvest and its continued production requires no labor
on the part of the farmer since the plant "crece veloz, y cuando exhausto
acaba, / adulta prole en torno le sucede" (*OCP*, 67) ["grows with swiftness,
and when it is outworn its full-grown children take its place" (*SW*, 30)].
Nevertheless, as in Landívar's poem, this glimpse of the Golden Age is
short-lived and provides a context for the poet's apparent call for agricultural progress. Whilst Landívar locates his Golden Age in an indigenous
past, for Bello, as Antonio Cussen notes, the "easy sustenance" provided by
the nonnative banana tree is associated with the servitude of the colonial
era and an unhealthy indolence that needs to be tempered by agricultural
endeavor.[32] Much of the remainder of Bello's poem, on the surface at least,
attempts to contain the profuse nature extolled in the opening stanzas,
with a focus on hard work and the ordering and control of plants.

Work is one of the central themes of both poems. Indeed, in the allegorical Book 6 of the *Rusticatio Mexicana*, Landívar's geographical focus
widens substantially to include "the cold north" (*RM*, 162) in his adoption
of the North American beaver as an embodiment of the work ethic necessary for making the tropical environs productive.[33] The closing lines
of the *Rusticatio Mexicana* are directed to the youth of America whom
it invokes to esteem their land and make it productive: "Let another,
like the beasts, go with unseeing eyes through the fields gilded by the
golden sunlight, and let him indolently waste his time in play. But you,
on the contrary, who have great keenness of mind, abandon old ideas
and adopt the new, and with a high resolve to uncover the mysteries
of nature, bring into the search the full vigor of your mind, and with
joyful work uncover your treasures" (*RM*, 258). Here Landívar's poem
seems to gesture toward a new order—the rejection of "old ideas" and
the embracing of new ones—that supports a reading of the poem as

a "political statement." As Browning argues, it is hard to believe that Landívar would not have been aware of the import of this declaration: "A more prosperous Guatemala would have been a more independent Guatemala, and such independence would have weakened the imperial structure."[34] Higgins has more recently shown that Landívar's work constituted part of a "Criollo Archive," a repository of information about the nature and culture of the Americas amassed by its inhabitants in the face of growing dissatisfaction with Bourbon reforms.[35] Landívar's appeal to the youth of his far-off homeland to renounce play in favor of work somewhat contradicts the message of the previous book, "Sports," in which the poet declares himself "inclined to add amusements to wearisome toil and to repair broken strength with gentle relaxation" (RM, 247), but it fits with the writer's classical and religious training. In Book 9, which focuses on one of the preeminent American plantation crops—sugarcane—first introduced to the Caribbean by Columbus in 1493, Landívar warns of the dangers of lulls in production, which dry out and destroy the sugar presses and demoralize workers.[36] Landívar's debt to Virgil and his view of agriculture as a means of establishing civic order is clear, but for the Jesuit poet the biblical context is no less important. Even in Genesis there is reference to the work of tilling the Garden of Eden, as John Hughes has noted—wholesome, productive work that contrasts with the "toil and sweat" meted out after man's disobedience.[37]

Just as Virgil schooled the farmer, stating that "Toil triumphed over every obstacle, unrelenting Toil, and Want that pinches when life is hard," so too does Landívar's poem set out step-by-step the gruelling processes that farmers in Central America needed to engage in to make the land productive.[38] In Book 5, which concerns the planting and harvesting of the native species *Indigofera suffruticosa*, also known as Guatemalan indigo, the poet offers advice about the ground best suited to the crop, the different tools used to work the soil, the sowing of the seed, and the appearance of young shoots—a moment that, Landívar warns, should not produce complacency: "be not too fast to congratulate yourself, for a long road lies ahead for the farmer" (*RM*, 157). Later in the same book, Landívar shows how the farmer must contend with the challenges of harvesting and processing indigo dye and with the threat of rain and insect bites.[39] Although the inclusion of minutiae about farming methods was characteristic of the classical georgic, Landívar's insistence on how the successful outcome of the crop was dependent upon the precise accomplishment of each step of cultivation is also reminiscent of pre-Columbian agricultural rituals. Wake regards the Mexica myths surrounding maize cultivation as an explanation for the "advent of the Agricultural Age": "Based on the observation of nature and its impact on the development of the maize plant (the gods and their acts), gradually the knowledge necessary to ensure the correct conditions for its growth and care during each stage of its cycle would have been acquired."[40] In this way Landívar's careful enumeration of farming tasks might be taken as evidence of superstition rather than good husbandry. Once again, native ecologies infuse and disturb Landívar's classically informed account of agricultural production.

Bello's poem is also concerned with the theme of work and his *silva* has been read by a number of critics to be proposing Rome as a model for Latin America, with agriculture at the center of future prosperity.[41] The second half of the poem calls on the citizens of the new Latin American republics to turn their backs on the vices of the city and go to the countryside where they will enjoy "la solitaria calma" (*OCP*, 69) ["solitary calm" (*SW*, 32)] of rural life—a peace contrasted both with the "festín beodo" (*OCP*, 68) ["foolish revels" (*SW*, 31)] of the city and the recent chaos of war:

> Id a gozar la suerte campesina;
> la regalada paz, que ni rencores
> al labrador, ni envidias acibaran; . . .
> El aura respirad de la montaña,
> que vuelve al cuerpo laso

el perdido vigor, que a la enojosa

vejez retarda el paso,

y el rostro a la beldad tiñe de rosa. (*OCP*, 69–70)[42]

Although the city is imbricated in a discourse of disease and contagion, with its "ocio pestilente" (*OCP*, 67) [pestilent idleness] and "infecto caos" (*OCP*, 69) [infected chaos], the countryside is health-giving, restoring lost vigor to the body and peace to the mind.[43] The poet is clear that the price to pay for such peace is work: "Allí también deberes / hay que llenar" (*OCP*, 70) ["There too are duties to perform" (*SW*, 33)]. This is the wholesome work of Genesis, which breeds satisfaction rather than sin. In contrast to the "indolente habitador" (*OCP*, 67) ["indolent dwellers" (*SW*, 30)] of the city, given to a range of vices, Bello calls on the farmer to take nature in hand, and nurture the soil that has grown "áspero . . . y bravo" (*OCP*, 70) ["harsh and wild" (*SW*, 33)] during the years of military conflict. In a series of abrupt imperatives, the poet calls on Latin Americans to domesticate their surroundings through the elimination of wild plants:

El intrincado bosque el hacha rompa,

consuma el fuego; abrid en luengas calles

la oscuridad de su infructuosa pompa.

Abrigo den los valles

a la sedienta caña; . . .

adorne la ladera

el cafetal; . . .

aquí el vergel, allá la huerta ría . . . (*OCP*, 70–71)[44]

This vision is one of both destruction (the cutting down and burning of native forests) and of construction (the tending of orchards, vegetable gardens, and plantations of nonnative crops).[45] The metaphorical encoding of this shift seems straightforward enough: as the jungle is cut down, dark gives way to light and the land is shaped into ordered, containable, and economically prosperous space. Nevertheless, there is something disturbing about all of this, for the clearing of forests in Bello's poem, far from evoking a sylvan scene of productive farming corresponding to the georgic mode, is akin to a military exercise and therefore reminiscent of the recent wars of independence. In spite of its Virgilian framework, the view of agriculture in "La agricultura de la zona tórrida" emerges as ambivalent. In both Bello's and Landívar's poems, the break with the Golden Age of vegetative plenty not only entails hard work but also ecological devastation.

Book 9 of the *Rusticatio Mexicana* is dedicated to sugarcane, from the ploughing of the land in preparation for the seed through to its harvesting, processing, and storage. Just as Bello seeks tropical equivalents for Old World victuals, comparing agave syrup to wine or yucca to bread, so does Landívar liken sugar to the "sweet honey" (*RM*, 188) of Sicily, with its glistening cones metaphorically compared to the "marble pyramids" (*RM*, 197) of Egypt.[46] Although drawing on classical forms and imaginaries, Landívar's poem shows pride and confidence in his tropical agricultural products, anticipating José Martí's affirmation in "Nuestra América" (Our America) that "El vino, de plátano, y si sale agrio, ¡es nuestro vino!" [Wine, from bananas; and even if it's bitter, it's our wine!].[47] Although sugar was not a native plant, it soon had "immeasurable commercial importance" in the Americas and was exactly the kind of treasure that Landívar advocated that the youth of his homeland uncover in the closing lines of the *Rusticatio Mexicana*, discussed above.[48]

Nevertheless, the process of producing sugar is not an easy one and is consistently likened to a military exercise. The poet describes how African slaves are forced to undertake the arduous task of digging irrigation ditches and burying the cuttings of sugarcane in trenches to produce further shoots. The slaves arrange the cuttings carefully, in what Landívar calls "phalanges" (*RM*, 9.46), a term used originally by the ancient Greeks to denote a military formation composed of warriors armed with interlocking shields and spears: "they join these stalks to one another in a straight line putting them end to end, and section to section, as a general, forced by the peril of battle, draws up with remarkable skill his heavily-armed lines, wisely dividing them and assembling them in a triple line of battle" (*RM*, 189).[49] The military metaphor develops as the cane grows, producing "long spears" ["hastis"] and "arrows" (*RM*, 190) ["sagittis" (9.88–99)], which are described as "frondere," translated by Graydon W. Regenos into English as "stiff" but more accurately rendered as "leafy," thus forming a kind of metal-vegetal composite. Landívar continues: "As once a company of armed men, born from the teeth of a serpent, sprang out of the earth, having broken through with the point of their spears, and brandished in their hands first the gleaming tips, then lifted into the air the steel shafts until at last spears were rising up all over the middle of the greensward, yielding a terrifying crop and a menacing forest of weapons" (*RM*, 190). Once again, plants and weapons combine in this metaphorical jungle of arms. This description, as Andrew Laird notes, resembles Ovid's version of the Argonautic myth in Book 7 of the *Metamorphoses* when, from the sown earth, emerge "forms of men": "up they rose / From the whole teeming field and each came forth / Clashing— most wonderful—the arms of war."[50] Unlike Virgil's call for agriculture to supplant war, in Landívar's poem the two are combined, creating an atmosphere of fear and foreboding not only through the extended military metaphor but also through the adjective "Horrentemque" (*RM*, 9.95) [terrifying] and, a few lines earlier, the verb "horrere" (*RM*, 9.88). Regenos translates "horrere" as "bristling," but it literally denotes how the hair stands on end in fear—a fact that compounds the sense of plants as animate beings in the poem and adds weight to a reading of Landívar's work as inflected with indigenous American imaginaries.[51]

Despite the importance of sugar to the plantation economy of tropical America, Landívar presents the nonnative crop as singularly dangerous and difficult to manage. Indeed, sugarcane was a remarkably destructive crop in the Americas; growing it is described by Shawn William Miller as "one of agriculture's most ravenous activities," both through

its sapping of the soil's fertility and through the large-scale forest clearance required to free up land for plantations and to fuel sugar mills.[52]
Although these environmental concerns were unlikely to have figured
explicitly for Landívar, writing in the late eighteenth century, his unease
about some of the side effects of intensive agriculture is revealed through
violent imagery. Throughout Book 9 he invests the soil with a number of
human characteristics, arousing the reader's pathos for one of the casual-
ties of this bloody agrarian assault by describing the land as a "teeming
mother-earth" (*RM*, 190) ["faecunda ex matre" (9.85)], whose "bowels"
(*RM*, 189) ["Viscera" (9.60)] risk being ripped open by flooding and whose
"belly" (*RM*, 189) ["ventrem" (9.68)] is pierced by the swelling seeds of
cane. Harvest time sees an intensification of the violent imagery. Slaves
"assail with sickles these armed divisions, and devastate all the land with
grievous destruction," spilling the "blood" ["sanguine"] of the cane on
the "pale earth" (*RM*, 190) ["Pallida arundineo" (9.106)]. As Daniel H.
Garrison notes in a discussion of the Latin poet Catallus: "paleness in
the Mediterranean is not so much the lack of color as a sickly yellowish,
sallow complexion. . . . Sappho compared it to the color of dead grass."
Indeed, the adjective "pallida" was used by Horace in his personification of death—"pallida Mors"—in the well-known ode "Solvitur acris
hiems."[53]

Landívar's evocation of the paleness of the landscape, in combination
with the metaphorical "slaying" of the sugar crop, strikes an elegiac note
in what purports to be a celebration of agricultural promise. Elsewhere
in the poem, he betrays a form of "imperialist nostalgia"—defined by
Renato Rosaldo as "mourning for what one has destroyed"—in the face
of agrarian change.[54] In Book 13, "Birds," and Book 14, "Wild Beasts," the
poet enumerates for the reader not only much of the fauna of his homeland but the best strategies for its annihilation. Wolves should be caught
in nets or shot in the head (*RM*, 240), the porcupine can be dispatched by
the force of a "stout club" (*RM*, 242), and the "tiger" (*RM*, 238) ["Tigrum"
(15.87)]—a local name for the jaguar—should be stabbed and beheaded.

In Book 13 Landívar describes in markedly human terms the "love" (*RM*, 228) between male and female peafowls and the care that the mother bird lavishes on her offspring before he goes on to detail how to disable the birds by cutting off both their feet or catching them with a noose "until you have stripped the tall tree of all its peafowl" (*RM*, 229). The image of the maimed birds lying "moaning on the grassy field" (*RM*, 228) is one of the most poignant of the entire poem.

Agriculture is presented in the *Rusticatio Mexicana* as directly and indirectly responsible for the mass slaughter of animals, since it necessitates the clearing of forests, the protection of crops from predators, and the provision of game for the farmer's table. Despite his inside knowledge of hunting, Landívar's ambivalence toward the sport is exemplified in his treatment of the stag—an animal that, the poet explains again through recourse to the language of battle, "Mother nature has deprived . . . of fierce weapons by failing to gird its mouth with hard teeth or its feet with claws or to provide its horns with fierce might" (*RM*, 242). In other words, unlike the hunter's battles with the wolf or the jaguar, the slaying of the stag does not conform to the rules of *jus ad bellum*. The section of the poem outlining the death of a stag establishes a link between the bellicose eagle, the bird of Jupiter, and the deadly huntsman whose attack on the vulnerable stag is likened to that of a bird of prey against a peace-loving dove:

> As the bird, sacred to Jupiter, sometimes swoops down with a great whirring of wings from a thick-leafed mountain-ash upon an affrighted dove, and the gentle bird, quaking with fear, beats the clear air with her wings, darts this way and that, and weaves countless circles in her yearning to find a safe retreat, yet Jove's armor-bearer presses upon the bird with his swift wings and soon brings bitter death to the innocent creature, in like manner the fierce dogs pursue the peace-loving stag, they hold him with their teeth, and inflict deep wounds. The hunter quickly unsheaths his deadly knife and buries it in the animal's soft breast. (*RM*, 243)[55]

In Book 13 Landívar has also previously outlined in gory detail the killing of a real dove by an eagle. Landívar's analogy of the hunter slaying the stag to an eagle killing a dove recalls both this earlier episode and Virgil's use of the figure in Book 11 of the *Aeneid*, when the murder of the son of Aunus by the violent female warrior Camilla is compared to the gruesome disemboweling of a dove by a hawk.[56]

Through these mythological references, Landívar evinces sympathy not only for the stag but for other victims of violence in Spanish America, specifically those who have suffered as a result of colonial agriculture. In his presentation of the production of cochineal, a dye extracted from a scale insect that feeds on the nopal or prickly pear (*Opuntia*), Landívar draws out the violence of intensive agricultural practices by way of a sometimes comic exploration of the "bitter fate" (*RM*, 151) awaiting the heavily personified insects. Cochineal production was of great commercial importance in colonial Latin America, and was part of a global trade that stretched to Europe, the Middle East, and Asia.[57] Seventeenth- and eighteenth-century pictorial depictions of cochineal insect cultivation and harvesting invariably show plantations of cacti being tended by indigenous workers, denotative of the inextricable colonial nexus of native peoples and native plants (see figure 1).[58]

Throughout Book 4, "Cochineal and Purple," Landívar arouses the reader's pity for the cochineal insects through anthropomorphism and emotive language. He describes the family structures of the insects as well as the development of the young into adults and consistently emphasizes their fragility and vulnerability, as in his mock-heroic account of the slaughter of the insects by predators:

> Suddenly a turbulent mob rises up in the wide fields, approaches the branches in a fierce line of battle, and attacks these young defenseless creatures with deadly weapons. The cruel spider winds her web around the insect, and having torn apart its belly, sucks out the reeking entrails;

FIGURE 1. "The manner of propagating, gathering & curing ye Grana or Cochineal, done by an Indian in the Bishoprick of Guaxaca in the Kingdom of Mexico in America." From Hans Sloane, *A Voyage to the Islands Madera, Barbados, Nieves, S. Christophers and Jamaica, with the Natural History . . . of the Last of those Islands*. Vol. 2, plate ix. London, 1707–1725. Reproduced by kind permission of The Huntington Library, San Marino, California (95867).

or a villainous chicken snatches them up in her greedy mouth. . . . Thus a greedy wolf, driven by madness, assails a sheepfold and wages war upon the lambs. Having snatched the young lambs from their mothers' sides, he savagely tears them to pieces, and raging through the fields with bloody mouth he devours the defenseless creatures amidst the bleating of the rest. (*RM*, 151)

Later, the poet outlines the manner of extracting cochineal, again presented hyperbolically as a pitiless murder, this time carried out not directly by the Creole farmers but, rather, by their skilled indigenous laborers who are portrayed as experts in this complex process and who achieve their end by dipping the insects in hot water until they are sure the "innocent creatures" (*RM*, 153) have expired, baking them alive, or scorching them with fire. Arnold Kerson compares the description of the cochineal insects under attack from all sides to the sack of Troy in Virgil's *Aeneid*, with the creatures themselves comparable to the "sleeping, inebriated Trojans."[59]

Although he also identifies Virgil as the source of the simile of wolves carrying off lambs, a more local parallel can be found in Bartolomé de las Casas's *Brevísima relación de la destruición de las Indias* (*A Short Account of the Destruction of the Indies*; 1552), in which he adopts the same metaphor to convey the cruelty of the Spanish toward the indigenous people: "En estas ovejas mansas, . . . entraron los españoles desde luego que las conocieron como lobos y tigres y leones crudelísimos de muchos días hambrientos" ["It was upon these gentle lambs, . . . that from the very first day they clapped eyes on them the Spanish fell like ravening wolves upon the fold, or like tigers and savage lions who have not eaten meat for days"].[60] In this way, the pathos evoked for the plant and animal victims of agricultural advancement tacitly extends to the indigenous people who were also uprooted as a result of the dramatic changes to land use under the colonial administration. Although there is an unresolved tension in Landívar's comparison of the indigenous people to the cochineal insect (historically, and in Landívar's account, it was the indigenous people themselves who harvested the dye), the echoes of Las Casas's account are unmistakeable. Throughout Book 3 of the *Rusticatio Mexicana*, the insects are shown to have a peace-loving and gentle disposition that abhors murder and disorder—qualities that again Las Casas equated explicitly with the indigenous Americans.[61] And whilst the peaceful society of cochineal insects adheres to the rules of a just war in its engagement with others, since "it creates no strife; it does not in anger indulge in threats, nor does it wantonly attack a defenseless foe" (*RM*, 150), it receives no such consideration from its antagonists who, mirroring the violence of the Spanish aggressors of Las Casas's account of colonial mistreatment, put the insects to death in a range of bloodthirsty ways.[62]

Although Bello's poem is explicitly written in opposition to military force in its presentation of farming as foundational for the new Latin American republics, as in the *Rusticatio Mexicana*, the metaphor of farmers as soldiers taking up arms against nature is central to an understanding of how the poet viewed plantation agriculture. The culmination of Bello's vision of agricultural "progress" comes approximately halfway through the *silva*, with the obliteration of an area of "intrincado bosque" (*OCP*, 70) ["matted trees" (*SW*, 33)]—an episode that, as Jerry Hoeg notes, seems to advocate "a slash and burn policy" for the new republics.[63] Bello opts for an extended martial metaphor in his account of a "troop" of men, "armed" with farm tools, "invading" the forest like a belligerent army and hacking an ancient tree to the ground:

> Gime el ceibo anciano,
> que a numerosa tropa
> largo tiempo fatiga;
> batido de cien hachas, se estremece,
> estalla al fin, y rinde el ancha copa.
> Huyó la fiera; deja el caro nido,
> deja la prole implume
> el ave, y otro bosque no sabido
> de los humanos va a buscar doliente . . .
> ¿Qué miro? Alto torrente
> de sonorosa llama
> corre, y sobre las áridas rüinas
> de la postrada selva se derrama. (*OCP*, 71)[64]

This episode is jarring in a poem that, on the surface at least, is concerned with restoration and reconciliation. In Bello's *silva* the colonial trope of the "empty" landscape is repeatedly invoked in what is now a postcolonial context, as the poet describes how settlers in this wild natural frontier clear the land and depopulate it of animals and people before establishing a new natural and cultural order. The scene is one of devastation: the air is thick with smoke and the animals living in the tree flee in terror, recalling a similar episode in Book 2 of Virgil's *Georgics* when the poet speaks of a farmer leveling ancient woodland and destroying birds' nests.[65]

As in Landívar's account of the relationship between hunters and their prey, this encounter is hardly balanced: with a hundred axes the aged tree is felled, and then burned. At the moment of death, nature has never seemed more alive. As with Landívar's peafowls, the tree groans and shakes as it is hacked to the ground, and the reader's sympathy for nature is heightened not only by its personification but also by the disproportionate use of force. The detail of a bird fleeing her young in terror as well as the delineation of the desolate aftermath of the land clearance—"sólo difuntos troncos, / sólo cenizas quedan" (*OCP*, 71) ["only dead trunks, only ashes remain" (*SW*, 34)]—make it difficult for any reader to take the side of agricultural progress here. As Alex Regier affirms, anthropomorphism "poses some of the oldest and most fundamental philosophical and theological questions dealing with the relation and status of the human subject vis-à-vis the physical world."[66] Indeed, the endowing of plants with human qualities is centrally important to how Spanish American texts have, over hundreds of years, extended moral consideration to vegetal life (see chapter 4). Here, Bello's anthropomorphism insists that the felling of the tree is regarded not simply as a horticultural act but, in the words of the Peruvian Amazonian poet Javier Dávila Durand, as "arboricide," arousing the reader's pity and indignation.[67]

The tree in the poem is referred to as a "ceibo." However, Bello is referring not to the *Ceibo erythrina* or coral tree—also called the *bucare* (mentioned a few lines earlier in the poem) and not of large proportions—but to the *Ceiba petandra* or silk cotton tree, which can reach heights of seventy meters and diameters of up to three (see figure 2).[68] The ceiba is considered a cosmic tree in many parts of the Americas, known as the Tree of Life and appearing in Maya mythology as the axis that holds the world—the heavens and earth—together. In Central America, early modern Spanish settlers acknowledged the indigenous peoples' reverence for them by including the trees in many colonial urban centers.[69] Some one hundred years after Bello's poem, a ceiba tree was symbolically planted in soil from nations across the Americas during a 1928 inauguration ceremony for the Parque de la Fraternidad Americana in Havana, exemplifying its importance not only to pre-Columbian culture (the tree was associated closely with the indigenous population of the Caribbean, the Taíno people) but also to postcolonial identity. The ceiba continues to play an important role in Afro-Cuban religions, and even today one can find remnants of sacrifices made to the god Changó at the foot of the ceiba in the Parque de la Fraternidad.[70] The felling of the ceiba in Bello's *silva*, then, is more than a shocking instance of environmental destruction; it is an act of desecration.[71]

The fact that a tree held sacred to the pre-Columbian people is destroyed in such a way suggests that, despite the recent overthrow of the colonial order, Bello's new generation of farmers continues to engage in a "bárbara conquista" (*OCP*, 72) ["savage conquest" (*SW*, 35)] of the Americas, both of nature and of the cultural legacy of the indigenous people whom their forefathers had brutally overthrown. Bello's anthropomorphism invokes sympathy not only for a vanquished nature but also for the unacknowledged indigenous people, who are implicit in the reference to the wild animals and birds being forced into exile to make way for agricultural progress.[72] In Spanish the verb "desterrar" (to exile) derives from the Latin "terra," meaning "earth." According to the *Diccionario de la lengua española*, as well as political or legal exile, the term has the sense

FIGURE 2. Kapok or silk cotton tree (*Ceiba petandra*) growing by a village in Surinam. Colored lithograph by P. Lauters, ca. 1839, after P. J. Benoit. Courtesy of the Wellcome Collection, London.

of uprooting.[73] The toppling of the ceiba also suggests, therefore, a wider history of both uprooting and exile precipitated by agrarian development. And although the denizens of the forest are uprooted, the poet prays that "libertad" [freedom], the buzzword of the new political order, "se arraigue y medre" (*OCP*, 72) ["(will) root and thrive" (*SW*, 35)]. As Rudyard Alcocer observes, this image "metaphorically collapses the language of people and plants," a tendency throughout the poem that Alcocer considers related to Bello's attempt to "fashion a new and viable Spanish-American identity . . . through the richness and, more importantly, promise of local agriculture."[74]

By using a botanical metaphor to describe the political world and by attaching human characteristics to nature Bello blurs the boundaries between the human and the nonhuman in a manner more consistent with the beliefs of Latin America's indigenous population than with the georgic mode. While the clearing of forests in the poem gives way, in time, to new shoots, in this section of the *silva* the enduring image is of ruins. The poet says he wants agricultural endeavor to atone for Latin America's troubled past—the recent legacy of "muertes, proscripciones, suplicios" (*OCP*, 73) ["deaths, proscriptions, tortures" (*SW*, 35)], which he sees as having sated the spirits of Atahualpa and Montezuma—but it is ironic that this attempt results in the visitation of further violence against nature and the inciting of more supernatural ire, this time that of the powerful ceiba tree.

The likely failure of Bello's georgic vision of productive farming is elucidated, retrospectively, by Lydia Cabrera's 1950s ethnography, *El monte* (The mountain), which contains a chapter on the ceiba, "el árbol sagrado por excelencia" [the sacred tree, par excellence].[75] The fieldwork for this book was undertaken in Cuba more than a century after Bello completed his poem and among a population whose beliefs about the tree owed much to their African lineage, but the prognostications it contains about the fate of anyone who chops down a ceiba are suggestive for a reading of Bello's work:

Un oscuro terror le impide al campesino descargar su hacha sobre el tronco sagrado. . . . Sólo un temerario, un irresponsable, consentirá en cortar la ceiba, que materializa, más que simboliza, a sus ojos, la terrible omnipotencia de Dios. . . . Las ceibas se vengan. Las ceibas no perdonan. . . . "Prefiero pasar miseria, dejar a mis hijos sin comer, ¡antes morirnos de hambre! que tumbar una ceiba," es la exclamación invariable del hombre rústico cuando se trata de suprimir el "árbol de la Virgen María," del Santísimo, el de Oddúdua o Aggayú, el árbol de los espíritus.[76]

As Joe Hartman observes: "The true destructive force of *la ceiba* is evoked when one cuts down or defiles the tree."[77] Through the prism of such beliefs, the felling of the tree in Bello's poem is encoded not as an act of national consolidation, of the farmer's "arte bienhechora / que las familias nutre y los estados" (*OCP*, 72) ["noble toil, that nourishes / families and whole countries too" (*SW*, 35)], but as an act of cosmic defiance. If agriculture rests on man's superiority over nature, then these mythical beliefs suggest it is doomed to failure in tropical America, where plants are not only uncontrollable but also endowed with a dangerous animism.

If Landívar's *Rusticatio Mexicana* and Bello's "La agricultura de la zona tórrida" view the transformation of land as a prerequisite for social and political change, the jungle remains a potent force in both poems. Landívar's work contains mainly references to cultivated landscapes such as fields and gardens, but the jungle resurfaces throughout the poem as a reminder of the work yet to be undertaken by the nation's agriculturalists. Putzeys Álvarez observes that cultivated spaces are presented as bright and sunny in the poem whereas the forest is always shady, a dense and unknowable space, as in Landívar's descriptions of a "lofty mountain peak, its summit thickly covered with trees and hidden under the shade of foliage" (*RM*, 223) or of the coyote "[c]oncealed by the dark shadows of the forest" (*RM*, 241).[78] Such images suggest the persistence of the sublime in the poem despite Landívar's attempts at scientific rationalization. The contrast between forest and field—always presented as dark and light, respectively—has clear metaphorical overtones. In this sense, the poem's celebration of agriculture is seen to conform to the will of God, "who commanded the light to shine out of darkness."[79]

And yet, arguably, in the poem darkness prevails, spanning the *Rusticatio Mexicana* from the "dark forest" (*RM*, 127) surrounding the *chinampas* of Mexico City in Book 1 to the woods of Book 14, "thickly covered with heavy oaks and overgrown with bushes, the dark recesses of which Phoebus shrinks from penetrating with his golden chariot" (*RM*, 236). Here, the forest strikes fear not only in humans but also in the gods of antiquity. Such places consist of almost black vegetation, "dark branches" (*RM*, 230) ["ramis . . . nigrantibus" (13.129)] or "shady oaks" (*RM*, 137) ["Nigrantesque . . . quercus" (2.208)], an unwavering gloom that suggests the unknowability of nature throughout much of the extended tropical region. The imagery surrounding forests in the *Rusticatio Mexicana* disturbs the pastoral landscapes of Landívar's poem and marks the limits of the poet's modernizing discourse.

Likewise, for Bello, the forest is often presented as warmongering and anarchic—qualities that have no place in a civilized agrarian republic. In his "Alocución a la poesía" Bello speaks of the jungle's bellicose "verdes laberintos" [green labyrinths]:

> En densa muchedumbre
> ceibas, acacias, mirtos se entretejen,
> bejucos, vides, gramas;
> las ramas a las ramas,
> pugnando por gozar de las felices
> auras y de la luz, perpetua guerra
> hacen.[80]

Once more, Bello's account of nature is framed in military terms, with the jungle plants (including the iconic ceiba) at war over access to light and sun.

In line with this, despite the potentially fateful consequences of felling a ceiba, "La agricultura de la zona tórrida" moves breezily on from its disturbing account of deforestation to a satisfied vision of newly established plantations "en muestra ufana de ordenadas haces" (*OCP*, 71) ["that display their proud rows and orderly design" (*SW*, 34)]. The apparent orderliness of nature at the end of the poem has led Hoeg, for one, to propose the following reading of the *silva*: "Man and Nature reverse their relative positions in terms of freedom and slavery. Initially, Nature is free and supplies Man's needs without cultivation. It is Man who is a slave to Nature. But by the post-independence period, however, Nature has become a slave to Man who is now free thanks to his control over Nature."[81] Yet Bello's poem also lends itself to another interpretation. Far from being in control of nature, man's hold over it at the end of the work is arguably as tenuous as at the beginning. This reading is suggested not only by the tacit threat of the sacred ceiba but also by the form of the poem itself. Although the subject matter of the *silva* moves from disorder to order, its form does not. Unlike Landívar's choice of Latin hexameter verse, the *silva*, imported to the New World from Italy and consisting of hendecasyllables or heptasyllables, has no predictable rhyme scheme or strophic divisions. If Bello's "La agricultura de la zona tórrida" advocates the control of wild nature, the lack of structure in the poetic form works against the ordered vision to create a work of prosodic unpredictability—what Marsha Suzan Collins has called in relation to Góngora's use of the *silva*, a "structureless structure."[82]

It can be no coincidence that Bello selected a form that draws its very name from one of the poem's most important natural spaces—namely, the *selva* or jungle.[83] Bello's choice of the *silva* seems a prior admission that the tropical forests of South America cannot be contained by either the sickle or the pen, by the farmer or the poet. John Beverley has noted that, in Luis de Góngora's "Soledades" ("Solitudes"), the *silva* form "becomes on the page of the text the graphic embodiment of a confusion."[84] The *silva* represents the limits of agriculture in Bello's New World georgic.

Its confused, meandering imprint bears more resemblance to the "tup-idas plantas montaraces" (OCP, 71) ["savage, tangled plants" (SW, 34)] cleared by the farmer than the ordered rows that grow in their wake. Although Landívar's Rusticatio Mexicana succeeds in observing the metrical rules of Latin hexameter verse, in both works there is a misalignment between form and content. Landívar's dark and disordered forests belie the poem's prosodic regularity just as Bello's ordered vision of happy and productive farming is undercut by the chaotic structure of the silva, a literary reflection of the very entity the poet wishes to suppress—the jungle.

Although both poets call for a more rational organization of land, both these works end with references to the supernatural. In his appendix entitled "The Cross of Tepic," Landívar relates the miraculous appearance of a vegetal cross in a village along the Pacific coast of Mexico, which in winter remains green when the grass around it dies, and which fades in spring just as the surrounding vegetation recovers. Despite the characteristic precision of his account of the cross, particularly in relation to its dimensions and form, the appendix departs from the rational bent of much of the rest of the poem in an apparent return to pre-Enlightenment views of nature. Landívar declares the cross "wondrous" (RM, 257) and reports that, in the past, it was said to have issued a stream of water that could cure a range of ailments. Bello, at the end of his silva, likewise includes an invocation to God to protect "la gente agricultora / del ecuador" (OCP, 72) ["the Equator's farming folk" (SW, 35)]:

Intempestiva lluvia no maltrate
el delicado embrión; el diente impío
de insecto roedor no lo devore;
sañudo vendaval no lo arrebate,
ni agote al árbol el materno jugo
la calorosa sed de largo estío. (OCP, 72)[85]

A twenty-first-century reader of Bello might well make the connection between extreme weather or insect infestations and the harmful effects of deforestation on climate, but even without the benefit of modern science it is clear that the future of these Latin American farmers is not at all secure. The prayer at the end of the poem suggests not only the vulnerability of the agricultural project to natural forces but also its reliance on the goodwill of the supernatural—a goodwill that has been cast in serious doubt in Bello's poem by the farmers' pitiless sacrilege of the hallowed ceiba. In *The Golden Bough*, J. G. Frazer notes the belief that trees "exercise a quickening influence upon the growth of crops," thus explaining the custom in some parts of the world of making sacrifices to trees in order to secure good harvests.[86] In Bello's poem, the farmers not only fail to propitiate the ceiba but treat it with violence and derision.

In both Landívar and Bello, farming brings with it less security than the Golden Age of preagricultural plenty. Both poets seem, at first, to advocate agricultural progress, but it is clear that this transformation comes at a cost—the felling and burning of forests, the annihilation of birds and animals, and the implicit displacement of many indigenous people. Ultimately, both poems fail to live up to the Virgilian framework they invoke. In the case of the *Rusticatio Mexicana*, the pathos surrounding the flora and fauna destroyed in the name of progress attenuates the poem's agricultural agenda. Likewise in Bello, the poem's outward support for land clearance is undermined by its very form, which acts as a potent reminder that the botanical fecundity eulogized in much of the *silva* cannot be controlled.

Landívar's and Bello's poems anticipate later ecological concerns regarding deforestation across Latin America and the reduction of biodiversity through monoculture. The specter of infestation and disease that haunts both Landívar's and Bello's works also portends the widespread use of pesticides in years to come. The catastrophic consequences of pesticides is the central concern of the final text to be considered here:

Samanta Schweblin's *Distancia de rescate*, which marks the endpoint of
agricultural promise in Spanish American literature.

PLANT HORROR AND ENVIRONMENTAL APOCALYPSE

> Then a strange blight crept over the area and everything began to change.
> Some evil spell had settled on the community: mysterious maladies swept
> the flocks of chickens; the cattle and sheep sickened and died. Everywhere
> was a shadow of death. The farmers spoke of much illness among their
> families. In the town the doctors had become more and more puzzled by
> new kinds of sickness appearing among their patients. There had been
> several sudden and unexplained deaths, not only among adults but even
> among children, who would be stricken suddenly while at play and die
> within a few hours.[87]

Rachel Carson's "A Fable for Tomorrow," an apocalyptic prognostication
of the consequences of DDT which opens *Silent Spring*, is partially realized in the small town at the center of Schweblin's unsettling short novel,
Distancia de rescate. Set in the author's native Argentina, Schweblin's work
is a hallucinatory read, narrated in the first-person singular by a dying
woman, Amanda, who pieces together the moments leading up to her
illness, prompted by an unsympathetic interlocutor, David, who we learn
is a boy of around nine. The story centers on a holiday taken by Amanda
and her young daughter in the Argentine countryside and their acquain-
tance with a local woman, Carla. Early on, Carla confides in Amanda
that her son David—Amanda's interrogator—had been poisoned and
nearly died after playing in a stream on their stud farm as a toddler.
Although he was cured by a local healer, Carla believes that the process
led to his being possessed by a spirit. Although Amanda is sceptical
about the story, she decides to cut her holiday short after some unsettling encounters with the boy. Her fatal decision to call by the soy farm
where Carla works on her way out of town leads to the horrific finale

of the novel in which the eponymous "distancia de rescate" ["rescue distance"]—what the anxious mother Amanda glosses as "esa distancia variable que me separa de mi hija" ["the variable distance separating me from my daughter"]—is stretched beyond viable limits in the face of toxicity and death.[88]

At times, the rural setting of Schweblin's novel corresponds to an idealized view of the countryside as a peaceful health-giving retreat from the city. Amanda refers to Carla's youthful good looks and speaks of relaxing pursuits such as swimming and sunbathing as well as delicious products from the local farmer's market. Nevertheless, such associations are destabilized from the start of the novel by its chilling opening lines: "*Son como gusanos ¿Qué tipo de gusanos? Como gusanos, en todas partes*" (*DR*, 11; original italics) ["*They're like worms.* What kind of worms? *Like worms, all over*" (*FD*, 1)]. Although Amanda notes her pleasure at the surrounding countryside, the fields and farms near the holiday home are far from bucolic. The water is stagnant and undrinkable; the soil of the surrounding fields, almost uniformly soy plantations, is figured as "seca y dura" (*DR*, 122) ["dry and hard" (*FD*, 148)]; and despite her elegant clothes, Carla's house is distinctly shabby, full of "[c]osas . . . feas e inútiles" (*DR*, 99) ["ugly and useless things" (*FD*, 117)], including, in an abrupt break with the superabundant vegetation of Landívar and Bello, bunches of plastic flowers.

Unlike the Virgilian trope of the healthy farmer, the rural inhabitants of Schweblin's novel must also contend with sickness. As Carla notes of her son's poisoning by contaminated water: "Eso pasa, Amanda, estamos en un campo rodeado de sembrados. Cada dos por tres alguno cae" (*DR*, 70) ["It happens, Amanda. We're in the country, there are sown fields all around us. People come down with things all the time" (*FD*, 78)]. References to disease and contagion span the novel, not only through minute accounts of the afflictions of the first-person narrator but also through the deaths and illnesses she has heard of or personally witnessed during her stay in the small town, including those of children she sees being escorted to hospital early in the morning: "Son chicos extraños. . . . Chicos con deformaciones. No tienen pestañas, ni cejas, la piel es colorada, muy colorada, y escamosa también" (*DR*, 108) ["They are strange children. . . . Deformed children. They don't have eyelashes, or eyebrows. Their skin is pink, very pink, and scaly too" (*FD*, 129)]. In Schweblin's novel, close contact with the countryside leads not to well-being but abnormality bordering on the supernatural. We read of dying horses, miscarriages, and the poisoning of unborn children "*por algo que sus madres aspiraron en el aire, por algo que comieron o tocaron*" (*DR*, 104; original italics) ["*from something their mothers breathed in the air, or ate or touched*" (*FD*, 124)].

It becomes increasingly clear in the novel that much of the contamination can be traced back to pesticides used in the production of soy. Like sugar, soy is not native to the Americas but has become one of South America's most important export crops, covering more land there than in any other continent. As one of the world's leading producers of GM soy, Argentina has been at the sharp end of the devastation caused by this crop, which has led to widespread deforestation as well as spiraling pesticide use. As Gustavo Oliveira and Susanna Hecht argue: "In its complete destruction of pre-existing natures, agrarian and otherwise, and its use of land essentially as a substrate, soy represents almost more completely than any other biotic production system the construction of a 'neo-nature.'"[89] References to soy recur throughout the novel. Amanda notes the ubiquity of the plantations, the noise made by the wind blowing through them, and her sense of how the soy leans toward her as she sits in the countryside.[90] As in Landívar's and Bello's works, plants are personified in *Distancia de rescate*, yet in this novel anthropomorphism does not arouse pathos. References to the encircling soy fields register as increasingly menacing and claustrophobic, cementing the work's classification as horror, or more precisely "plant horror," which, as Dawn Keetley notes, often "marks humans' dread of the 'wildness' of vegetal nature— its untameability, its pointless excess, its uncontrollable growth."[91] At the end of the novel, Amanda is pushed by David to face the realization that her own ailment, which begins with the sensation of needling under the skin—the worms of the novel's opening lines—originated in a soy plantation after she and her daughter sat on contaminated grass while waiting to see Carla. One of the ironies of the novel is that Amanda has spent much of her life worrying about a tragedy befalling her child but fails to identify or circumvent it when it finally occurs.

The novel ends without the fate of Nina being explicitly revealed, and with the reader experiencing a growing horror surrounding her mother's inability to maintain the eponymous "rescue distance" at the moment of most need, especially when we learn of Carla's intention to take the sick girl to the same exorcist to which she had taken her son. In the final pages of the book, the dying Amanda has a posthumous vision in which her husband calls at Carla's house only to discover the woman has skipped town (perhaps with Nina). As he is leaving, Amanda's husband finds David strapped in his car in a position customarily adopted by his daughter, with his legs crossed and her favorite soft toy clasped in his hand. The dizzying possibility that David now conceals the spirit of Amanda's daughter brings some sort of closure to the narrative but this is far from a happy ending. The interminable traffic jam in which Amanda's husband finds himself trapped in the final paragraph of the novel as he joins a mass evacuation from the countryside to the city—a mechanical "plaga inmóvil" (DR, 124) ["motionless scourge" (FD, 151)], supplanting the swarming insects of Landívar's and Bello's poems and reversing Bello's call for a rural exodus in post-independent Spanish America—confirms for the reader that this ecohorror is not ending but has only just begun.

When asked about Distancia de rescate Pablo Messiez, the director of a 2016 theatrical adaptation of the novel, notes its evident preoccupation with high levels of pesticides in the Argentine countryside.[92] Pesticide use in Argentina dates back to the late nineteenth century, and a growing quantity of agrochemicals, primarily glyphosate, are used by the Argentine soy industry each year.[93] Schweblin's novel is not just a cautionary tale, like Carson's "A Fable for Tomorrow." Although replete with supernatural or science-fiction elements, *Distancia de rescate* is an account of the terrifying perils of agrochemicals in rural Argentina—the deformities, abortions, poisonings, and cutaneous cancers that are not the stuff of plant horror but the day-to-day reality for many people living in formerly rich agricultural belts such as Chaco.

Susan Sontag has discussed the power of illness as a metaphor in society. In Schweblin's novel, the figure of disease is both metaphorical, denoting the degradation of our relationship with nature that leads us to poison and destroy the world we inhabit, and also real, reminding us of the dangers of synthetic pesticides, what Carson calls "elixirs of death."[94] The documentary undercurrents of *Distancia de rescate* starkly reveal that Landívar's and Bello's reservations about the negative side effects of agricultural processes some two hundred years ago were not ill-founded. By the time Schweblin's novel was published, Bello's prayer for tropical agriculture to be delivered from insects had been answered, not by God but by international agrochemical firms. In this recent novel, the soy plantations are thriving, yet they do so at the expense of people and the environment.[95] In Schweblin's dystopian work, agricultural imagery has come full circle in Spanish American literature, from a poetics of plenty to a discourse of disease and contamination. In this sense, the title of Schweblin's novel does not just denote the proximity of the mother-child relationship but also demonstrates how close humans are to failing to protect a natural world on which they depend.

Although these three significant Spanish American literary works about agriculture emerge from different historical moments, are set in different places, and take different forms—the late colonial period, the early postcolonial period, and the present; tropical Central and South America and temperate Argentina; poems and a novel—these texts share a number of concerns and features that are characteristic of Spanish American writing about plants. They include a preoccupation with the ecological effects of large-scale agriculture; a tendency to anthropomorphize vegetal life; and an interest in native plant species, including sacred trees such as the *Ceiba petandra*. In the early poems, botanical knowledge also emerges as an important means through which to rework European literary traditions and to establish local poetic forms and tropes. In these texts, published just before and just after independence, Landívar and Bello appeal first and foremost to plants as a means to reflect upon their own identities and futures. Some two hundred years later, Schweblin continues to ponder the effects of agriculture in Latin America, particularly the social and environmental costs of large plantations of nonnative crops. The plantation holds a prominent place in Latin American literature, especially in the nineteenth-century novel where writers infuse European literary conventions with local plant knowledge and imaginaries to create a distinctively Spanish American aesthetic. Into the nineteenth century, botanical considerations continued to be at the forefront of how Spanish American writers negotiated not only the representation of the environment but also their own relationships to nature and their literary and national identities.

CHAPTER 2

PLANTS AND PLANTATIONS

Floriography, Femininity, and the
Horticulture of Hair in *Sab* and *María*

The plantation assumed an ambivalent position in post-independent Latin America. Although plantation agriculture offered the opportunity for economic prosperity and foreign investment, it had catastrophic social and ecological consequences, chiefly the introduction of slavery and widespread forest clearance. In his account of the "Columbian exchange," Crosby notes how plantations obliterated entire species of native plants: "In thousands and thousands of square miles of the Americas, the indigenous plants have been eliminated completely or restricted to uncultivated strips along the side of roads; and sugar, coffee, bananas, wheat, barley, and rye occupy the greater part of the land."[1]

Just as Landívar and Bello responded to shifts in land use in the late colonial and early postcolonial periods through their rewritings of the georgic, by the middle of the nineteenth century a number of Spanish American writers were engaging in literary accounts of the plantation. Among them were the Cuban poet and novelist Gertrudis Gómez de Avellaneda and the Colombian writer Jorge Isaacs. Avellaneda's *Sab* (1841) and Isaacs's *María* (1867)—two significant novels of the nation-building period following independence—intersect on many levels. Both texts are set on sugar plantations in tropical Latin America in the early to mid-nineteenth century; they both recount failed love stories that end in the deaths of the eponymous hero or heroine; and they both engage, sometimes controversially, with contemporary debates about slavery and femininity.[2] The novels are also marked by racial heterogeneity, including not only black and (in the case of *Sab*) putatively indigenous characters such as Martina but also Creole settlers of Jewish descent.[3]

Plants are fundamental to the action and imagery of both *Sab* and *María*. Throughout these novels Avellaneda and Isaacs engage with the nineteenth-century European predilection for floriography, the "Language of Flowers," that attached specific meanings to different plants and, as Seaton explains, used them to "communicate various moral and spiritual truths, as well as emotions connected with home, family, and romance."[4] Both authors include a preponderance of references to temperate and tropical flora as well as—the plantation setting notwithstanding—apparently Romantic descriptions of wild tropical terrains. In the eighteenth and early nineteenth centuries, Spanish American writers appealed to established literary tropes involving plants as a means to contest or disassociate themselves from European literary paradigms. In the same way, plant imagery facilitates an internal counterdiscourse in *Sab* and *María*, with both novels engaging the European floriographical tradition in ways that are ironic or counterdiscursive.[5] In the case of *Sab*, an extended botanical metaphor calls into question the standing of the central female character, Carlota, as the true heroine of the novel and instead extols the virtues of a triad of socially marginalized figures, including the slave Sab. Isaacs's *María* likewise draws upon floriographical motifs to contest the perception of the female protagonist as virginal and passive, including through the multiple references to human hair, once thought to share the physiology of plants.[6] Horticultural motifs support a reading of the novels as going against the contemporary status quo. *Sab* was banned in Cuba for its negative portrayal of slavery, which is unsurprising given the frequent denunciations of the practice across the novel. Both *Sab* and *María* are polemical and contestatory novels, resisting the views that underpinned nineteenth-century inequalities of race and gender and proposing, through the language of plants, ways of living beyond the confines and hierarchies of the tropical plantation.

SAB (1841)

Sab is widely considered a pioneering novel not only for its antislavery views but also for its incipient feminism.[7] Set on a sugar plantation halfway between the modern-day Camagüey and Cubitas in eastern Cuba, *Sab* relates a tragic tale of unrequited love between the eponymous slave and his Creole mistress, Carlota, who is engaged to a fickle and avaricious young man of English descent, whom her cousin Teresa also loves. At the end of the novel Sab is dead, physically consumed by his love for Carlota who, now married, has come to realize, all too late, the flaws of her husband, the limitations of her condition as a woman, and the nobility of the late Sab's character.

Although it was published in Spain, where Avellaneda moved in 1836 and spent most of her adult life, the novel is not only closely engaged with Cuban society of the first half of the nineteenth century but is also richly evocative of the tropical flora of the Caribbean. Avellaneda was born in Puerto Príncipe, a region known for its agricultural products, including sugar, coffee, rice, and tobacco, as well as flowers.[8] The novel includes references to a wide range of flowers and trees, many of them tropical, and a number of the important episodes (the midnight meeting between Sab and Teresa, for instance) take place beyond the plantation, in the midst of nature. Vacillating between Romantic accounts of the natural world, drawing on European writers such as Jean-Jacques Rousseau, Jacques-Henri Bernardin de Saint-Pierre, and François-René de Chateaubriand, as well as Avellaneda's tutor, the Cuban José María Heredia, on the one hand, and what Stacey Schlau has described as a neoclassical

bent for inventories of flora and fauna, on the other, discourses surrounding nature are central not only to the aesthetics of the novel but
to its ideological drive.[9] There has been much critical discord about the
"meaning" of *Sab*, especially vis-à-vis its status as an antislavery or feminist novel. Floral and arboreal imagery helps the reader to negotiate some
of the ambivalences of the text and determine its views on plantation
culture more broadly.[10]

The presence of flora in *Sab* corresponds to the growing popularity
of flower imagery in early nineteenth-century literature, originating in
France with Madame Charlotte de Latour's 1819 *Le Langage des fleurs* and
quickly spreading across Europe and beyond.[11] In *Sab* flowers are associated primarily with Carlota, the beautiful heroine, in line with the
novel's Romantic tendency to draw a comparison between humans and
nature, where one can detect a "mágica armonía entre la voz querida,
el susurro de los árboles, la corriente de los arroyos y el murmullo de
la brisa" ["magical harmony between the cherished voice, the whisper-
ing of the trees, the current of the stream, and the murmuring of the
breeze"].[12] As Claudette Sartillot has noted: "Because of their perfume,
shape, color, in short, because of their 'beauty,' flowers have traditionally
served as a common literary device to express human qualities." Appeal-
ing to floriographical motifs, Carlota is likened to a "flor de una aurora"
(194) ["dawn flower" (145)], her coloring is compared to the lily and the
local "clavellina" (96), which an earlier authorial footnote informs us is
a Cuban species quite unlike the "clavel" or carnation, and her lips are
said to resemble roses (96).[13] Seaton notes that, in the nineteenth century, flowers were often used to represent stereotyped female qualities
such as smallness, delicacy, and ephemeral beauty.[14] In the case of *Sab*,
the flower symbolism surrounding Carlota draws overwhelmingly on
nonnative temperate plants, causing a misalignment between Carlota
and her tropical environs.

Despite the feminist credentials of *Sab*, largely based upon Sab's powerful closing letter in which he compares married women to slaves, floral

discourse also seems to do little to advance the female cause. This is typified by the third-person narrator's extended botanical metaphor that describes Carlota's disappointment when she discovers the true nature of her rapacious husband: "Aquella atmósfera mercantil y especuladora, aquellos cuidados incesantes de los intereses materiales marchitaban las bellas ilusiones de su joven corazón. ¡Pobre y delicada flor!, ¡tú habías nacido para embalsamar los jardines, bella, inútil y acariciada tímidamente por las auras del cielo!" (182).[15] The metaphor of Carlota as a flower is picked up again later in the chapter when, on her deathbed, Teresa speaks of "el mal que marchita sus [Carlota's] años más hermosos" (185) ["the trouble that is debilitating (lit. "withering") her most beautiful years" (137)]. Although sympathetic in tone, the comparison of Carlota to a delicate flower appears to perpetuate the very tropes of female powerlessness and infirmity that many scholars believe Avellaneda is trying to contest in the novel. Women, whose beauty is all too quick to "wilt," are, according to this account, merely decorative and should be enclosed like flowers in a garden, precisely the space that Sab creates for Carlota (a point to which I will return below).[16]

Avellaneda's familiarity with the language of flowers is evidenced not only in *Sab* but also across her writing, including in her poetry and, centrally, in the 1852 play *La hija de las flores* (The daughter of flowers). Hugh Harter notes how, in contrast to her great formal virtuosity as a poet, Avellaneda's poetic imagery is often quite conventional and draws on European floral metaphors of the rose and violet to denote "brief moments of beauty and happiness."[17] *La hija de las flores*—which in three acts relates a complex tale of rape, illegitimacy, and madness, albeit in a comic mode—centers around a young woman, suggestively named Flora, who believes she is the offspring of flowers: "Mujer y flor, ¿no es igual? / Mujer me dicen que soy, / Y yo siento sin cesar / Que soy flor" [Woman and flower, are they not the same? / They tell me I'm a woman, / and I always feel / that I am a flower]. Although Ángel A. Rivera believes that Flora's marginal status in the play as part of nature rather than culture allows her to cast a critical eye on society, the floral discourse surrounding Avellaneda's Carlota gives her no such leverage.[18] Far from the nymph-like heroine of *La hija de las flores*, romping around her sylvan glade in an ecstasy of sensory delight, the comparison of Carlota to flowers serves only to accentuate her weakness and lack of freedom. Flowers, we are constantly reminded in *Sab*, may be beautiful but they are also painfully fleeting. As the narrator notes of summer blooms: "su perfume es más penetrante pero su existencia más pasajera" (58) ["their perfume is headier but their existence more fleeting" (40)]. And flowers are also part of a powerful ecosystem, which can be at once nurturing and ruthless, like a torrent that "tiende mansamente sus aguas sobre las yerbas del prado, y acaricia las flores que en su impetuosa creciente puede destruir y arrasar en un momento" (79) ["gently spreads its waters over the plants of the field and caresses the flowers which in its impetuous flood it is capable of destroying and uprooting in an instant" (57)]. As in *Sab*, throughout Avellaneda's poetry flowers are often employed in discourses of fragility and mortality, as in "La primavera" (The springtime), where the poet bemoans the fleeting life of man:

> Vuelves al árbol las flores
> El perfume y el color . . .
> ¡Mas no das al hombre las flores perdidas!
> ¡Mas no le revives la muerta ilusión![19]

In a later poem addressed to her husband-to-be, Pedro Sabater, who was nearing death, the author writes mournfully: "Yo no puedo sembrar de eternas flores / La senda que corréis de frágil vida" [I cannot sow with eternal flowers / the path your fragile life takes].[20] In *Sab* the sustained comparison of Carlota to a flower—particularly one that is wilting— therefore suggests the delicacy not only of her health but of her character. Despite the novel's forwarding of a belief in "Las almas grandes" (155) ["Great souls" (114)], which are capable of transcending race and sex and which Carlota is said to possess, floral discourse shows that she corresponds more closely to the clichéd figure of the "débil mujer" (188) ["weak woman" (140)], in contrast to Sab, who is endowed with "un cora-zón que se moría sin marchitarse" (186) ["a heart which died without withering" (138)].

The description of the "pequeño y gracioso jardín" (77) ["small and delightful garden" (56)] created by Sab for the pleasure of his mistress marks the most sustained use of floriographical imagery in the novel. One of few gardens in Puerto Príncipe in this epoch, we are told that its design is not constrained by English or French tastes—dominant in nineteenth-century garden design—but follows only the "caprichos" (77) ["fancy" (56)] of its progenitor and the inclinations of Carlota:

> Era un recinto de poca extensión defendido del ardiente viento del sur por triples hileras de altas cañas de hermoso verde oscuro, conocidas en el país con el nombre de pitos, que batidas ligeramente por la brisa formaban un murmullo dulce y melancólico, como el de la ligera corriente del arroyo. Era el jardín un cuadro perfecto, y los otros tres frentes los formaban arcos de juncos cubiertos por vistosos festones de cambutera y balsamina, cuyas flores carmíneas y doradas libaban zumbando los colibrís brillantes como esmeraldas y topacios. Sab había reunido en aquel pequeño recinto todas las flores que más amaba Carlota. Allí lucía la astronomía de pom-posos ramilletes morados, la azucena y la rosa, la clavellina y el jazmín, la modesta violeta y el orgulloso girasol enamorado del rey de los astros, la variable malva-rosa, la aleluya con sus flores nacaradas, y la pasionaria ofreciendo en su cáliz maravilloso las sagradas insignias de la pasión del Redentor. En medio del jardín había un pequeño estanque en el que Sab había reunido varios pececitos de vistosos colores, rodeándole de un banco de verdura sombreado por las anchas hojas de los plátanos. (77–78)[21]

Catherine Davies classifies the garden as "intrinsically Cuban," but the plants in Sab's plot are also notable for their botanical heterogeneity.[22]

Whilst Sab includes some native flowers such as the "clavellina," plants more often associated with temperate climates abound, especially the rose, lily, and violet. The backdrop of bananas confirms the transnational quality of Sab's garden since, although long naturalized in the Americas, they hail from Africa (like his maternal forebears) and are, in the words of Elizabeth DeLoughrey, a "product of the transatlantic slave trade and the subjugation of South American landscapes and laborers."[23] The mixture of flora included in the slave's planting scheme—native and nonnative, tropical and temperate, African and European—gives weight to arguments that the garden in *Sab* is a "mediating device between black and white" or a figure for transculturation.[24] The garden is a fusion of different locales and traditions, a horticultural hotchpotch that anticipates the eclectic style of Flora's garden in Avellaneda's *La hija de las flores* that includes "Los claveles de la China / Y heliotropos del Perú" [carnations from China / and heliotropes from Peru].[25] The flowers of Sab's garden also figure highly in the European floriographic tradition, not only roses and lilies (frequently adopted to denote beauty and innocence and closely associated, as Jennifer Bennett notes, with the Virgin Mary) but also violets and sunflowers, which are endowed by the narrator with their projected characteristics of modesty and pride, respectively.[26] Passionflowers, one of the native additions to Sab's plot, and the nonnative "aleluya" (a popular name for *Oxalis acetosella*) both have rich religious connotations, given their associations with Easter.[27]

Centrally, however, many of the flowers in Sab's garden are potent symbols of love. Davies likens Sab's creation of a garden for Carlota to the act of a husband providing a house for his wife.[28] Sab's inclusion of highly perfumed flowers, including violets, roses, and lilies—all three of which make up the perfumed garments worn by Aphrodite, the goddess of love, in the ancient Greek epic the *Cypria*—show that Sab's garden is designed expressly as a space of seduction and sensuality. Indeed, in Avellaneda's *La hija de las flores*, Flora conjoins these very flowers as symbols of the key attributes of the female lover: "Violeta, rosa, azucena, /

Juntitas habéis de estar; / Que forman bello conjunto / Candor, modestia y beldad" [Violet, rose, lily, / You have to be together; / Since you form a beautiful group / Honesty, modesty and beauty].[29]

Despite the narrator's stress on the artlessness of his garden design, Sab's choice of significant plants from the floriographical tradition as well as his careful arrangement of space reveal a man with substantial horticultural experience and intent. He is, after all, the manager of a large, if declining, sugar plantation and is credited by his owner with the single-handed improvement of the outlaying estates, which, before Sab's intervention, were "casi abandonadas" (94) ["practically abandoned" (68)]. Although including some wild flowers and grasses, the garden is a controlled and ordered place that contains a number of impressive specimen plants. Its perfectly square shape conforms to the Neoplatonic preference for geometric garden design from antiquity onward and it also contains an ornamental fishpond, a popular feature of the formal garden that dates back to the ancient Egyptians.[30] Rogelia Lily Ibarra suggests that Sab's plot implies a "constraining of nature." The garden was a favored topos in colonial representations of place, and as John Thieme notes, there are "significant similarities between horticulture and cartography."[31] As such, the particular form that the garden takes—its highly artificial and ordered construction and the profusion of nonnative plants—emphasizes Sab's ambivalent role in relation to nature. Like Landivar's and Bello's poetic personae, Sab both resists and embraces plantation agriculture—a system that relies upon the restraining not only of nature but also of human bodies. Sab's garden also reveals something of his view of women. Although the garden has no walls, the sense of seclusion and containment created by the tall plants forming its perimeter is directly suggestive of the metaphor of the virginal woman as a *hortus conclusus.*[32]

Most striking about this garden, however, are the repeated references to its luster, particularly the comparison of its showy flora and fauna with precious gems and minerals such as emeralds, topaz, gold, and mother-of-pearl. As well as suggesting the Jewel Garden of the *Epic of Gilgamesh*, where trees bear precious stones as fruit, the invocation of plants as gems explicitly relates Sab's garden to Eden: "Thou hast been in Eden the garden of God; every precious stone *was* thy covering, the sardius, topaz, and the diamond, the beryl, the onyx, and the jasper, the sapphire, the emerald, and the carbuncle, and gold: the workmanship of thy tabrets and of thy pipes was prepared in thee in the day that thou wast created."[33] Ibarra has argued that Sab's garden appropriates colonial models to create a new transcultural space that "challenges the definition of nature, Cuba as Eden," yet the narrator's allusion to the biblical jeweled garden shows that Edenic imagery remains preeminent in this botanical space.[34] What is unsettling to the status quo in Sab's garden is not so much its design but the identity of its Adamic creator. When railing to Teresa against the condition of slavery, Sab poses the powerful rhetorical question: "¿No tienen para él [the slave] conciertos las aves, ni perfumes las flores?" (133) ["Do not the birds sing for him and the flowers emit their perfume?" (97)]. As well as a statement of Sab's love for Carlota, the garden therefore becomes the material proof of his intelligence and aesthetic sensibility, even if it also signals his ability to dominate nature, just as the bodies of slaves and the Cuban landscape had been dominated for years under the colonial, and later postcolonial, plantation system.

Sab's garden is styled by the narrator as a mere corner of the "vasto y magnífico vergel formado por la naturaleza" (77) ["vast and magnificent garden which nature had made" (56)] that is Cuba—a botanical image that, as Adriana Méndez Rodenas notes, has clear Edenic impulses. The trope of the tropics as a fertile garden was a cornerstone of tropical Romanticism, a mode favored throughout much of the early to mid-nineteenth century as a means to convey the beauty and superabundance of tropical environs, particularly from a European perspective. Avellaneda began writing *Sab* before setting off to live in Spain, but the voice of the omniscient third-person narrator vacillates between that of an insider and that of an outsider, displaying, as Méndez Rodenas notes, a "detached and an engaged perspective, as if the novel was written with both a *criollo* and a peninsular audience in mind."[35] Accounts of the tropical landscape display both an intimate knowledge of nature, a lived experience of a landscape seen close up over many years, and a foreigner's point of view. This last perspective is embodied early in the novel by Carlota's husband-to-be, Enrique Otway, who finds himself in an unfamiliar part of the island when visiting the estates of the heroine's father and then again, most emphatically, when Carlota and her family go on an excursion to the remote Cubitas.[36] According to Rivera-Barnes, while living in Spain Avellaneda "began to think like a Spaniard and [to] construct the Cuban environment just as a Spaniard would," with awed reverence for an exotic tropical world. Both Rivera-Barnes and Thomas Ward compare the tendency of the novel's narrator to enumerate features of the natural world to the same technique in colonial tracts such as Gonzalo Fernández de Oviedo's *Sumario de la natural historia de las Indias* (Natural history of the Indies).[37] This is particularly true of Avellaneda's treatment of plants. *Sab* contains a number of botanical footnotes to guide the foreign reader, including glosses of Cuban flowers and shrubs, such as the "yarey" (41), used locally to make hats and baskets; the "clavellina cubana" (78), as mentioned above; and the wild bellflower, "campanilla" (97). The postcolonial context of these footnotes, however, allows us to position Avellaneda's recording of the specific details of local plants not as part of the colonial botanizing tradition but as a first step toward a Creole understanding and appreciation of native flora.

The Romantic elements of the novel also contribute to this dual native/nonnative perspective. Like her literary progenitor Carlota was born on the island, but her views of the Cuban landscape are often modulated through literary discourses of the sublime or the picturesque. They are also redolent of the French Romantics, as in the following passage, which follows Sab's account of the murder of the indigenous Cacique Camagüey at the hands of Spanish colonizers: "Aquí vivían felices e inocentes aquellos hijos de la naturaleza: este suelo virgen no necesitaba ser regado con el sudor de los esclavos para producirles: ofrecíales por todas partes sombras y frutos, aguas y flores, y sus entrañas no habían sido despedazadas para arrancarle con mano avara sus escondidos tesoros. ¡Oh, Enrique! Lloro no haber nacido entonces y que tú, indio como yo, me hicieses una cabaña de palmas en donde gozásemos una vida de amor, de inocencia y de libertad" (102).[38] As with Sab's garden, there is a return to Edenic discourse in Carlota's construction of Cuban nature as a virginal milieu that does not require toil. From the first European accounts of tropical America, its construction as a paradise was predicated on the lack of a necessity for work. The abundance of uncultivated food found by European travelers in the Caribbean contributed to its popular image as Eden—a bountiful space where nature yielded its products freely, as in the agricultural epics of Landívar and Bello. Nevertheless, Bello's "La agricultura de la zona tórrida" glosses over the hand of the slave required to harvest the fruits of the celebrated "fecunda zona" ["fertile zone"], just as Carlota suppresses the reality of slavery that sustains her family's bountiful plantations.[39]

Here Carlota's idealized view of life before the Conquest fuses Edenic discourse with the Enlightenment myth of the noble savage, residing simply and in a state of innocence. Harter notes that, while she was writing *Sab*, Avellaneda was reading Chateaubriand's *Atala*, a novel that also recounts a doomed, interracial love affair. The traces of this reading can be detected in particular in Carlota's reference to a palm hut, reminiscent of Chactas's plea to the Christian heroine of *Atala* that they build a hut and hide themselves away in the wilderness.[40] Carlota's empathetic response to the death of Camagüey—whom she regards as a metonym for a "raza desventurada" (101) ["unfortunate people" (73)]—suggests clear differences between her outlook and Enrique's view of nature as a space to be plundered. Rivera-Barnes argues that the ideas underpinning Carlota's Romantic vision of tropical superfluity are "at the root of a colonial myth of Eden that has not only silenced and damaged the Caribbean landscape but has also interred a violent and unjust history that equally contributed to the degradation of this landscape."[41] In other words, Carlota's and Enrique's views of nature are not so opposed, which is made clear in the narrative by the fact that earlier in the same chapter he adopts a similar discourse with respect to "la prodigiosa fertilidad de aquella tierra privilegiada" ["the prodigious fertility of this exceptional country"]—albeit a discourse that explicitly relates Cuba's fertility to "el grado de utilidad que podía sacarse de ella" (97) ["the degree of profit that could be gained from it" (71)]. Elsewhere, Carlota's treatment of nature also coincides with Enrique's more unequivocally utilitarian view. Carlota is described in her garden both chasing and finally capturing a butterfly and also picking and then pulling apart some flowers before throwing them in the pond.[42] In a parallel gesture, Enrique later plucks and then peels an orange from a tree, which, in line with the novel's theme of tropical superabundance, "doblegaban sus frutos" ["was bowed down with fruit"], only immediately thereafter to throw it away "con impaciencia" (90) ["impatiently" (65)].

In contrast to their conduct, which demonstrates a wasteful disregard for nature, Sab is shown to be a meticulous horticulturalist in his role as overseer and gardener. In the novel such behavior is repaid in kind. Whilst the eponymous hero is protected by nature, Enrique suffers the full brunt of its power during a tropical storm that he insists on traveling through, attended by Sab, on a matter of business: "el árbol bajo el cual se hallaba cayó abrasado por el rayo, y su caballo lanzándose por entre los árboles, que el viento sacudía y desgajaba, rompió el freno con que el aturdido jinete se esforzaba en vano a contenerle. Chocando su cabeza contra las ramas y vigorosamente sacudido por el espantado animal, Enrique perdió la silla y fue a caer ensangrentado y sin sentido en lo más espeso del bosque" (70–71).[43] Here the trees doubly conspire against Enrique, first falling on his horse and then knocking him off his saddle. In contrast Sab is unharmed, just as he later admits to surviving hurricanes and lightning, which he has implored to strike him, while beside him "ha caído . . . la altiva palma, reina de los campos" (135) ["the

proud palm, the queen of this land, has crashed down" (99)]—the tree
vicariously taking the place of the lovesick slave. Such imagery is somewhat heavy-handed, failing to acknowledge Sab's own (albeit imposed)
contributions to the dismantling of native ecologies and the production
of capitalist space as a plantation manager and horticulturist. Yet it is
an important means through which to establish the links between Sab
and plants, particularly native tropical plants, unlike the metaphorical
encoding of Carlota through reference to the clichés of the European
floriographical tradition.

Throughout the novel Sab is consistently shown to be at one with
the surrounding flora, particularly through repeated images of him
concealed amid trees or greenery, as when he hides from Teresa amid
sugarcane and twice spies on Carlota from behind plants in his garden.[44]
As well as merging with flora, Sab is frequently likened to trees, particularly what Anderson has called "big old trees."[45]

Arboreal discourse is widespread in the novel and is of great metaphorical significance. Flower imagery in *Sab* tends, in line with the
European floriographical tradition, to draw on clichés of women as
fragile and beautiful, blunting the credentials of Carlota as a feminist
heroine of the text. Arboreal discourse, on the other hand, disrupts the
colonial status quo by revealing the nobility and endurance of not only
Sab but also the impoverished Martina, who claims to be of indigenous
descent, and also Carlota's poor illegitimate cousin, Teresa. This triad of
characters, whose racial or social lineage places them on the very margins
of plantation society, are elevated to the center of the narrative through
tree imagery. Although earlier in the novel Sab remarks on his impervi-
ousness to storms and other natural phenomena, on Sab's deathbed the
narrator adopts a tree metaphor to compare the slave's demise to that of
an "encina a las tempestades del cielo" (168) ["oak before the tempests
of heaven" (125)]. The only oaks native to Cuba are evergreen, like the
iconic live oak or *Quercus virginiana*, which grows widely in the southern
United States and is associated with Native Americans, for whom it was

an important source of food and shelter. Although the cultural symbolism of oaks varies from culture to culture and from species to species, Anderson's comments on the live oak help to elucidate the significance of this tree in *Sab*: "They speak of isolation, endurance, self-sufficiency, romance, and the harmony of nature."[46] Oaks are known for their grand stature and resilience, and the comparison of Sab to this tree acts not only as further confirmation of the protagonist's noble character but as a point of contrast between the slave and the morally feeble Enrique—whose body, in turn, is likened to "una lijera paja" (71) ["weightless piece of straw" (51)].

Tree imagery also proliferates in relation to Martina and Teresa. Jenna Leving Jacobson has recently described Martina as "one of the most enigmatic yet least studied characters" of *Sab*—a marginality that she aims to reverse by reading the novel against the grain of Doris Sommer's paradigm of national romance in order to show that Martina's vision of the vengeance of her alleged forebear, the cacique Camagüey, foretells not a future of national reconciliation but one of violence and retribution.[47] Although Martina's putative Amerindian origins are by no means certain and her "aire ridículamente majestuoso" (115) ["ridiculously majestic air" (83)] registers at times as comically theatrical, the arboreal imagery in *Sab* confirms Martina's close relationship to the slave Sab and by extension her nobility of character.[48] The narrator's opening description of Martina is as "derecha y erguida, como una palma" (108) ["erect and upright as a palm tree" (78)]. Shortly afterward Martina herself adopts an extended botanical metaphor that compares herself and Carlota's equally aged father to ancient trees, surrounded by the next generation of young trees and saplings:

> El árbol viejo del monte, cuando ya seco y sin jugo sólo alimenta curujeyes, ve pasar años tras años sin que ellos le traigan mudanza. El resiste a los huracanes y a las lluvias, a los rigores del sol y a la aridez de la seca; mientras que el árbol todavía verde sufre los ataques del tiempo y pierde poco a

poco sus flores, sus hojas y sus ramas. Pero he aquí . . . tres hermosos árboles en todo el vigor de su juventud, con todos los verdores de la primavera,
y cuatro tiernos arbolitos que van creciendo llenos de lozanía. (108–9)[49]

Like Sab's image of the oak, Martina's appeal to the metaphor of an
ancient tree speaks of strength of character and of deep roots.[50] Martina
treats Sab as her son, and Sab embraces her as his "madre adoptiva"
(113) ["adoptive mother" (82)], with the two further conjoined through a
persistent arboreal discourse, which reveals them as sharing a nobility of
spirit although they are divergent in race and ancestry. Although Teresa
at first appears to have an "alma apática" (51) [lit. "apathetic soul"],
exhibiting a lack of empathy and emotion toward, for instance, the plight
of Martina and her ailing grandchild, Luis, Sab sees Teresa as a twin
spirit and "mujer sublime," "grande y fuerte, ennoblecida por los sacrifi-
cios" (188) ["sublime woman," "great and strong, ennobled by sacrifices"
(140)].[51] This is most vividly conveyed through Sab's comparison of Teresa
to a ceiba, one of the most significant trees of the Americas, and particularly Cuba: "Así cuando precipita el huracán su carro de fuego sobre
los campos, la ceiba se queda erguida, iluminada su cabeza vencedora
por la aureola con que la ciñe su enemigo; mientras que el arbusto, que
ha querido en vano defenderse como ella, sólo queda para atestiguar el
poder que le ha vencido. El sol sale y la ceiba le saluda diciéndole:—veme
aquí—, pero el arbusto sólo presenta sus hojas esparcidas y sus ramas
destrozadas" (188).[52] The ceiba was considered sacred by the Ancient
Maya and remains a central point of reference for Afro-Cuban culture,
including, as Hartman notes, among practitioners of Palo Monte/May-
ombe, a religion thought to have originated with Congolese slaves on the
island. Although professing to be a Catholic, Sab informs Enrique that
his mother was a princess from the Congo. Sab's choice of the ceiba tree
as a metaphor and his references to hurricanes and lightning strikes,
here and elsewhere, certainly bear traces of Afro-Cuban religious beliefs
given the ceiba's connection to Oyá, the orisha or deity of hurricanes,

and Changó, the orisha of lightning who would fight his enemy Oggún, the orisha of war and iron, underneath its bowers.[53]

As well as testament to Teresa's strength and nobility, which Sab regards as being epitomized in her forbearance of Enrique's love for Carlota, tree imagery again advances an alternative form of kinship. Like Martina's "adoption" of the orphan Sab, Teresa disregards blood ties in her repeated declaration that she is the slave's sister.[54] Tree imagery cements the bonds between this triad of characters of different races and backgrounds, united by their strength of character. In contrast, although the narrative voice, as well as Sab, lauds Carlota for her spiritual elevation, throughout much of the novel she registers as immature and "pueril" (79) ["childlike" (57)]. In the passage above, the significance of the contrast between the sturdy ceiba tree and the storm-ravaged bush may be lost on its author, Sab, who continues until his death to hail Carlota as a "visión celeste" (191) ["celestial vision" (143)], but the distinction succeeds in reminding the reader of the images of botanical decay and fragility surrounding the apparent heroine of the novel and the implications of these images for an understanding of her character. Excuses are often made for Carlota, not only by the narrator—who indulgently attributes her thoughtless butterfly catching to the fact that "conviene a las almas superiores descender de tiempo en tiempo de su elevada región" (79) ["for superior souls it is necessary to descend from time to time from their elevated heights" (57)]—but also by critics such as Harter, who describes Carlota as a perfect Romantic heroine, although he does concede that she might be seen as, "by today's standards, insipid, shallow, and in her emotional myopia, inconsiderate of the needs and feelings of those around her." Schlau notes how Carlota develops from "a flighty, capricious young girl into a mature woman" following her anagnorisis about Enrique's unworthiness. Rivera-Barnes's characterization of Carlota as a "study of inattention, of good intentions that pave the way to hell" is somewhat less forgiving.[55] Nevertheless, botanical imagery in *Sab* facilitates a reading between the lines, by drawing attention to the discrepancies between the actions of people in the novel and what is said about them either by the narrator or by other characters. Floriography acts counterdiscursively in *Sab* to underline the weakness of the presumed heroine, Carlota, the beautiful daughter of the plantation class who is associated with delicate European flowers and, in contrast, the "fortaleza" (189) ["strength" (141)] of the treelike Teresa.

Flowers tend to be associated with ephemerality and mortality; trees are denotative of permanence and strength, but they are not invulnerable: in the end, even Sab, the towering oak, is struck down as if by lightning. Indeed, the three characters most closely associated with trees all die, and they all fail to leave any offspring. Carlota's father also perishes, and Carlota herself inhabits a kind of half life—taking refuge with Teresa in a convent while her cousin is still alive and afterward standing vigil by Sab's grave.[56]

The preponderance of death in *Sab* is related to a broader botanical discourse of withering and sterility pervading the novel. Martina, for instance, metaphorically speaks of her ailing grandson, who later dies, as "la última hoja marchita que se desprenderá de este viejo tronco" (110) ["the last withered leaf that will fall from this trunk" (79)], and Sab refers to his "estéril y triste juventud" (135) ["barren and unhappy childhood" (98)] and compares the life of a slave to "la planta estéril" (193) ["the barren plant" (145)]. Carlota too remains childless at the end of the novel, a fact that Evelyn Picon Garfield ascribes to her resistance to an extractive economy where women, like the Cuban landscape, are valued for their productive yield.[57]

Images of dead trees and wilting flowers are also important reminders of the decline of the natural environment in Cuba in the nineteenth century. Although Avellaneda's novel speaks nostalgically of the island's superabundant and "lozana vegetación" (39) ["luxuriant vegetation" (27)], this is tempered by references to the ephemerality of flowers and dying trees. Carlota's family plantations—much to Enrique's chagrin—are declining, but at the very moment when the novel was first published, sugar production and the concomitant program of state-sanctioned forest clearances were gaining momentum across Cuba. Antonio Benítez-Rojo regards the sugar industry, established in Cuba in the sixteenth century, as the single greatest cause of deforestation in the country, a process that accelerated in the nineteenth century when Avellaneda was writing.[58]

The Galician botanist Ramón de la Sagra, who was director of the Botanical Garden of Havana between 1822 and 1836, wrote evocatively of forest clearance in his 1831 *Historia económico-política y estadística de la isla de Cuba* (Economic, political and statistical history of the island of Cuba)—published before Avellaneda departed for Spain—describing the transformation of the land into sterile plains, and the concomitant rise in temperature and decrease in rainfall: "desaparecerán los benéficos y abundantes rocíos, que en la época de la seca suplen á la falta de aguas, en las comarcas de grandes arboledas, condenando al estermenio las plantas y los animales en los meses a noviembre á marzo, y en los calurosos, no se percibirá el soplo vivificador de los bosques ni el olor balsámico de las flores silvestres. En fin, donde se aniquilen los árboles, una escena de soledad y muerte se sostituirá a risueño espectáculo de una naturaleza jóven y agreste."[59] De la Sagra regards the sugar industry's environmental record as not only destructive but short-sighted. As Reinaldo Funes Monzote argues, in the first decades of the nineteenth century, Cuba's forests were seen as "no more than lumber to build sugar mills, firewood to fuel them, and sources of stunningly fertile soil," ignoring their important role in conservation. By the late 1850s, when Avellaneda returned to live in Cuba for a period of five years, forest covered only 40 percent of the island.[60] Toward the end of the century the plantation heartland of Cuba was, in Manuel Moreno Fraginals's words, "a treeless land. The death of the forests was also, in the medium term, the death of the island's fabulous fertility."[61]

In *Sab*, glimpses of forested "prados coronados de palmas y gigantescas ceibas" (39) ["pasturelands crowned by palms and gigantic ceiba trees" (28)] seem like wishful thinking amid the "inmensos cañaverales" (130) ["immense cane fields" (95)], where tropical fecundity is channeled into agro-industrial ends. Such images invoke imperialist nostalgia, which Rosaldo sees as revolving "around a paradox: A person kills somebody, and then mourns the victim. . . . At one more remove, people destroy their environment, and then they worship nature."[62] At the end of *Sab*, only the amoral Enrique has prospered, and the sugar plantations have succeeded in uprooting the native flora—the delicate wildflowers and mighty trees—that forms the symbolic bedrock of the novel. As such, in spite of the counterdiscursive posturing in *Sab*, the novel ends darkly, with little visible progress in terms of black—or female—liberation. Slavery would not be abolished on the island of Cuba until 1886.[63] Twenty-five years later, Jorge Isaacs's *María* once again appeals to botanical discourse for emancipatory ends.

MARÍA (1867)

The protagonist and first-person narrator of Jorge Isaacs's *María* (1867), Efraín, draws extensively on floral imagery as a means to convey a lost love—that of the eponymous heroine, his cousin and wife-to-be, who dies while he is completing his studies abroad.[64] Tapping into the Romantic predilection for wild nature, Isaacs sets the novel in the lush Cauca valley in a period before the abolition of slavery in Colombia, and plants, particularly flowers, inform much of the novel's imagery. Rightly identified as encoding female eroticism, flowers propel the tragic love affair between the narrator and María, who spends much of her time in the family's walled garden, collecting and arranging blooms as love tokens for Efraín.[65] At the end of *María*, after the heroine's death, the flowers picked in the throes of young love are described as "marchitas y carcomidas" [withered and worm-eaten] encoding her untimely passing as well as intimating the waning of plantation culture in South America.[66]

As in *Sab*, Isaacs makes reference to a wide range of flowers and trees in *María*, including carnations, lilies, roses, poppies, mallow, violets, honeysuckle, jasmine, orange trees, weeping willows, tamarinds,

cedars, ceibas, and palms. As well as contributing to the realism of the
novel, flora has an important symbolic dimension, in part echoing the
nineteenth-century interest in the "Language of Flowers," allowing lovers
to enter into passionate exchange through a seemingly chaste botanical
metalanguage.[67] In *María* flowers are endowed with multiple meanings,
primarily romantic but also moral and religious. From the first chapter
of the novel, María's love for Efraín is persistently sublimated in the
picking and arranging of blooms—"las flores más lindas" (75) [the pret-
tiest flowers]—with which she ornaments his bedroom and bath. And,
as well as the giving of flowers, their withholding is important to the
plot. On one occasion, María shows her displeasure with Efraín by not
picking him fresh flowers. Efraín is grieved by the absence—"Si hubiese
encontrado enrollada sobre la mesa una víbora, no hubiera yo sentido
emoción igual a la que me ocasionó la ausencia de las flores" (73) [If I
had found a snake coiled up on the table, I would not have felt as much
emotion as that occasioned by the absence of the flowers]. He responds
by throwing away a bunch of wild lilies he had been given on a trip to
the countryside and that he had intended for María, and which she later
reclaims illicitly.

Lilies and roses are two of the most important floral intercessors in
the love affair of María and Efraín. These flowers are not only connected
to love in floriographical terms but, as in *Sab*, are also symbols of the
Virgin Mary—a figure that the heroine of Isaacs's novel is related to not
only through her name but her religious devotion and virginity. In Western art Mary is often pictured alongside lilies and/or roses (see figure 3),
and she has variously been called the Mystic Rose, the Rose of Sharon,
and the Peerless Rose. Roses also lend their name to the rosary, from the
Latin *rosarium* meaning "rose garden."[68] María is twice compared to the
rose of Castille (111, 137), and her coloring is often described as "rosy"
("sonrosado" [53, 142, 281], "sonroseado" [96], "de color de rosa" [76]),
while her skin is likened more than once to white lilies, with the flowers
employed, as in *Sab*, in line with the clichés of popular romance.[69]

FIGURE 3. Francisco de Zurbarán, *The Young Virgin*, ca. 1632–1633. Courtesy of the Metropolitan Museum of Art, New York.

Roses and lilies are often used as symbols of love. When Efraín is about to set off on his fateful journey to Europe, María speaks explicitly of the romantic import of the rose: "'¿Ves este rosal recién sembrado? Si me olvidas, no florecerá; pero si sigues siendo como eres, dará las más lindas rosas'" (240) [Do you see this recently planted rose? If you forget me, it will not blossom; but if you continue as you are, it will bear the most beautiful roses]. María explains that by including wild lilies in her letters (propagated from the branch that featured in their early lovers' quarrel), she could communicate "muchas cosas que algunas veces no deben escribirse" (242) [many things that sometimes one ought not to write]. True to her word, María includes part of the calyx of a lily in her first letter to Efraín, a chaste anatomical choice, since the calyx of a plant has been compared in function to a girdle, supporting and concealing the internal organs of a flower.[70] Nevertheless, in the same epistle her account of the final bunch of flowers she left in Efraín's bedroom—"marchitas ya" [now withered], and of a personified rose bush, clawing at his window "como a buscar[le]" (287) [as if in search (of him)]—is suggestive of her despair at her lover's absence, prefiguring the tragic outcome of the novel. The semantic shift of roses in *María* from tokens of romance to symbols of death anticipates Georges Bataille's commentary on the flower in "The Language of Flowers," where he argues that, despite the rose's metaphorical association with love and prettiness, its interior "does not at all correspond to its exterior beauty; if one tears off all the corolla's petals, all that remains is a rather sordid tuft." For Bataille, the rose becomes a symbol of indecency, perversion, and ultimately death.[71] In the final chapters of *María*, when Efraín revisits the family home, abandoned in the wake of his lover's illness, flowers continue to feature, but now they represent death rather than love. The rose bushes by the waterfall under which the couple used to commune are the site of Efraín's suicidal anguish and "las más bellas flores del jardín" (320) [the most beautiful flowers of the garden], once reserved by María for her lover, have recently been used to festoon her deathbed. When Efraín places a wreath of lilies and roses on her grave, the symbolic remit of these flowers turns full circle from love to death.

María is associated not only with flowers but with the site of their cultivation—the enclosed walled garden of the family home. Like the lily and rose, the walled garden, or *hortus conclusus*, is an important Marian symbol, and as with the lily and rose this imagery originated in the Old Testament in the Song of Solomon: "A garden inclosed *is* my sister, *my* spouse; a spring shut up, a fountain sealed." As Elizabeth A. Augspach explains, it was St. Jerome who first connected the enclosed garden of the Song of Solomon with the Virgin Mary, establishing "a correspondence between the perfect divine garden and the perfect woman not blighted by original sin."[72] María's garden is, on the surface, a symbol of the young woman's chastity, but it is also a pleasure garden, a sensual space rather like Sab's garden for Carlota where the "azahares, albahacas y rosas daban al viento sus delicados aromas" (138) [the delicate scents of orange blossom, basil, and roses were carried in the wind].

Although the garden is largely a female space where María and her sisters grow and pick flowers, it later becomes a key meeting place for the lovers, when the plants are shown to be complicit in concealing them in their intimate colloquies, as when Efraín describes how "un grupo de jazmines nos ocultaba a todas las miradas" (275) [a group of jasmines hid us from sight]. And, despite being enclosed, María's garden is not impregnable. On a number of occasions Efraín scales its walls (124, 139). On the morning after his arrival from Bogotá he spies on María in the garden from his bedroom window while she is picking fresh roses, barefoot and bare shouldered. Efraín describes her response on becoming aware of his attention: "cayó de rodillas para ocultarme sus pies, desatóse del talle el pañolón, y cubriéndose con él los hombros, fingía jugar con las flores" (59) [she fell on her knees to hide her feet, untied the shawl from around her waist and, draping it over her shoulders, pretended to play with the flowers]. This disruption of María's prelapsarian artlessness has echoes of the biblical fall and casts some doubt on the encoding of the garden as an unremitting Eden in the novel.[73]

Indeed, it is not the garden but its uncultivated hinterlands that are explicitly associated with Eden, as when Efraín muses on why he is reminded of María while he is traveling through the wild tropical forests beyond the plantation: "Aquellas soledades, sus bosques silenciosos, sus flores, sus aves y sus aguas, ¿por qué me hablaban de ella? ¿Qué había allí de María? en las sombras húmedas, en la brisa que movía los follajes, en el rumor del río. . . . Era que veía el Edén, pero faltaba ella" (72) [Those solitary places, the silent forests, the flowers, birds and streams, why did they speak to me of her? What was there of María amid the humid shadows, in the breeze that rustled the leaves, in the sound of the river . . . ? It was as if I was looking at Eden, but she was missing]. Here Efraín, however reluctantly, associates María not with a cultivated garden but with the native forests surrounding the family home. Within Christian iconography, as Augspach notes, the metaphorical shift from garden to jungle is equivalent to the move from virgin to whore: "Both garden and woman must be restrained so that neither of them becomes a whore. The garden may do so metaphorically by becoming a forest or jungle. The woman may do so quite literally, by giving herself to someone other than her husband, or, if she is unmarried, to someone other than her father wishes."[74] Since one of the primary characteristics of the jungle is its humidity, it is not inconsequential that the lachrymose heroine of *María* is frequently described in terms relating to moisture.[75] Throughout the novel, María's cheeks, "salpicadas de lágrimas" [bedaubed with tears] are likened to dew-spangled flowers: "eran idénticas a aquellas rosas frescas humedecidas de rocío, que ella recogía para mí por las mañanas" [they were just like those fresh roses wet with dew, that she used to pick for me in the mornings].[76]

María is also frequently associated with wild rather than cultivated flowers, including not only mountain lily, which is so symbolically reso-nant, but "Campanilla morada" (*Ipomoea purpurea* or morning glory, part of the Convolvulaceae family), a purple-blue flower native to tropical America that grows wild on the riverbanks of the forests surrounding the family estates. "Campanilla morada" is included in the first bunch of flowers María picks for Efraín, and the purple-blue color of their blooms is connected to María's clothing when Efraín dreams of her wearing a "falda de muselina vaporosa salpicada de florecillos azules" (58) [gauzy muslin skirt covered with small blue flowers] and, after her death, "un traje blanco vaporoso" [a gauzy white dress] with a "delantal azul" (326) [blue apron]. Elaine Scarry includes the gauziness of flowers as one of four defining characteristics which make them easy to imagine: "The gossamer quality of many flowers (columbine, campanula, foxglove, sweet pea, rose of Sharon), the thinness and transparency of the petals (that lets one see the sunlight through them or see the shape of another overlapping petal coming from behind), gives them a kinship with the filmy substance, the substancelessness, of mental images."[77] The color and the transparency of María's clothes persistently present her as flowerlike, while also revealing Efraín's (at least subconscious) view of her as part of nature rather than culture—as wild and unconstrained as "los montes . . . limpios y *azules*" (285; my emphasis) [the clean and *blue* . . . mountains] by the family home. The Aztecs associated a plant closely related to "Campanilla morada"—*Turbina corymbosa* or *ololiuqui* in Nahuatl, also a species of morning glory—with Macuilxochitl, the god of dancing and sport. Although the hallucinogenic seeds of the plant are popularly known as "seeds of the Virgin" and hence (in name at least) are in line with the Marian symbolism surrounding Isaacs's heroine, the Aztecs notably used them as an aphrodisiac.[78] Latent native plant mythologies here and elsewhere in the novel disrupt the stereotyped depiction of the heroine within the European floriographical tradition and facilitate alternate, feminist readings of *María*.

Despite the predominance of horticulture and agriculture (both prac-tices that transform wild nature into domesticated, productive spaces), the novel is steeped in the Romantic tradition.[79] Chateaubriand's *Atala* and Bernardin de Saint-Pierre's *Paul and Virginia* are important source texts and provide a blueprint for how the lovers should approach tropical nature. Efraín introduces María to Chateaubriand's *The Genius of Christianity* (1802) as part of a program of reading set by his mother, and María is deeply moved by this book, especially the interpolated novella relating the tragic love story of Atala and Chactas.[80] She rejects two didactic anthologies—*Veladas de la Quinta* (Soirees at the country estate) and *Tardes de la Granja* (Evenings on the farm), the very names suggestive of their compatibility with the contained world of the plantations—in favor of *Atala*.[81] Efraín and María decide to read the book in the midst of sublime nature, at the top of a steep hill, from which they are able to see "las corrientes bulliciosas del río, y teniendo a nuestros pies el valle majestuoso y callado" (78) [the turbulent current of the river and, below, the majestic and silent valley], which compounds the impact of the Romantic tract and leaves María upset and darkly anticipating her own death.

Much of the lovers' affair is conducted in the garden of the family home, though even this environment has elements of wildness in it, especially the deep pool by the rose bushes, which Efraín calls an "abismo" (325) [abyss] at the end of the novel when resisting the urge to commit suicide. This moment directly recalls the struggle of Goethe's eponymous protagonist in *The Sorrows of Young Werther*: "Ah, there I stood, arms outstretched, above the abyss, breathing: plunge! plunge!"[82] Likewise, the importance of flowers to their courtship follows the example of other Romantic or proto-Romantic lovers, such as Adam and Eve in Milton's *Paradise Lost* who, as Chateaubriand recalls in *The Genius of Christianity*, lie down together on a bed of flowers or Paul and Virginia who exchange bouquets as symbols of their love.[83] The aesthetics of *María* are firmly Romantic, borne out by María's destiny. As a Romantic heroine she must die, as her reading of Chateaubriand (by way of the Bible) reminds her: "She hath passed away like the grass of the field: this morning we beheld her in all her graceful bloom; this evening her charms are withered."[84] In the same way, nature in the novel tends to wildness—botanical recalcitrance that works against not only Efraín, as he desperately travels back from Europe to the Cauca valley when María is on her deathbed, but also the orderliness of plantation agriculture itself.

María's associations with the humid jungle or wildflowers such as the wild lily or morning glory are part of a widespread floral counterdiscourse that disturbs the narrator's (at least professed) view of the heroine as pure and contained, as well as the primacy of European floriographical discourse. By drawing more consistently on native plant imagery, as well as native imaginaries of people as coextensive with vegetal life, *María* confirms the importance of plants to the formation of Spanish American poetics in the nineteenth century. By disturbing the dichotomy of jungle/garden, *María* casts doubt on the robustness of other symbolic oppositions—sexuality/chastity, black/white, and civilization/barbarism, supporting Sommer's observation that the behavior of Isaacs's heroine often slips "into the 'barbarity' of uncontrolled femaleness."[85] Floriographical motifs such as the lily support the characterization of María as chaste, but other floral emblems point in a different direction, highlighting María's connections to impure sexuality. As in *Sab*, the semantic stability of European floriographical motifs is shaken in this postcolonial novel, as are idealized models of femininity and of nature.

In his essay on flowers, Bataille reminds us that smell is an important aphrodisiac aspect of plants. In *María*, olfactory and erotic pleasures often coalesce, not least in Efraín's daily baths, which are strewn by María with sweet-smelling flowers and likened by the narrator to "un baño oriental" (60) [an oriental bath], with its connotations of steamy sexuality.[86] Later in the novel María's rival, the sultry Salomé, Custodio's daughter, also adds flowers to Efraín's bath—not the cultivated flowers of María's garden but wild tropical blooms—when he joins her family for lunch. She gives him a perfumed towel as part of her efforts to seduce him:

Y dándome a oler la sábana que llevaba colgada en un hombro, añadió:

—¿Qué olor tiene?

—El tuyo

—A malvas, señor. (262)

[And letting me smell the towel that she carried over her shoulder, she added:

"What does it smell of?"

"You"

"Of mallow, sir."]

Although the variety of mallow is not specified, its strong smell suggests it is musk mallow, *Abelmoschus moschatus*, a tropical plant from the Malvaceae family that is known for the aphrodisiac qualities of its scent.[87] Diane Ackerman notes that a "flower's fragrance declares to all the world that it is fertile, available, and desirable, its sex organs oozing with nectar. Its smell reminds us in vestigial ways of fertility, vigor, life force, all the optimism, expectancy, and passionate bloom of youth."[88] In the same way, the scented flowers picked by María are explicitly tied to sex and are interpreted by Efraín as a substitute for the body of his beloved, as when he relates how, on finding fresh flowers in his room: "las ajé con mis besos; quise aspirar de una vez todos sus aromas, buscando en ellos los de los vestidos de María" (64) [I crushed them with my kisses; I wanted to draw in all their aromas at once, seeking in them the smell of María's clothes]. Later he describes how the fragrance of flowers "había llegado a ser algo del espíritu de María que . . . se mecía en las cortinas de mi lecho durante la noche" (73) [had become part of the spirit of María that . . . wafted through my bed curtains at night].

One of the scents that María is persistently associated with is basil. After her death Efraín has a dream in which her hair smells of the herb (327), and earlier, she fans herself with a branch of the plant (244). Such associations may well derive from the fifth tale on the fourth day of

Boccaccio's *The Decameron*, in which basil plays a central role in the tragic love affair of Lisabetta and Lorenzo. In this tale, after the heroine's brothers murder her lover, Lisabetta digs him up and plants his head in a pot of basil, which she waters with her own tears.[89] John Keats later retold this in his narrative poem "Isabella; or, The Pot of Basil" (1818), and just a year after the publication of *María*, the English Pre-Raphaelite artist William Holman Hunt completed a painting on the same subject while in mourning for his own wife who had died just two years before. Basil can be seen to betoken death and failed love in *María*, as well as, potentially, madness, given the popular belief developed in the Middle Ages that, if smelled, pounded basil left under a stone or pot could cause a scorpion to develop in the brain.[90] Plants and flowers are not without their dangers in *María*, as Efraín reminds his cousin early in the novel when he responds to the first bouquet she leaves for him by rather ungallantly informing her of the latest medical thinking about the dangers of having flowers in the bedroom overnight: "son nocivas en la pieza donde se duerme" (57) [they are dangerous in the room where you sleep].

Besides the virginal rose and lily, morning glory, and aromatic basil, carnations are another important symbolic plant. During Efraín's first evening at home, María wears a carnation in her hair, and carnations are included in the first bouquet she picks for her cousin. Later Efraín surprises her when she is arranging flowers in the garden, holding a carnation between her lips:

> —Buenos días, María—le dije apresurándome a recibirle las flores.
>
> Ella, palideciendo instantáneamente, correspondió cortada al saludo, y el clavel se le desprendió de la boca. Entregóme las flores, dejando caer algunas a los pies, las cuales recogió y puso a mi alcance cuando sus mejillas estaban nuevamente sonroseadas.
>
> —¿Quieres—le dije al recibir las últimas—cambiarme todas éstas por el clavel que tenías en los labios?
>
> —Lo he pisado—respondió bajando la cabeza para buscarlo.

—Así pisado, te daré todas éstas por él.

Permanecía en la misma actitud sin responderme.

—¿Permites que vaya yo a recogerlo?

Se inclinó entonces para tomarlo y me lo entregó sin mirarme. (96)[91]

Here the carnation acts for Efraín as a sexual go-between, rather like the cup in Ovid's *Art of Love*: "Whene'er she drinks, be first to take the cup, / And where she laid her lips, the blessing sup."[92]

Carnations carry many different meanings in both religious and secular domains, but they are especially associated with love, femininity, sexuality, and forthcoming marriage.[93] In Shakespeare's *Romeo and Juliet* the carnation, or pink, is the source of a sexual pun between Romeo and his cousin when Mercutio describes himself as a courteous "pink," to which Romeo responds by boasting that his "pump is well flowered," linking, according to Holly Dugan, the "carnation's color to female genitalia and the tactility of 'pinking' or perforating something to the physical act of sex."[94] Freud also discusses the significance of the carnation in connection to the dream of a young woman who, like María, is on the cusp of marriage. Freud muses on the meaning attached to carnations, which in the dream are included in a centerpiece alongside violets and lilies of the valley:

> In connection with *"pinks,"* which she went on to call *"carnations,"* I thought of the connection between that word and "carnal." But the dreamer's association to it was *"colour."* She added that *"carnations"* were the flowers which her *fiancé* gave her frequently and in great numbers. At the end of her remarks she suddenly confessed of her own accord that she had not told the truth: what had occurred to her had not been *"colour"* but *"incarnation"*—the word I had expected. Incidentally, *"colour"* itself was not a very remote association, but was determined by the meaning of *"carnation"* (flesh-colour). .... The dreamer's comment to the effect that her *fiancé* frequently gave her flowers of that kind was an indication not

only of the double sense of the word "*carnations*" but also of their phallic meaning in the dream.[95]

According to Freud, the genitals are often symbolized by flowers, "the sexual organs of plants": "It may perhaps be true in general that gifts of flowers between lovers have this unconscious meaning."[96] Links between human and plant sexuality have long been established in botanical texts. Botanical treatises on plant reproduction in the late seventeenth and early eighteenth centuries, for instance, led to a popularization of discourses of plant sexuality and even "phytoerotica"—ribald literary texts that drew on plant physiology as a substitute for human genitalia.[97] The carnal connotations of the name "carnation" are absent in the Castilian "clavel," which derives, via Latin, from the Catalan for "clove" (which smells similar to the flower), but the fleshy overtones are preserved through its combination with the epithet "encarnado" (56) [incarnate].[98] In the conversation between María and Efraín, the carnation has clear erotic overtones, invoking the female sexual organs—the flowerlike genitalia—as well as the penis by way of the phallic description of the stem between María's lips. This particular carnation has been trampled underfoot; just as when María wears a "clavel marchito" (64) [withered carnation] in her hair earlier in the novel, the destroyed bloom here is suggestive of the loss of female chastity, with María literally and metaphorically "deflowered."

One of the primary indicators of María's sexuality is her increasingly unkempt hair, which is also firmly connected to horticultural motifs. Efraín refers to María's hair frequently, almost obsessively: he includes references to its color (which shifts from dark brown to black) and the way in which it is styled (normally in braids or ringlets [59, 64, 77, 132, 240]).[99] Like flowers, hair takes on a symbolic role as part of the lovers' amorous exchanges. Before Efraín departs for England, they cut off locks of hair for one another, and when María dies she makes sure that Efraín's hair is returned to him in a locket also containing the locks of her late mother. In addition, she insists that her braids are posthumously given to Efraín. When her lover first sees them, he is shocked by the braids' uncanny qualities: "Un grito se escapó de mi pecho, y una sombra me cubrió los ojos al desenrollarse entre mis manos aquellas trenzas que parecían sensibles a mis besos" (325) [A cry escaped me, and a shadow covered my eyes as those braids that seemed to feel my kisses unrolled in my hands]. As Carol de Dobay Rifelj notes: "Severed hair is a part of the body that retains its appearance—texture, shape, and color—after death or after being cut from the living body. The hair is dead, yet it has powerful iconic force."[100]

Superstitions surrounding the hair of the dead can be related to a number of cultural traditions that regard hair as a vital vegetal force. The Greek physician Galen argued that the growth of human hair, as of plants, was regulated by moisture levels—an idea that was reinvoked by medical writers in the early modern period.[101] Efraín's sense that María's hair was somehow living also recalls the concept of the "Vegetative soul," which in Aristotle's tripartite division of the soul denoted the most basic physical functions, attributed to plants as well as animals and humans, such as growth and reproduction. As Edward J. Geisweidt explains, the concept of the Vegetative soul often focused on the way in which hair could—apparently—continue to grow after death, as in the following seventeenth-century anatomy book:

> Hair is form'd and stirr'd up, being endu'd with a particular Soul and Life distinct from the rest of the Parts . . . ; Now that they live by virtue of another peculiar Vegetable Soul, that has no Communion with the other animated Parts of the Body, is apparent from hence: for that they do live only while a man is alive, but after his Decease, are nourish'd and encreas'd, after the same manner as *Polypody-Moss*, &c. grow upon old Trees, both before and after the Tree dies; because they have each a proper Soul, distinct from the Form and Soul of the Tree, out of which, and wherein they grow.[102]

If the comparison of hair to plants relies, as Geisweidt notes, on Aristotle's distinction between animal and plant life, "[i]nsofar as hair was thought to be constituted by a vegetable soul," it also challenges the clarity of such distinctions. As Garrett A. Sullivan Jr. notes, the concept of the tripartite soul "both explains man's difference from animal and plant and articulates ontological connections among all three"—ontological fluidity that characterizes, in particular, non-European conceptions of vegetal life.[103]

The vital qualities that Efraín ascribes to María's hair can be explained not solely through recourse to the European philosophical and literary tradition in which Isaacs's novel is grounded, then, but also through indigenous American views of plant life. Viveiros de Castro has used the term "multinaturalism" to describe indigenous American beliefs in a "metaphysical continuity" between humans and all living things, including animals and plants.[104] For the Aztecs, the hair of Tlaltecuhtli, an earth deity, was often depicted as grass, establishing the figure's fertility and regenerative powers.[105] The insistent allusions to the vegetative soul in the dead María's hair serve only, in the end, to undermine Aristotle's ideas of a secure division between people and plants and to reorient the novel toward indigenous American beliefs in the continuities between human and plant anatomy. María's association with flora is conveyed not only through the European floriographical tradition—descriptions of her rosy red cheeks or lily-white skin—but a persistent "plantification" of her hair.

In the course of the novel María's at first neat tresses become wilder. Within the Judaeo-Christian tradition, hair has often been associated with sex and sin, and frequently concealed by women. As Galia Ofek affirms, this view continued into the nineteenth century when many "treated unkempt or disheveled hair as a sign of unbridled libidinal drives."[106] For the Aztecs too, the orderliness of Tlaltecuhtli's grassy locks denote the figure's positive centering influence, and depictions of her hair as untidy or entangled with insects suggest "impurity and pollution," as well as death.[107] While María's braids conform to nine-teenth-century plantation society's predilection for tightly controlled tresses, her passion for Efraín is represented by her hair hanging loose. In chapter 34, for example, Efraín returns from a trip with his father to discover María not engaged in her usual "womanly" pursuits of gar-dening or sewing but on top of a high boulder, taking in the view of the valley below. Slightly taken aback by her unconventional behavior, Efraín describes her wild appearance, including her hair, which "suelta en largos y lucientes rizos, negreaba sobre la muselina de su traje color verde-mortiño" (179) [fell in long, shining curls, black against the muslin of her *mortiño*-green dress]. Here María is doubly plantlike, with her flowing locks and the green dress, likened to the color of "mortiño" or *Vaccinium meridionale*, a fruit-bearing shrub that grows wild in Colombia. Her black hair anticipates the black bird of ill omen that first appears just a few pages later, and which at key moments in the novel prefigures the family's misfortunes.[108] In this episode, as elsewhere, María's hair is charged with sexuality and suggests disorder and rebellion. When Efraín and María meet in the garden shortly before he departs for England, he notes how her hair is "destrenzada hasta el suelo" (241) [falling to the ground unbraided]. Later, when she is verging on death and distraught at her lover's absence, "los bucles desordenados de la cabellera casi le ocultaban el rostro" (319) [her disordered curls almost hid her face].

María's wild hair points to her burgeoning sexuality and often coin-cides with her epileptic fits, as when Efraín describes the aftermath of his cousin's first seizure: "Estaba como dormida; su rostro, cubierto de palidez mortal, se veía medio oculto por la cabellera descompuesta, en la cual descubrían estrujadas las flores que yo le había dado en la mañana" (80) [She seemed like she was sleeping; her face, wearing a deadly pallor, was half covered by her disheveled hair, in which could be seen the flow-ers, now crushed, that I had given her in the morning]. Discounting her deathly pale complexion, María's disheveled hair strikes a certain postcoital pose and for nineteenth-century readers would have evoked a constellation of associations between epilepsy and aberrant sexual behavior. Galen compared epileptic fits to the spasms of orgasm, and in the eighteenth century many believed that libidinal excess, including masturbation, were causes of the disease.[109] Up to the early twentieth century, as Jeannette Stirling explains, doctors believed that epilepsy had a "disinhibiting effect on the libido and those sexual drives normally held in check by socialisation and the conventions of propriety."[110] Efraín's parents at first discourage the love affair between María and their son precisely because they fear María's passion will exacerbate her epilepsy.[111] María eventually succumbs to the opposite affliction: unable to bear the four-year wait for the consummation of their marriage, María dies of her condition before Efraín is able to return. As she is laid out in her coffin, her hair is once again suitably coiffed, with her braids wrapped under a headdress of white gauze—a picture of purity and containment that contrasts with the wild-haired heroine just before her death.[112] Hair not only encodes a struggle between female control and female sexuality but, by consolidating María's oneness with plants, suggests the erosion of ontological categories such as human/nonhuman and self/other.

As in *Sab*, floriographical motifs are ambivalent in *María*. Despite the heroine's association with the temperate rose and the *hortus conclusus* (both potent symbols of female chastity and containment), by the end of the novel, European floriographical motifs have been resemanticized and many of the flowers bound up with a discourse of disease, death, and transgressive sexuality. Domesticated vegetal loci such as the garden or plantation also accede to wilder tropical spaces such as the forests Efraín traverses in his attempt to reach María before she dies. In London Efraín is filled with longing for his native "montañas americanas" (286) [American mountains], yet it is this American nature that works against him on his journey home—the mosquitoes, snakes, vampire bats, waterfalls, and dense vegetation that slow him down and propel the novel to its tragic dénouement.[113] Far from the beautiful gardens of the family home, María's final resting place is in a rural cemetery bordering the jungle.

The graveyard is fringed by thorny brambles and tangled branches, and María's gravestone is surrounded by grass, overgrown trees, and opium poppies, a flower commonly associated with death.[114] From the start imbricated in the language of flowers, at the end of the novel María has left behind the temperate gardens of the family plantation and become one with the wild plants of this tropical dell.

After her passing, her garden has also been transfigured, since, although still tended, it is now in the hands of Tránsito and Braulio, local smallholders and friends of the family who, unlike the nonproductive union of María and Efraín, have borne "fruto" (325) [fruit] in the form of a beautiful six-month-old baby. Ileana Rodríguez has noted how the leitmotif of the "garden-gone-bush" is related to nationhood in Latin America: "when a garden goes wild, bush, this image . . . also stands for maroonage, for guerrilla warfare under colonialism, and therefore as metaphor for liberation, self-determination, and national formation."[115] Although María's garden has not yet turned wild, on his final walk around it Efraín considers how it might change now that the family estate has been left empty, adopting the favored Romantic trope of anthropomorphism: "Frondosos naranjos, gentiles y verdes sauces que conmigo crecisteis, ¡cómo os habréis envejecido! Rosas y azucenas de María ¿quién las amará si existen? Aromas del lozano huerto, no volveré a aspiraros" (326) [Leafy orange trees, gentle and green willows that grew up alongside me. How you will have aged! María's roses and lilies. Who will love them if they exist? Fragrances of the luxuriant garden, I will not smell you again]. The image of the garden gone wild becomes a metaphor not only for the heroine's transcendence of sexual or even ontological restraints but also for the wider changes to take place in Colombia in the coming years, including a series of devastating civil wars, the abolition of slavery, the waning of plantation culture, and as Erika Beckman notes, the country's incorporation into expanding global markets. Ana María Mutis and Elizabeth Pettinaroli note that at the moment Isaacs was writing *María*, Colombia was undergoing "tremendous economic and industrial development," which they relate to "nascent ecological pre-occupation."[116] María's death is one of many endings in the novel, most significantly that of a social order underpinned by slavery. The beautiful garden with its scented flowers and venerable trees will, in time, become for Efraín, like María, simply a memory.[117] The poetics of plants encode in *María* not only the heroine's burgeoning and ultimately fatal sexuality but the decline of plantation culture itself.

These readings of the novels show that Avellaneda and Isaacs were fully aware of the limitations of the floriographical tradition in a Spanish American context. Both novelists engaged with the "Language of Flowers" critically in order to disturb clichés of female beauty or delicacy and to allow for counterdiscursive readings of their works, where marginal social figures such as slaves or women are able to adopt positions and personalities otherwise denied to them. Through the introduction of native flora such as the hallowed ceiba or the wild lily, the European tradition of floriography is also subtly adjusted to fit local conditions.

Another important feature of these nineteenth-century Spanish American literary engagements with plants is the continuation of an animistic discourse surrounding trees and flowers, already discernible in Landívar's and Bello's agricultural poems. Comparisons between people and plants in much Spanish American literature draw on indigenous understandings of the ontological slipperiness between humans and nonhumans and advocate a way of engaging with nature that is respectful and nonexploitative, in stark opposition to the capitalist ideology underpinning plantation culture. The fact that the eponymous protagonists of both *Sab* and *María* are associated most often with tropical plants and environments reveals the authors' recognition of a misalignment between the aims of the European floriographic tradition and a Latin American genre concerned with the establishment of local culture and forms.

One of the significant features of European floriography that both novels continue to embrace, however, is its "flowery" aesthetic—a romantic overblown style that twentieth- and twenty-first-century readers of *Sab* and *María* have tended to regard with some suspicion. If Avellaneda and Isaacs refused the wholesale mapping of European plant meanings onto a Latin American context, they enthusiastically adopted flower imagery to produce a (literally) florid and extravagantly sentimental prose style. Such a style became, in the twentieth century, one characteristic of the New World baroque. The incipient "baroqueness" of *Sab* and *María* demonstrates that a recourse to flowers not only facilitated a critique of female subjugation and/or slavery in the plantation romance but also introduced an aesthetic breach between an inherited European literary tradition and an emergent Spanish American form. Plants became an important source of literary as well as political contestation in these works, a means of disrupting the status quo but also of asserting cultural and literary difference.

CHAPTER 3

"NACIDO DE ÁRBOLES"

Carpentier's Vegetal Baroque

Nuestro arte siempre fue barroco: desde la espléndida escultura preco-
lombina y el de los códices, hasta la mejor novelística actual de América,
pasándose por las catedrales y monasterios coloniales de nuestro conti-
nente. . . . No temamos, pues, el barroquismo en el estilo, en la visión de los
contextos, en la visión de la figura humana enlazada por las enredaderas
del verbo y de lo ctónico, metida en el increíble concierto angélico de
cierta capilla (blanco, oro, vegetación, revesados, contrapuntos inauditos,
derrota de lo pitagórico) que puede verse en Puebla de México, o de un
desconcertante, enigmático árbol de la vida, florecido de imágenes y de
símbolos, en Oaxaca. No temamos el barroquismo, arte nuestro, nacido
de árboles, de leños, de retablos y altares.[1]

Alejo Carpentier's "Problemática de la actual novela latinoamericana" ("Questions concerning the Contemporary Latin American
Novel"), which contains this central statement of the New World
baroque, both performs and articulates some of the predominant features

of the style for the twentieth-century Spanish American writer, including its abstruseness, its prolixity, its love of lists, and its *horror vacui.*[2] The baroque was a European phenomenon that originated in the seventeenth century as a Catholic response to the Reformation and was readily exported to the New World. Yet even in its earliest days the American baroque differed from its European sources. This distance between the Old and New World baroque intensified in the twentieth century when Carpentier and other postwar Spanish American intellectuals such as José Lezama Lima and Severo Sarduy adopted the form as a "postcolonial strategy," transforming it into a means of "cultural recuperation and revitalization."[3] Eugenio d'Ors espoused this view in his influential work *Lo barroco* (The baroque), in a section that Carpentier highlighted in his personal copy: "el estilo Barroco puede renacer y traducir la misma inspiración en formas nuevas, sin necesidad de copiarse sí mismo servilmente" [The baroque style can revive and translate the same inspiration in new forms, without the need to copy itself servilely].[4] Carpentier's baroque transcends the ideological limitations of the seventeenth-century form and draws on its inherent aesthetic modernity, a fact made clear by the author's aligning the folk baroque of colonial Mexico with the mid-twentieth century Latin American novel.[5]

In "Problemática," Carpentier traces his baroque style back not only to the syncretic religious art of the early colonial period and the pre-Columbian codices but also to American flora. The baroque, he says, is "arte nuestro, nacido de árboles" ["our art, born from trees"].[6] The quotation above is itself replete with botanical references: Carpentier describes a human figure wrapped in vines and his examples from Mexican colonial art focus on vegetal-inspired motifs. The word "florecido," which Carpentier uses to describe the ornate symbolism of the Tree of Life design on the ceiling of the Iglesia de Santo Domingo in Oaxaca, is derived from the Latin *floreo* (to flower) and shares the same etymology as *florido*, florid, an epithet frequently applied to baroque art, which in Spanish signifies not only "having flowers" but also an elaborate language or style.[7] The church in Oaxaca is expounded upon in the essay "Lo barroco y lo real maravilloso" ("The Baroque and the Marvelous Real"), exemplifying Carpentier's fascination with the intertwining of the human and the vegetal that characterizes much of his baroque imaginings. In this essay he describes the ornamentation in the church as "un gran árbol que se expande y con cuyas ramas se entremezclan figuras de ángeles, de santos, figuras humanas, figuras de mujeres, confundidas con la vegetación" ["a great, expanding tree whose branches are entwined with figures of angels, saints, human figures, figures of women, all blending into the vegetation"].[8] Carpentier's baroque is concerned with what, in his celebrated prologue to *El reino de este mundo* (*The Kingdom of This World*), he calls the "desenfrenada creación de formas de nuestra naturaleza" ["the unbridled creativity of our natural forms"], the slippery morphology between things—between plants and animate and inanimate objects, in particular—that dominates art in tropical America, from the indigenous sculptures in colonial churches to the paintings of the Afro-Cuban artist Wifredo Lam.[9]

Few commentators have noted the vegetal underpinnings of Carpentier's writings or discussed connections between baroque aesthetics and the botanical motifs that often abound in baroque art.[10] In their discussions of the baroque, including of Carpentier's baroque writings, however, many critics have had recourse to botanical analogies. In d'Ors's *Lo barroco*, a book Carpentier owned and annotated extensively, the Catalan art critic parodies the Linnaean system of binomial nomenclature in his adoption of a table of baroque stylistics, "A estilo del vocabulario de los botánicos" [In the style of a botanical lexicon], headed with the genus "Barocchus" and including such "species" as "*Bar. vulgarus*" and "*Bar. officinalis*."[11] Pál Kelemen, who wrote an important account of baroque art in Latin America which Carpentier was probably influenced by, also draws on botanical language when he compares the hybrid qualities of the Latin American baroque to a tulip bulb replanted in a new horticultural context.[12] Carpentier's near contemporary Lezama Lima likewise defined the baroque as a style that is "arraigadísimo" ["firmly rooted"] in Spanish America, and Julio Cortázar, reflecting in turn on the work of Lezama Lima, spoke of the "complejas raíces" ["complex roots"] of the baroque.[13] Indeed, with specific reference to Carpentier, an influential early account of the boom generation appeals to a gardening metaphor in its unfavorable account of his baroque prose: "a veces no es más que un elegante jardinero, sofocado por sus flores" [at times he is nothing more than an accomplished gardener, suffocated by his flowers]. More recently, Gonzalo Celorio has characterized the New World baroque as a form that privileges "las ramas sobre el tronco" [the branches over the trunk].[14]

All these writers and critics, without quite realizing it, have identified the significant continuities between the New World baroque—its hybridity and excessive ornamentation—and vegetal life. Plants were central to Carpentier's conception of the New World baroque—fundamental not only to the imagery of his fictional and theoretical writings but to the formulation of concepts such as hybridity, metamorphosis, and the marvelous real.

ARBOREAL ARCHITECTURES

Although often celebrated for his evocations of nature—the jungles of *Los pasos perdidos* (*The Lost Steps*) or Caribbean beaches in *El siglo de las luces* (*Explosion in a Cathedral*)—Carpentier was, in his later years in particular, a writer of cities.[15] His interest in architecture is well-known. His father, Jorge Julián Carpentier, was an architect, and Alejo had trained briefly at the School of Architecture at the University of Havana before the breakdown of his parents' marriage caused him to abandon his studies and pursue a job as a journalist.[16] His interest in buildings, and in their erection and demolition in particular, is evident across his work, from his account of the construction of the Citadelle Laferrière in *El reino de este mundo* to his persistent appeal to the image of collapsing pillars in a painting by François de Nomé, which acts as a leitmotif throughout *El siglo de las luces*. Alexis Márquez Rodríguez has even pointed to Carpentier's architectural training in a discussion of the novelist's stylistics: "Hay en la sintaxis carpenteriana una monumentalidad arquitectónica que es un rasgo eminentemente barroco" [There is in Carpentier's syntax an architectural monumentality that is an eminently baroque trait].[17]

For Carpentier, architecture is one of the best instantiations of the New World baroque.[18] Not only are many of the buildings he includes in his fictional and nonfictional writings baroque per se, but many also exemplify baroque characteristics such as the trope of *engaño* or deceit, when what seem to be man-made structures turn out to be natural forms and vice versa—a trope that further destabilizes the human/nonhuman binary in the author's work.[19] Carpentier also consistently establishes the combined importance of architecture and plants for the New World baroque. In his essay "Lo barroco y lo real maravilloso" he states: "Nuestro mundo es barroco por la arquitectura—eso no hay ni que demostrarlo—, por el enrevesamiento y la complejidad de su naturaleza y su vegetación, por la policromía de cuanto nos circunda, por la pulsión telúrica de los fenómenos a que estamos todavía sometidos."[20]

Although, as Carpentier himself concedes, Cuba is not a match for some other Latin American countries in terms of grand baroque buildings, Havana is central to his formulation of the vegetal baroque, and the city's buildings and monuments—raised, as Steve Wakefield notes, "to the level of protagonistic significance" in a number of his fictions—provide fruitful examples of the coalescence between plants and the built environment.[21] For Carpentier, the baroque surfaces as frequently in modest domestic settings in Havana as it does in grand colonial churches: "Cuba es barroca en sus rejas, sus cristalerías, sus muebles, la vegetación tradicional de sus patios" [Cuba is baroque in its window grilles, its glassware, its furniture, the traditional vegetation of its patios].[22]

His essay "La ciudad de las columnas" ("The City of Columns")—first published in 1964 as part of the collection *Tientos y diferencias* (Gropings and differences) and later alongside a collection of photographs by Paolo

Gasparini (1970)—is a paean to Havana.[23] From the start of the essay, Havana's baroque cityscape is imagined in botanical terms as a living entity, "germinando, creciendo" [lit. germinating, growing] over the years, beyond its original walled limits.[24] In the essay, Carpentier develops his theory of the New World baroque as a process of symbiosis, hybridity, and endless proliferation: "el barroquismo cubano consistió en acumular, coleccionar, multiplicar, columnas y columnatas en tal demasía de dóricos y de corintios, de jónicos y de compuestos, que acabó el transeúnte por olvidar que vivía entre columnas, que era acompañado por columnas, era vigilado por columnas que le medían el tranco y lo protegían del sol y de la lluvia" (Cdlc, 73) ["The Cuban baroque consisted in accumulating, collecting, and multiplying columns and colonnades in such an excess of Doric and Corinthian, Ionic and composite capitals, that they ended up making the pedestrian forget that he lived among columns, that he was accompanied by columns and observed by columns that measured his stride and protected him from (sun) and rain" (CC, 257)].[25]

Columns are an important feature of the baroque proclivity for repetition. Sarduy notes that, in the baroque, "lo que cuenta son las series, el alineamiento obsesivo, la repetición de columnas y molduras" ["What counts are the series, the obsessive alignment, the repetition of columns, moldings"].[26] Carpentier likewise speaks of the baroque as a style in which "núcleos proliferantes" ["proliferating foci"] multiply around a central axis.[27] Carpentier's meandering and repetitive prose both describes and reenacts the pedestrian's walk through the ubiquitous and varied colonnades of Havana—a baroque proliferation of columns that, both in this essay and elsewhere in his fiction, are interspersed with and frequently indistinguishable from their arboreal precursors and doubles.

Carpentier dwells at length upon the intersection between the column and the tree trunk in "La ciudad de las columnas," including in the internal patios of Havana houses, "donde el tronco de palmera . . . convivió con el fuste dórico" (Cdlc, 64) ["where the trunk of the palm tree coexisted with the Doric shaft" (CC, 246)]. Throughout the essay, the author notes how trees and columns provide much-needed shade in the city and also have a striking physical resemblance. The proliferation of columns in Havana are figured as a "selva" (Cdlc, 64) ["jungle" (CC, 247)] and the columns themselves are likened to "troncos de selvas posibles" (Cdlc, 73) ["tree trunks of imagined jungles" (CC, 258)].[28]

The relationship between the tree and the column is also fundamental to Carpentier's 1955 novella *El acoso* (*The Chase*), a fictional antecedent to "La ciudad de las columnas." The story of the final days of a revolutionary (who, in an autobiographical flourish, is also an architect) on the run in 1930s Cuba, the novella presents trees and columns as interchangeable, acting as a source of cover for the young protagonist as he makes his way on foot through the city: "De sombra en sombra alcanzó el término de los árboles, pasando al mundo de las columnas" ["from shadow to shadow, he reached the end of the trees and passed into the world of columns"].[29] Later, shortly before his death, the revolutionary takes refuge in a church and, in an attempt to conceal himself as he approaches the altar, moves "de pilar a pilar—como antes hubiera andado de un árbol a otro árbol" ["from pillar to pillar—as before he'd gone from tree to tree"].[30]

The arboreal origins of the pillar have been studied primarily in relation to classical architecture. Dainis Dauksta describes the classical column as "a metaphor made concrete, its tapered form recalling the stem of a tree."[31] The columns of the first Greek temples were, in fact, made from wood, so any wooden temple column, as George Hersey argues, could in a sense be regarded as a sacred tree or tree trunk.[32] Carpentier's knowledge of and interest in the history and design of columns can be seen in a number of books in his personal library, which included a Spanish edition of Frazer's *The Golden Bough* as well as an array of illustrated works on ecclesiastical architecture (on Westminster Abbey, Paris's Saint-Alexandre-Nevsky, Notre Dame Cathedral, and Barcelona Cathedral among others).[33] Carpentier also owned a French edition of Roger Cook's beautifully illustrated esoteric art book *The Tree of Life*, in which the Cuban author turned down a page marking a section on the "Tree of Fertility," which includes an account of the ancient Egyptian myth of Osiris and Isis and a corresponding sketch of the Djed Pillar.[34] According to Plutarch's rendering of this tale, the Djed Pillar formed when a tree grew around a chest containing the body of the slain Osiris and was later used to hold up the roof of a palace.[35]

Carpentier also approached the question of the telluric underpinnings of the column via modern art and literature, particularly cubism and surrealism.[36] "La ciudad de las columnas" ends with a partial quote from the poem "Correspondances" from Charles Baudelaire's *Les Fleurs du mal*, widely acknowledged as an important precursor of the surrealist movement: *"temple où de vivants piliers / laissaient entendre parfois de confuses paroles"* (Cdlc, 73; Carpentier's italics).[37] In a section not quoted in Carpentier's essay, these lines go on to speak of "forêts de symbols"—an explicit reflection on the intersection between nature and architecture, which was a common theme in early twentieth-century avant-garde movements.[38] Spyros Papapetros, who has written on the organicism of twentieth-century art and architecture, draws attention to the miniature columnar structures in Fernand Léger's 1910 Cubist painting *Nudes in the Forest*, for instance, which he connects to other "arboreal monuments" in fin-de-siècle art.[39] The increasingly abstract tree series (1908–1913) of Piet Mondrian, an artist with whom Carpentier was familiar, also shows a marked interest in the coalescence of trees with the built form.[40]

One way in which architects inscribe remembrance of the arboreal origins of the pillar is by adding vegetal embellishments such as fluting to represent bark and foliation such as acanthus leaves on capitals.[41] For Carpentier, such embellishments instantiate the baroque by blurring the line between living plant and nonliving object: "Lo barroco existe cuando el retablo de iglesia se puebla de tantas yedras y guirnaldas, de tantas flores y festones, que la madera, lo labrado y dorado, adquiere una nueva existencia vegetal" ["The Baroque exists when the church reredos is so covered with ivy and garlands, and with so many flowers and wreaths,

that the wood, worked and golden, acquires a new vegetal existence"].[42]
In "La ciudad de las columnas" Carpentier notes the preponderance of
botanical motifs in the domestic architecture of the Havana suburbs,
including in the decorative window grille, "enrevesada, casi vegetal por
la abundancia y los enredos de sus cintas de metal, con dibujos de liras,
de flores" (Cdlc, 66) ["with its profusion of metal ribbons entangled like
vegetation, ensnaring figures of lyres, flowers" (CC, 249)]. Carpentier's
own house in the Vedado district of Havana boasts just such vegetal
embellishments on its window grilles as well as plaster festoons of flowers, foliate Doric columns, and voluted consoles flanking its grand front
steps (see figure 4). The photographs accompanying the 1970 edition of
La ciudad de las columnas that Gasparini worked on, alongside Carpentier, accentuate the interplay between plants and architecture through
an excess of floral grilles, foliate capitals, and transom windows with
bold silhouettes of flowers and leaves. In one double-page photograph
of a particularly ornate façade—partially hidden behind a wall covered
with an undulating vegetal rinceau design and flanked by Corinthian
columns clad with acanthus leaves—the conjoining of the vegetal and
architectural is heightened by the intrusion of the branches of an actual
tree in the upper right-hand corner.[43] Such a photograph, in which neoclassical architecture encounters tropical nature, reminds the reader of
Carpentier's arresting description of the buildings of Havana in the same
essay: "ágora entre manglares, plaza entre malezas" (Cdlc, 63) ["an agora
among mangroves, a plaza in the underbrush" (*CC*, 246)]. Carpentier's
baroque architectures are only ever one step away from their botanical
forerunners.

Buildings in Carpentier's fiction easily revert to nature, compounding
the sense of ontological instability between living plants and material
culture. In the short story "Viaje a la semilla" ("Journey Back to the
Source")—which, in line with Carpentier's view of time as nonlinear
and malleable, relates a life in reverse from the demolition of a house to
the death, illness, manhood, childhood, and birth of its final owner, Don

FIGURE 4. A volute by the steps leading up to Alejo Carpentier's Vedado home. Photo by the author.

Marcial. The proclivity of architectural forms to regress to their natural states is also foregrounded. Consistent with the narrative's reverse chronology, the botanical underpinnings of buildings are reanimated in the description of masonry on the wasteland where the house once stood: "varios capiteles yacían entre las hierbas. Las hojas de acanto descubrían su condición vegetal. Una enredadera aventuró sus tentáculos hacia la voluta jónica, atraída por un aire de familia. Cuando cayó la noche, la casa estaba más cerca de la tierra" ["Several capitals lay in the grass, their acanthus leaves asserting their vegetable status. A creeper stretched adventurous tendrils toward an Ionic scroll (volute), attracted by its air of kinship. When night fell, the house was closer to the ground"].[44] Here the

FIGURE 5. The volute shape of an unfurling fern. Photo by the author.

acanthus decoration, widely used on Greek and Roman pillars, intermingles with the surrounding foliage, and the volute, a scroll often included in the capital of columns (identified elsewhere by Carpentier as a key component of baroque decoration), attracts a creeper, which detects a resemblance between itself and the spiral form.[45] Although in architectural history there is uncertainty about the source of the volute, it has been suggested that it derives from the shape of the ovule of a common species of Greek clover and has also been compared to the unfurling of fern fronds (see figure 5).[46] In *El siglo de las luces* the botanical origins of the volutes adorning the iron window grilles are so self-evident as to render them "claras vegetaciones de hierro prendidas de las ventanas" ["more like iron vegetation twining around the windows"].[47]

Later in the novel, in a reversal of this imagery, the narrator observes how the flowers and plants in the house's patio "parecían de metal" ["might have been made of metal"], taking on "una pesadez de hierro forjado" (*SL*, 57) ["the heavy look of wrought iron" (*EC*, 53)]. Here Carpentier marks the radical interchangeability of plants and architecture: buildings mimic natural forms, but plants and trees also resemble the built environment. During the significant narrative sequence in *El siglo de las luces* when the protagonist Esteban climbs a tree, the narrator figures the jungle canopy in stark architectural terms, referring, for instance to the "suntuoso sotechado" (*SL*, 174) ["sumptuous roof" (*EC*, 161)]. And in Carpentier's autobiographical account of a trip to the Venezuelan interior, "Visión de América" (Vision of America), he compares tree trunks to marble and describes them as "más obeliscos que árboles" [more obelisks than trees].[48] This image is reinvoked in *Los pasos perdidos* when the narrator glimpses tree trunks "de antiquísimas selvas muertas, blanquecidos, más mármol que madera . . . como los obeliscos cimeros de una ciudad abismada" (*PP*, 167) ["of the ancient dead forest, whitened until they seemed more marble than wood, . . . like the towering obelisks of a drowned city" (*LS*, 164)]. The mineral-like appearance of these tree trunks—the opposite of dendritic crystallization, where the fractal growth of crystals takes on an arboreal shape—is presented as a process of petrification, further detailed for the reader in a passage that explicitly draws a comparison between trees and architecture: "Las maderas le encanecían, tomando consistencia de granito rosa y quedaba erguido, con su ramazón monumental en silenciosa desnudez, revelando las leyes de una arquitectura casi mineral, que tenía simetrías, ritmos, equilibrios, de cristalizaciones" (*PP*, 168) ["Its wood aged, acquiring the texture of pink granite, and it stood erect, its monumental skeleton in silent nakedness revealing the laws of an almost mineral architecture, with symmetries, rhythms, balances of crystallized forms" (*LS*, 165)]. Carpentier's persistent signaling of the correspondences between plants and architectural forms throughout his work not only establishes tropical America as a natural home for the baroque but also erodes ontological divisions between nature and culture, plants and things. Carpentier's vegetal-infused theories of the New World baroque draw on animistic pre-Columbian imaginaries, absent in the European formulation of the baroque, in order to attune it to Spanish American landscapes and cultures.

The intersections between nature, especially trees, and the built environment in Carpentier's work reaches its fullest expression in *El siglo de las luces* through repeated references to a painting by François de Nomé (also known as Monsú Desiderio). In the novel this painting is called *Explosión en una cathedral* (*Explosion in a Cathedral*) but the painting on which it is based is catalogued—by the Fitzwilliam Museum in Cambridge, England, where it resides—as *King Asa of Judah Destroying the Idols* or *King Asa of Judah Destroying the Statue of Priapus* (c. 1620). The narrator of *El siglo de las luces* hazily refers to the artist of the painting as an anonymous Neapolitan master.[49] In reality little is known of de Nomé, other than that he was born in what is now the Lorraine region of France in 1593, and that in the early seventeenth century he moved to Naples where he produced strange architectural paintings, often showing interiors in a state of fragmentation and collapse.[50] The painting of interest to Carpentier enacts just such a scene (see figure 6). An inscription in the upper left-hand corner, not visible in the small black-and-white reproduction of the painting that Carpentier taped into the front cover of his bound typewritten manuscript of the novel, reveals that it depicts a biblical episode from Kings 1.15, which tells of King Asa of Judah's purging of idolatry.[51] The painting, showing the nave of an imposing cathedral, is

FIGURE 6. King Asa of Judah Destroying the Idols, painting by François Didier de Nomé. © The Fitzwilliam Museum, Cambridge.

split between a scene of (almost total) order on the left-hand side, consisting of grand, richly decorated columns, and one of chaos and disorder on the right, where the eponymous explosion has severed the columns and is sending shards of masonry, broken statues, and other debris flying through the air.[52] In among (and seemingly unperturbed by) the devastation of their surroundings, people commit acts of human excess and cruelty. In the bottom left-hand corner two men are engaged in dismantling a statue; in the center is, apparently, an execution that calls to mind Francisco de Goya's famous 1814 painting *The Third of May, 1808*.[53] De Nomé's work is mentioned some six times in *El siglo de las luces*, and it migrates from the New World to the Old first being located in the home of the central characters in Havana and later moving to Madrid where the novel ends.[54]

Most critics of *El siglo de las luces* regard the painting as a metaphor for the revolution at the center of the novel. Donald Shaw, for instance, argues that the "cathedral stands primarily for the old, traditional, theo-centric view of life and society, which . . . the French Revolution blasted apart."[55] This reading is supported by Esteban's meditations on the painting in chapter 35 of the novel:

> Si la catedral era la Época, una formidable explosión, en efecto, había derribado sus muros principales, enterrando bajo un alud de escombros a los mismos que acaso construyeran la máquina infernal. Si la catedral era la Iglesia Cristiana, observaba Esteban que una hilera de fuertes columnas le quedaba intacta, frente a la que, rota a pedazos, se desplomaba en el apocalíptico cuadro, como un anuncio de resistencia, perdurabilidad y reconstrucciones, después de los tiempos de estragos y de estrellas anunciadoras de abismos. "Siempre te gustó mirar esa pintura—dijo Sofía—. ¡Y a mí que me parece absurda y desagradable!" (*SL*, 268–69)[56]

Sofía's dismissal of the painting emerges, at the end of the novel, as ironic, since it holds within it a prognostication of her own death. The parallels between de Nomé's oil painting and Goya's series of prints *Desastres de la guerra* (*The Disasters of War*; 1810–1820) that catalogues the horrors of the Peninsular War following the May 2 uprising are made explicit by Carpentier's inclusion of thirteen titles from the Goya series as epigraphs to the novel's chapters.[57] Indeed, this uprising is the historical endpoint of Carpentier's novel, which concludes with the disappearance of Sofía and Esteban, engaged in the revolutionary violence in Madrid. Esteban's use of the word "estragos," translated here as "destruction" but also meaning "ravages," "wastes," or even "disasters," is notable given that the noun is not only a near synonym of the title of the Goya series as a whole but part of the designation of the Spanish artist's thirtieth etching, *Estragos de la*

Guerra (*Wastes of War*), which forms the epigraph to chapter 18 of *El siglo de las luces*.[58] Catherine E. Wall has noted the "striking" correspondence between the epigraph and the action of this particular chapter, which relates the taking of Basse-Terre from the English: "Chaos reigns in both text and engraving. Visually we see a room in a shambles: bodies tumble round in mid-air, and a chair, a stationary object, appears to fall from the ceiling."[59] More significant for the purposes of this discussion of the vegetal baroque, however, is the coincidence between the etching and de Nomé's painting, both of which foreground tree-like broken pillars or beams in their representation of the collapse of a building following an explosion.

De Nomé's painting certainly plays an allegorical role in the novel as a graphic embodiment of the leveling force of revolution on society, but it is also significant for its representation of columns—structures that are central to Carpentier's conception of the New World baroque, and in particular of its telluric underpinnings. The columns in de Nomé's painting are divided into imposing and ornate Corinthian pillars to the left of the canvas and fractured tumbling structures to the right. The apparently dyadic organization of the painting can be interpreted, in terms suited to the Enlightenment context of the novel, as representing order/disorder or reason/unreason. The picture might also be seen as depicting the aesthetic split between the classical and the baroque. Yet viewing the painting in this way does not pay sufficient attention to a third element of the canvas—the epicenter of the explosion in the far right-hand corner. Here the viewer is confronted not with the unnaturally clean breaks of the exploding fluted pillars but, rather, with splintered log-like structures, which have an organic arboreal appearance accentuated by the use of thickly applied brown paint that produces a striking chromatic and textural similarity to bark.[60]

Carpentier's mindfulness of the tree-like underpinnings of de Nomé's pillars is revealed a number of times in *El siglo de las luces*, not least in the book's closing sentence, where the painting is described as melting into

the background of the room as "mera sombra" (SL, 371) [mere shadow]—
one of the foremost functions of the pillar and the tree in works such
as El acoso and "La ciudad de las columnas."[61] Earlier in the novel, Esteban contemplates the painting's depiction of "grandes trozos de fustes,
levantados por la deflagración" (SL, 316) ["huge fragments of column,
sent into the air by the deflagration" (EC, 296)], before throwing a stool
at the work in frustration. The noun "fuste" is defined by the Diccionario de la lengua española primarily in botanical terms as "madera, parte
sólida de los árboles cubierta por la corteza" ["wood, the solid part of
trees covered by bark"]. It is also an architectural term, designating the
part of the column between the capital and the base.[62] Carpentier uses
this word elsewhere in his work, usually as a synonym for column, yet
often in a manner that recalls the arboreal origins of columnar structures. This is the case in "La ciudad de las columnas" when Carpentier
speaks of the similarity between palm trunks and "el fuste dórico" (Cdlc,
64) ["Doric shaft" (CC, 246)] and again in Los pasos perdidos, when the
narrator notes how the locals employed Greek techniques when building the Adelantado's jungle city: "Para servir de pilastras se eligieron
troncos de un mayor diámetro en la base, en virtud de una instintiva
voluntad de remedar el fuste dórico" (PP, 142) ["Treetrunks wider at the
base than at the top were selected for pilasters in an instinctive desire
to imitate the Doric column" (LS, 139–40)]. And the noun "fuste" is also
employed early in El siglo de las luces in the description of the aftermath
of a cyclone, where furniture from Havana is carried by the storm: "más
allá de las murallas de la ciudad, más allá de las huertas, allá donde
centenares de palmeras yacían, en el desbordamiento de los arroyos
crecidos, como fustes de columnas antiguas derribadas por un terre-
moto. Y, sin embargo, a pesar de la magnitud del desastre, las gentes,
acostumbradas a la periodicidad de un azote que era considerado como
una inevitable convulsión del Trópico, se daban a cerrar, a reparar, a
repellar" (SL, 63–64).[63]

As well as clearly alluding to de Nomé's painting through the simile comparing the trunks of torn-down palm trees to buckled columns, this significant passage arguably anticipates the ending of the novel. The "escenografía de cataclismo" (*SL*, 65) ["scene of the cataclysm" (*EC*, 60)] following the storm foreshadows the chaos in Madrid, where "[r]einaba . . . la atmósfera de los grandes cataclismos, de las revulsiones telúricas" (*SL*, 370) ["some great cataclysm or telluric convulsion prevailed" (*EC*, 348)]. The noun "desastre" (disaster), which in the passage above denotes the devastation of the cyclone, also prefigures the references to Goya's print series later in the novel and establishes a firm connection between natural and political catastrophe.

In this way de Nomé's disintegrating columns do, as Shaw and others have noted, symbolize political revolution in the novel, but they also confirm Carpentier's conception of the New World baroque as closely related to plants. The tree-like appearance of the broken masonry in the right-hand corner of the canvas facilitates an allegorical reading of the painting as representing not only a split between classical and baroque aesthetics but also the emergence of a neo-baroque stylistics underpinned by vegetal forms.

Throughout his oeuvre Carpentier's columns—whether the elegant colonnades of Old Havana or the crumbling residues of de Nomé's apocalyptic painting—are an instantiation of his theory of the vegetal baroque, which sees plants as the cornerstone of cultural expression in Latin America. One of the recurrent themes of the Latin American writer's engagement with plants has been the rejection of a clear separation between humans and nonhumans—a separation that has been fundamental to, for instance, colonial appropriations of nature and even agricultural endeavor. The continuities between plants and buildings foregrounded by Carpentier's fictional and nonfictional writings are one way in which the author destabilizes the idea of human culture as separate from nature. The intersections between humans and plants are presented even more clearly by the author in his formulation of the neo-baroque tropes of hybridity and metamorphosis.

BOTANICAL HYBRIDS

In "La curiosidad barroca" ("Baroque Curiosity") Lezama Lima writes about what he regards as the "gran hazaña del barroco Americano" ["greatest achievement of the American Baroque"]: the carvings on the façade of San Lorenzo Cathedral in Potosí by the indigenous sculptor José Kondori that combine "la hoja americana con la trifolia griega, la semiluna incaica con los acantos de los capiteles corintios."[64] For Carpentier as well, the New World baroque was characterized by the fusion of disparate elements—the vegetal and the architectural; the European and the American; the human and the nonhuman—that in combination produced "new worlds, new cultures, new collective identities, and new forms of expression."[65] As Carpentier puts it: "toda simbiosis, todo mestizaje, engendra un barroquismo" ["all symbiosis, all *mestizaje*, engenders the baroque"].[66]

Carpentier's writing is awash with examples of these baroque blends. He discusses the symbiosis of tropical nature in Lam, for instance, and draws attention to how the artist invests plants "con formas humanas" [with human forms].[67] In his most famous painting, *The Jungle* (1942–1943), Lam's abstract human shapes intertwine with their vegetal surroundings so as to erase the boundaries between people and plants—a persistent fascination of Spanish American writers and artists. A profusion of cane or bamboo stalks and dense foliage form the backdrop to the voluptuous composite figures of this painting, whose buttocks and breasts have been compared to tropical fruits such as mangoes and papayas, whose knees are like tree trunks, and whose lips resemble open seed pods.[68] Other compositions from the same period, such as *Goddess with Foliage* (1942) and *The Murmur* (1943), highlight the connections between plants and people in a myriad of hybrid forms that are bereft of any sense of hierarchy between the human and the nonhuman.[69]

Although not solely relating to botany, the term "hybrid" is often used in relation to plants to refer to the outcome of cross-pollination,

whether intentional or not, between two different varieties.[70] Throughout
Carpentier's fiction, human-plant hybrids frequently appear as ciphers of
the vegetal baroque, especially in *El siglo de las luces*, where early on there
is a reference to Esteban's liking for "pinturas de autores recientes, que
mostraban criaturas, caballos espectrales, perspectivas imposibles—un
hombre árbol, con dedos que le retoñaban" (*SL*, 19) ["pictures by modern
artists representing monsters, spectral horses, or impossible scenes—a
tree-man with fingers sprouting from him" (*EC*, 18)].[71] Throughout the
novel, the third-person narrator frequently reminds us how close humans
are to plants, culminating with dark humor in the placing of the trunk of
banana trees in a guillotine when the machine is taken by the authorities
on a tour around Guadalupe: "nada se parece más a un cuello humano,
con su haz de conductos porosos y húmedos" (*SL*, 165) ["nothing looks
more like a human neck . . . , with its cross-section of moist, porous
ducts" (*EC*, 153)]. The coincidence between human and botanical forms
is also clearly foregrounded in the sequence in which Esteban climbs a
tree—a pivotal moment in the novel almost exactly midway through the
text: "Trepar a un árbol es una empresa personal que acaso no vuelva a
repetirse nunca. Quien se abraza a los altos pechos de un tronco, realiza
una suerte de acto nupcial, desflorando un mundo secreto, jamás vistos
por otros hombres. La mirada abarca, de pronto, todas las bellezas y
todas las imperfecciones del Árbol. Se sabe de las dos ramas tiernas, que
se apartan como muslos de mujer, ocultando en su juntura un puñado
de musgo verde" (*SL*, 174).[72] Esteban's encounter with the tree is sexu-
alized, with its limbs and bifurcations compared to the breasts, thighs,
and pubis of a female lover who is being "deflowered"—a term, in this
context, with both literal and metaphorical implications. By climbing the
tree, the protagonist is not only brought closer to nature (specifically, the
tropical nature of his Cuban childhood and adolescence) but elevated in
his understanding of the world and the Revolution. As Adam Sharman
notes, this episode reenacts the "classic Enlightenment topos of detach-
ment-as-objectivity," where "nature gives perspective, understanding,

cosmic vision, clarity to the place of the smallest detail in the order of things."[73]

The coming together of the human and the vegetal does not always precipitate a feeling of well-being in *El siglo de las luces*. When, during one of its many reversals, the Revolution restores slavery in the Caribbean, Sofía witnesses scenes of human cruelty and barbarism in Cayenne, including "racimos de cadáveres" (*SL*, 342) ["corpses hung in bunches" (*EC*, 321)] on the leafy tropical trees. Such an image emphasizes less the oneness of people and plants than their radical disjuncture, as humans enlist nature as a means of inflicting pain on others. Just a few pages later, plants themselves are exposed to revolutionary violence, when Víctor Hugues, a leading proponent of the French Revolution in the New World, oversees forest clearances to facilitate the construction of his new estate:

> En los siempre retrocedidos linderos del humus caían troncos centenarios, copas tan habitadas por pájaros, monos, insectos y reptiles, como los árboles simbólicos de la Alquimia. Humeaban los gigantes derribados, ardidos por fuegos que les llegaban a las entrañas, sin acabar de calar las cortezas; iban los bueyes de los hormigueantes campos al aserradero recién instalado, arrastrando largos cuerpos de madera, aún repletos de savias, de zumos, de retoños crecidos sobre sus heridas; rodando raíces enormes, abrazadas a la tierra, que se desmembraban bajo el hacha, arrojando brazos que aún querían prenderse de algo. (*SL*, 345)[74]

The persistent use of vocabulary that is more commonly applied to humans than trees—the plural nouns "cuerpos" (rendered as "corpses" in the English translation, but literally denoting bodies), "entrañas," "brazos," and "heridas" (entrails, arms, wounds) and the verbs "abrazar" (to hold) and "desmembrar" (to dismember)—anthropomorphizes nature and arouses pathos for the uprooted vegetation, a pathos accentuated not only by the age of the trees or the fact that cutting them down dislodges myriad animals, birds, and insects but also by their tenacious attempts to cling to life. Like the felling of Bello's ancient ceiba in "La agricultura de la zona tórrida," the lexical field established by Carpentier presents the forest clearance as an act of arboricide, where an animate and supernatural flora (as with Bello's cosmically significant ceiba, there is a reference to magical plants above) is violently slain in the name of progress. The arms ("brazos") of the personified trees are emphasized in Carpentier's account of deforestation, including through the use of the etymologically cognate verb "abrazar." Earlier in the novel, Esteban comes across a group of runaway slaves who have been sentenced to the loss of their left leg. This scene of amputation prefigures Hugues's dismembering of the trees above, specifically through the surgeon's earlier deadpan comment to Esteban: "También se amputan brazos" (*SL*, 257) ["They cut off arms as well" (*EC*, 241)]. The tree that Esteban climbs in the novel is also described as having "brazos," which Carpentier added in pen to a typewritten manuscript, deleting the original more neutrally botanical "palos" (branches).[75] In Carpentier's baroque universe, the revolutionary zeal for cutting off legs, arms, and heads is not limited to human victims but extends to their arboreal doubles and hybrids.

The proximity of human flesh to vegetal fiber often produces a sense of revulsion in Carpentier's work, as when Esteban encounters a plant with leaves "de una suavidad tan semejante a la de la piel humana, que las manos no atrevían a tocarlas" (*SL*, 176) ["so like human skin in their smoothness that one's hands were afraid to touch them" (*EC*, 163)] or sees figures of Jesus made from sugarcane, whose flesh so closely resembles human skin that "la mano, al tocarlos, retrocedía ante una ilusión de pálpito aún viviente en la herida de Lanza" (*SL*, 238) ["the hand recoiled when it touched them, under the illusion that life still throbbed in the spear-wound in their sides" (*EC*, 224)].[76] Such images correspond to Julia Kristeva's definition of the abject in *Powers of Horror* where the breakdown of boundaries—the end point of Carpentier's baroque hybrids—can leave the subject reeling at the lack of distinction between self and other, subject and object.[77] Mary Douglas, on whom Kristeva draws, notes that "all margins are dangerous. . . . Matter issuing from them is marginal stuff of the most obvious kind. Spittle, blood, milk, urine, faeces or tears by simply issuing forth have traversed the boundary of the body."[78] In the account of Hugues's felling of the trees, references to their "savias, . . . zumos" (*SL*, 345) ["sap and juices" (*EC*, 324)], the botanical equivalents of blood, are obvious examples of this marginal matter, as is Esteban's fear of touching the fibrous open wounds of the woven figures of Christ.

Metamorphosis is closely related to hybridity in Carpentier's writings and also determinedly vegetal in its figuration. Indeed, in his philosophical account of plants, Coccia regards them as models of metamorphosis: "Plant life is nothing but the cosmic alembic of universal metamorphosis, the power that allows any form to be born."[79] In one of the most significant accounts of metamorphosis in Carpentier's writings, the anonymous narrator of *Los pasos perdidos* describes the jungle as "el mundo de la mentira, de la trampa y del falso semblante" (*PP*, 169) ["the world of deceit, subterfuge, duplicity" (*LS*, 166)]—a place in perpetual flux between one form and another: "Aquí todo parecía otra cosa, creándose un mundo de apariencias que ocultaba la realidad, poniendo muchas verdades en entredicho. . . . los bejucos parecían reptiles y las serpientes parecían lianas, . . . junto a la falsedad de un camaleón demasiado rama, demasiado lapizlázuli, demasiado plomo estriado de un amarillo intenso" (*PP*, 169).[80] In this section of the novel, the jungle is presented as an animate force whose proclivity for subterfuge and deception divests onlookers of any sense of reality. According to Carpentier's narrator, in the Amazon animals not only resemble plants and vice versa but, in their attempt to appear Other, become hyperreal, losing their original identity, like the chameleon that too closely resembles a plant or a mineral to seem like an animal at all.[81] In *The Botany of Desire*, Michael Pollan notes how plants often rely on symbolism and subterfuge, pretending through sight or smell to be something they are not: "flowers by their very nature traffic in a kind of metaphor, so that even a meadow of wildflowers brims with meanings not of our making."[82] The absence of a conjunction in Carpentier's defining statement of vegetal metamorphosis in this section of *Los pasos perdidos*, "allí todo era disfraz, estratagema, juego de apariencias, metamorfosis" (*PP*, 169) ["everything there is disguise, stratagem, artifice, metamorphosis" (*LS*, 166)], drives home the infinite mobility of the jungle environment—what d'Ors terms, in a section again highlighted in the margin in Carpentier's copy, "el *dinamismo*, característico de toda obra barroca" ["*dynamism*, characteristic of every Baroque work"].[83]

Carpentier's human-plant hybrids in *Los pasos perdidos* often adopt an in-between state, that of the "lagarto-cohombro, la castaña-erizo, la crisálida-ciempiés" (*PP*, 169) ["lizard-cucumber, the chestnut-hedgehog, the cocoon-centipede" (*LS*, 166)]. González Echevarría speaks of how, in Carpentier, the hyphen designates "the continuous act of changing, of being transformed."[84] Such transformations for Carpentier are characteristically baroque, as is made explicit in his definition of the style as "un arte en movimiento, un arte de pulsión, un arte que va de un centro hacia afuera y va rompiendo, en cierto modo, sus propios márgenes" ["art in motion, a pulsating art, an art that moves outward and away from the center, that somehow breaks through its own borders"].[85]

In *El siglo de las luces* it is not the jungle but the sea that best embodies this interstitiality, although even here the botanical remains paramount in descriptions of jellyfish "aún suspendidas entre lo vegetal y lo animal" (*SL*, 83) ["suspended half-way between the vegetable and animal kingdoms" (*SL*, 77)] and coral reefs where "toda delimitación entre lo inerte y lo palpitante, lo vegetal y lo animal, quedaba abolida" (*SL*, 187) ["all delimitation between the inert and the palpitant, the vegetal and the animal, was abolished" (*EC*, 176)]. In terms deeply redolent of *Los pasos perdidos*, Carpentier defines the reefs as an underwater forest where there is "una perenne confusión entre lo que era de la planta y era del animal" (*SL*, 189) ["a perpetual mingling of the animal and the plant kingdoms" (*EC*, 177)]. Once more the hyphen serves to yoke together the animal and the vegetal kingdoms, the "peces-vegetales" and "setas-medusas"

(*SL*,189) ["vegetable-fish" and "mushroom jelly-fish" (*EC*, 177)], creating equilibrium between two states in constant flux.

Such acts of metamorphosis correspond to the baroque device of "metonymic displacement," where, as Lois Parkinson Zamora explains, "compositional elements permutate as they move through fictive space . . . ; elements grow out of one another or dissolve into one another; ideas and images associate and accumulate in patterns that become the basis for the structure as a whole."[86] In "Lo barroco y lo real maravilloso," Carpentier dwells on another botanically grounded example of metonymic displacement when he compares the proliferating figures on Indian bas reliefs to entwined flora, creating "(en grupos y en figuras sueltas, danzantes y siempre unidas, ligadas unas con otras como vegetales) una serie de focos proliferantes que se prolongan al infinito" ["a series of proliferating foci—in groups and individually, dancing and always united, interlocked like plants—foci that extend to infinity"]—a statement that is central to an understanding of the kinetic and boundless qualities of the author's vegetal baroque.[87]

Gilles Deleuze has theorized the constant movement of the baroque structure as a fold that "unfurls all the way to infinity," an idea that can be regarded as analogous to the figures of proliferation and metamorphosis in the works of Hispanic baroque writers such as Lezama Lima, Sarduy, and especially Carpentier.[88] Carpentier shares with Deleuze and his fellow Cuban writers a belief in the dynamism of the baroque, but his use of the term is distinguished by its determinedly botanical perspective. The baroque for Carpentier is best embodied by plant life, whether the "barroca proliferación de lianas" ["baroque proliferation of lianas"] in the Amazon basin or the vegetal-animal hybrids of Caribbean coral reefs.[89] Carpentier's vegetal composites are often contestatory and unnerving, enlisting a surrealist penchant for vegetal human appendages as well as indigenous ideas about the interconnectedness of all living things in the search for new hybrid forms of expression to convey American reality. One of these hybrids is Carpentier's celebrated term "lo maravilloso real" or "the marvelous real," also firmly connected to plants.

SPECIMEN PLANTS

In "Problemática de la actual novela latinoamericana," Carpentier attempts to define a Spanish American stylistics: *"un tercer estilo*: el estilo de las cosas que no tienen estilo. O que comenzaron por no tener estilo" [*a third style*: the style of things that do not have a style. Or which do not have a style to start with].[90] Among the examples of what emerges as a characteristically baroque aesthetic, Carpentier includes the curiosity cabinet, or wunderkammer, a baroque conceit par excellence.[91] Beginning in the medieval period with collections of disparate objects, often combining the arts and the sciences and frequently including items considered strange or bizarre, the wunderkammer was a precursor to the modern museum.[92] In his essay "The Cabinet of Wonder," Giorgio Agamben has argued that, despite the miscellaneous appearance of such collections, they functioned as "a sort of microcosm that reproduced, in . . . harmonious confusion, the animal, vegetable, and mineral macrocosm."[93] The paradoxical term "harmonious confusion" coincides with Carpentier's definition of the "third style" above: coherence is developed over time when objects take on new meanings through their arrangement and "acercamientos fortuitos" [fortuitous approximations].[94] Just as the twentieth-century Spanish American writer was able to retool the baroque of seventeenth-century Europe, so too are articles contained in a wunderkammer disassociated from their original function or significance through their radical juxtapositions.

Carpentier's fictions abound in curiosity cabinets. Charlotte Rogers has studied the trope in relation to Carpentier's penchant for collecting as well as in its connection to neo-baroque aesthetics.[95] In a 1937 article, Carpentier wrote about his own extended wunderkammer—the study in his Paris home, which was full of "juguetes mexicanos, cerámicas andaluzas . . . y ponchos venezolanos" [Mexican toys, Andalusian ceramics, . . .

and Venezuelan ponchos].[96] Rogers argues that Carpentier's accruing of objects, particularly American items, functioned as a kind of fetish and a means for Carpentier to elide his own European birth, the fact of which he sought to deny throughout his life.[97] Rogers also sees collecting as an instantiation of Carpentier's baroque stylistics, more generally—a means through which he tried "to gather the endless diversity of Latin America into a single unifying aesthetic."[98] Many of Carpentier's fictional protagonists share this zeal for collecting. The amassing of so-called primitive musical instruments is central to *Los pasos perdidos*, and at the start of *El siglo de las luces* the young protagonists take delivery of "Un Gabinete de física" (*SL*, 26) ["a physics laboratory" (*EC*, 24)], which includes a vast array of scientific implements. Guillermina de Ferrari has noted how this particular collection functions as a form of baroque proliferation in the novel, with the significance of the instruments emerging through their juxtapositions rather than through their intended use.[99] Another such baroque assortment appears in Carpentier's short story "El camino de Santiago" ("The Highroad of Saint James") when the protagonist encounters a man selling marvels that have been brought back from Spain's newly discovered American territories, including two stuffed alligators, a monkey, a parrot, and stones that ease headaches.[100] Such a collection highlights the New World baroque's preference for proliferation and strange juxtapositions as well as revealing the baroque's proximity to the marvelous through the reference to medicinal stones. As Márquez Rodríguez has argued, Carpentier's conceptions of "lo maravilloso real" and the New World baroque are closely interrelated, not least in their attempt to formulate a Latin American stylistics predicated on the non-assimilation to European norms.[101]

In a number of Carpentier's fictional works the wunderkammer takes the form of a collection of plants, often presented—in line with the cabinet's role as a repository of wonder—as a source of the marvelous. The epitome of such botanical collections comes in *El recurso del método* (*Reasons of State*) when "una rara colección de raíces-esculturas, de esculturas-raíces, de raíces-formas, de raíces-objetos" ["rare collection of root-sculptures, sculpture-roots, root-forms, root-objects"] is enumerated over the course of several pages:

> Raíces barrocas o severas en su lisura; enrevesadas, intrincadas, o noblemente geométricas; a veces danzantes, a veces estáticas, o totémicas, o sexuales, entre animal y teorema, juego de nudos, juego de asimetrías, ora vivas, ora fósiles. . . . Raíces arrancadas de sus suelos remotos, arrastradas, subidas, trajinadas, por los ríos en creciente; raíces trabajadas por el agua, volcadas, revolcadas, bruñidas, patinadas, plateadas, desplateadas, que de tanto viajar, dando tumbos, chocando con las rocas, peleando con otros maderos acarreados, acababan por perder su morfología vegetal, desprendidas del árbol-madre, árbol genealógico, para cobrar redondeces de tetas, aristas de poliedro, cabezas de jabalíes o caras de ídolos, dentaduras, garfios, tentáculos, falos y coronas.[102]

This fragment epitomizes Carpentier's baroque prose style, which employs anaphora in its repeated use of the plural noun "raíces" (roots) followed by a proliferation of qualifying epithets.[103] This collection of roots—explicitly characterized as baroque—embodies many of the traits of the New World baroque as set out elsewhere in Carpentier's writing: the form's tendency to decorative excess; its ludic propensities; and its privileging of metamorphosis and hybridity, especially between animals and plants. In the passage above, this morphological slipperiness is accentuated by the addition of a suffix to the past participle: "volcadas, revolcadas" and "plateadas, desplateadas."[104] In the case of the latter pair, the slipperiness is heightened by the preceding orthographically related word—"patinadas"—that makes the sentence read like a kind of word-morph puzzle, in which one successively changes a single letter to produce a new term.

Carpentier continues with an account of the physical appearance of the various roots included in the collection and their geographical origin—a taxonomy that registers as comic through not only the excessive level of detail but the unlikely names attached to many of the plant specimens, including *Humpty-Dumpty* (given to a root resembling the nursery rhyme figure) and the "bailadora liana" ["liana ballerina"], Anna Pavlova.[105] The bizarre collection also includes a number of mandrakes (*Mandragora officinalis*); one is enormous and barbed, and the other more human-like, with bulging eyes and a hat. Bataille has discussed mandrakes in "The Language of Flowers," where he characterizes roots in general as "a perfect counterpart to the visible parts of a plant." The leaves and flowers give the impression of beauty or dignity, and the "ignoble and sticky roots wallow in the ground," becoming, for Bataille, symbols of debasement and evil.[106] Michael Taussig has also written at length about the mandrake, noting the plant's hallucinogenic properties and its importance in witchcraft. In line with Carpentier's botanical hybrids, the mandrake, Taussig explains, has long been regarded as inhabiting an interstitial condition between the human and the vegetal: "Part plant, part human, the mandrake is an astonishingly precise instance of something hovering between an art of nature and an art in nature, and surely this is what accounts, in part, at least, for its magical powers. . . . the foot-long blackish root, often forked, and said by many—but not all—to have a human form, even with a male sexual organ, which juts out as a subsidiary root" (see figure 7).[107] Such is their resemblance to human anatomy that throughout history superstitions have abounded regarding the digging up of mandrakes, which were said to shriek and groan when disturbed (traditionally, dogs were used as intermediaries so that people could avoid the supposedly fatal task of uprooting them themselves).[108]

Carpentier may well have been drawn to the image of the mandrake because of the root's hybrid human-like appearance, but the superstitions surrounding it would also have been compelling for a writer so steeped in plant lore. Carpentier owned a copy of Frazer's *The Golden Bough* and an extensively annotated copy of Cabrera's *El monte*, which included an array of information about Afro-Cuban herbal medicine.[109] Although

FIGURE 7. *Mandragora mas. Mandragore.* Mandrake root by Abraham Bosse. From N. Robert, A. Bosse, and L. de Chastillon, "Estampes pour servir à l'histoire des plantes. 1ère [-2de] partie." Vol. 2. Courtesy of the Wellcome Collection, London.

a temperate plant, and therefore not included in Cabrera's work, the mandrake was also known for its miraculous powers. Frazer had produced a paper on the cultural history of the mandrake for the British Academy in 1917, which opened with a discussion of beliefs surrounding the plant's supposed role in human fertility.[110] Mircea Eliade, who was an important influence on Carpentier, notes that in terms of its "magical or medicinal virtues" the mandrake was unparalleled in Romanian culture, where it was believed to exert influence on a wide range of situations, from luck in love to the stimulation of bovine milk production.[111] As such, the mandrake can be positioned within Carpentier's fiction as one of a large number of marvelous plants—botanical specimens with curative or psychotropic properties.

Often such plants are presented en masse, as a kind of living wunderkammer or miniaturized botanical garden (a space singled out by d'Ors as an important site of the baroque).[112] In *El reino de este mundo*, Carpentier draws on this trope when he portrays the rebel slave Makandal foraging for botanical specimens in order to concoct a powerful poison: "La mano traía alpistes sin nombres, alcaparras de azufre, ajíes minúsculos, bejucos que tejían redes entre las piedras; matas solitarias, de hojas velludas, que sudaban en la noche; sensitivas que se doblaban al mero sonido de la voz humana" ["His hand gathered anonymous seeds, sulphury capers, diminutive hot peppers; vines that wove nets among the stones; solitary bushes with furry leaves that sweated at night; sensitive plants that closed at the mere sound of the human voice"].[113] Here the marvelous quality of the plants does not reside only in their capacity for destruction but in their mysterious and recondite habits. These plants are nameless, scarcely visible to the naked eye, and isolated. And like the mandrake, some are endowed with remarkably human characteristics, such as auditory consciousness or perspiration. Other examples of botanical collections in Carpentier's fiction include the herbalist Montsalvaje's basket of dried herbs in *Los pasos perdidos*—the smell of which precipitates, like Proust's madeleine, involuntary memories of childhood for the narrator—and

Remigio's secret physic garden in *El siglo de las luces*, containing "perejiles y retamas, ortiguillas, sensitivas y hierbas de traza silvestre, en torno a varias matas de reseda, esplendorosamente florecidas" (*SL*, 47) ["parsley, nettles, mimosa and woodland grasses . . . around several very flourishing mignonette plants" (*EC*, 44)]—discovered, and subsequently destroyed, by the Haitian physician Doctor Ogé when tending to Esteban's asthma. Ogé's belief that illnesses are mysteriously connected to the proximity of certain plants or trees draws out the esoteric dimensions of vegetal life, although, as González Echevarría has observed, "we can easily discover the 'scientific' foundation of Ogé's diagnosis—allergies are the cause of Esteban's asthma."[114] Like other botanical collections in Carpentier's fiction, this "minúsculo jardín" (*SL*, 47) ["miniature garden" (*EC*, 44)] in *El siglo de las luces* also acts as a living wunderkammer—an amalgam of marvelous plants, many of which played important roles in Afro-Cuban herbal medicine. Carpentier would have known about these plants from his reading of *El monte*, which includes entries on all of those mentioned in Remigio's plot.[115] Cabrera records how the locally named *ortiguilla* was a singularly malign plant, which, for instance, when combined in a potion with hair follicles, finger nails, and a donkey's nose was believed to cause impotence in anyone who imbibed it.[116]

A number of commentators have stressed the mutuality of ideas of the baroque and "lo maravilloso real," although they are often seen as separate, even contradictory terms.[117] Zamora, for one, argues that the marvelous real "is itself a Baroque *coincidentia oppositorum*: the marvelous opposes the real and also resides within it."[118] Carpentier also spoke of the significant overlap of the two terms in his essay "Lo barroco y lo real maravilloso."[119] It is my contention here that collections of plant specimens are an important meeting point for the baroque and the marvelous in Carpentier's work. In her discussion of early European botanical gardens, Lucia Tongiori Tomasi observes how some of the central concepts of the baroque such as the marvel and metamorphosis were embodied in "rare, exotic and teratogenic specimens that were cultivated in the botanical garden" as well as "the life-cycle of the plants themselves, which were undergoing constant renewal and could sometimes generate unexpected mutations."[120] Carpentier's plants embody the marvelous not only through their potent curative or toxic effects and bizarre morphology but also by way of their religious and cultural associations, like the shrieking mandrake root. This is also the case for the highly symbolic ceiba tree—the single most important botanical reference for Carpentier.

CEIBA, THE APOTHEOSIS OF THE NEW WORLD BAROQUE

If there is one plant that embodies the vegetal baroque for Carpentier it is the *Ceiba petandra*.[121] The ceiba is a significant tree across tropical America and plays an important role in Afro-Cuban religious practices as well as in Maya mythology, where the tree is considered the *axis mundi* whose trunk goes through the Middleworld, whose roots traverse the Underworld, and whose branches reach the heavenly realm of the Otherworld.[122] In one of Carpentier's late novels, *La consagración de la primavera* (The consecration of spring), completed two years before his death, the character Enrique speaks of the identification of the ceiba with the Earth Mother and indigenous Caribbean cosmogonies involving the "Árbol de la Vida, Árbol-centro-del-Mundo, Árbol-del-Saber, Árbol-del-Ascenso, Árbol-Solar" [Tree of Life, Tree at the Center of the World, Tree of Knowledge, Tree of Ascent, Solar Tree].[123] Such reflections echo the language used to describe the ceiba in the *Chilam Balam*, a text that Carpentier knew well.[124] The Cuban poet Oscar Hurtado included a passage from this Mayan book as an epigraph to a long poem on the ceiba (*La seiba*, 1961) that he presented to Carpentier. He dedicated a typed manuscript of the work to his "amigo Alejo . . . por haber probado la fruta de este árbol" [friend Alejo . . . for having tried the fruit of this tree]:

> Y la Gran Madre Seiba se levantó entre
> los recuerdos de la destrucción de la

tierra. . . .

Y con sus ramas y sus raíces

llamaba a su señor.[125]

Colonial texts focus on the tree's shade-giving properties, an association that would not have been lost on Carpentier, who accords such prominence to this arboreal function in "La ciudad de las columnas." In the Florentine Codex, for instance, the tree is persistently associated with shade: "shady, shadowy. It shades; it gives shade, it gives shadow; it shades one. Under it, one is shaded."[126] Fray Diego de Landa, who compiled his *Relación de las cosas de Yucatán* (*Account of the Affairs of Yucatán*) in 1566, also reports how the shade of the ceiba (locally known as the *yaxché*) came to be figured in myths of the afterlife as a space of eternal repose.[127]

Carpentier's interest in the ceiba stemmed largely from his affinity with the Afro-Cuban movement that began in the 1920s and 1930s.[128] Cabrera confirms the significant role played by the ceiba in Afro-Cuban culture in a chapter on the tree in *El monte* in which she catalogues beliefs about the ceiba among Cubans of Yoruba and Congolese descent, not least the injunction against cutting one down.[129] This sanction was experienced firsthand by Carpentier when he was involved in the establishment of a museum in Ernest Hemingway's house in Cotorro, in the Havana suburbs, after the American's death in 1961. Some year later Carpentier recalled how the transformation of the house into a museum had necessitated the felling of a ceiba: "Había que cortarla; pero me costó grandes problemas encontrar quién lo hiciera. La gente en Cuba no cortan las ceibas. Creen que ella es 'la madre de todos los árboles'" [We had to cut it down, but it was very difficult to get someone to do it. People in Cuba do not cut down ceibas. They believe that it is "the mother of all trees"].[130] Even in the twenty first century, in streets a gentle stroll away from Carpentier's Vedado home, the understories of ceiba trees remain scattered with animal sacrifices as well as broken religious artefacts, bananas, and seed pods (see figure 8).[131]

FIGURE 8. Understory of a *Ceiba petandra* in Havana, 2017. Photo by the author.

Within Carpentier's fictional and nonfictional writings, the ceiba emerges not only as an important repository of pre-Columbian or Afro-Cuban beliefs but also as a symbol of the New World baroque. In "Problemática de la actual novela latinoamericana," Carpentier chooses the ceiba as a significant metonym for the Otherness of vegetal nature in tropical America and the difficulty of conveying such nature through language. The section dealing with the ceiba, "Del estilo" ["On Style"], is some four pages long and is in many senses the culmination of the essay. Carpentier begins by reflecting on universally recognizable trees such as the pine or the palm, where the utterance of the arboreal signifier is sufficient to "definir, pintar, mostrar" ["define, paint, and illustrate"] the object in question. Not so with the ceiba, Carpentier contends:

La palabra *ceiba*—nombre de un árbol americano al que los negros
cubanos llaman "la madre de los árboles"—no basta para que las gentes de
otras latitudes vean el aspecto de columna rostral de ese árbol gigantesco,
adusto y solitario, como sacado de otras edades, sagrado por linaje, cuyas
ramas horizontales, casi paralelas, ofrecen al viento unos puñados de hojas
tan inalcanzables para el hombre como incapaces de todo mecimiento.
Allí está, en lo alto de una ladera, solo, silencioso, inmóvil, sin aves que
lo habiten, rompiendo el suelo con sus enormes raíces escamosas. . . . A
centenares de metros de allí (porque la ceiba no es árbol de asociación
ni de compañía) crecen unos papayos, herbáceas salidas de los primeros
pantanos de la creación, con sus cuerpos blandos, cubiertos de medal-
lones grises, sus hojas abiertas como manos de mendigos, sus ubres-frutas
colgadas del cuello. . . . Esos árboles existen. Son árboles americanos que
forman parte, por derecho y presencia, de la novelística americana. Pero
no tienen la ventura de llamarse *pino*, ni *palmera*, ni *nogal*, ni *castaño*, ni
abedul.[132]

Here Carpentier employs a richly baroque prose to convey the wonder
of these American trees—the ceiba and the papaya—presented as relics
from a far-removed time. Shalini Puri and Debra A. Castillo have noted
that the first tree in each of the paired botanical juxtapositions in this
passage—pine and palm, ceiba and papaya—corresponds to "a symbol
linked to primordial sacred practices, while the second tree provides
exotic or everyday fruit, depending on the geography."[133] The ceiba's
links to the sacred are foregrounded by its lack of correspondence to
"normal" arboreal habits and appearance: the tree is unnaturally straight
and upright, its leaves do not rustle, it is strangely isolated from others of
its species, and it does not act as a habitat for birds. In *La consagración de
la primavera* Carpentier also observes that it is impossible to climb a ceiba
because of the sharp spines that normally cover its trunk (see figure 9).[134]

   The essay "Problemática de la actual novela latinoamericana" was
first published in 1964 in *Tientos y diferencias* alongside "La ciudad de las

FIGURE 9. Spiny trunk of a *Ceiba petandra*. Photo by Lalo Vazquez, licensed under CC BY-SA 2.0

columnas"—an essay in which Carpentier sets out his baroque theory of the arboreal underpinnings of the column. As Carpentier's alter ego in *La consagración de la primavera* makes clear in his description of the ceiba as an "árbol arquitectónico" [architectural tree] and, in superlative terms, "el más monumental . . . de *mis* árboles" [the most monumental . . . of *my* trees], the ceiba epitomizes the coalescence between trees and buildings.[135] In "Problemática" and again in *El siglo de las luces*, Carpentier stresses the architectural qualities of the tree through reference to its "rostral column," a term denoting a type of scaled victory pillar originating in ancient Rome to commemorate maritime battles and sometimes appended to the front of boats.[136] Interestingly, the adjective "rostral," which derives from the Latin "rostrum" for "beak" or "nose," is also used for the plates just above the mouth in snakes, the so-called rostrum scale—a connection Carpentier seems to evoke via his reference to the ceiba's "raíces escamosas" ["scaly roots"] in "Problemática."[137] Figuring the ceiba as having scales augments the bizarre qualities of this tree, making it an ideal (if rather large) fit for the baroque wunderkammer or curiosity cabinet.

The reptilian aspect of the tree also links it to other hybrids in Carpentier's oeuvre—those hyphenated baroque amalgams in *Los pasos perdidos* and the interstitial reef world evoked in *El siglo de las luces*, where a tree, submerged in a mangrove swamp, also developed "escamas" (*SL*, 189) ["scales" (*EC*, 177)] after it was colonized by oysters. Such baroque blends, according to the narrator of *El siglo de las luces*, necessitate a new language—"la aglutinación, la amalgama verbal y la metáfora" (*SL*, 189) ["agglutination, verbal amalgams and metaphors" (*EC*, 178)]—in order to convey the unfamiliarity of the nature of tropical America. These strategies have been a constant, as Carpentier knew, of the writer's experience of translating the so-called New World for a universal readership. Colonial writers such as Oviedo (the official chronicler of the Indies for Charles V who referred to the ceiba a number of times) or the Spanish Jesuit and naturalist José de Acosta provided an important blueprint for

Carpentier with respect to the question of naming American plants.[138] Carpentier alludes to such forerunners when describing how, in the colonial period, the comparative impulse often involved the combination of botanical and nonbotanical morphemes to coin names for newly discovered flora such as "'acacia-pulseras,' 'ananás-porcelana,' 'madera-costilla,' 'escoba-las-diez,' 'primo-trébol,' 'piñón-botija,' 'tisana-nube,' 'palo-iguana'" ["'acacia-bracelets,' 'pineapple-porcelain,' 'wood-rib,' 'ten o'clock broom,' 'cousin clover,' 'pitcher-pine-kernel,' 'tisane-cloud,' and 'iguana-stick'"].[139] Such agglutinations register as baroque fantasies rather than actual plant varieties.[140] Real or not, however, these amalgams bear out Carpentier's view that, when faced with the unfamiliar, "La descripción es ineludible, y la descripción de un mundo barroco ha de ser necesariamente barroca" ["Description is inescapable, and the description of a baroque world is necessarily baroque"].[141] In the case of the ceiba, the baroque tree par excellence, the task for the writer is to render it through "palabras cabales, pertenecientes al vocabulario universal" ["words that belong to a universal vocabulary"].[142] Within Carpentier's conception of the vegetal baroque there is no contradiction between the need for precision and accuracy, implied by the adjective "cabal," meaning "exact" (a word omitted in the published English translation), and the necessarily baroque prose that results. The towering ceiba, with its scaly buttress roots and spines and its manifold associations in Meso-American and Afro-Cuban culture, exists. For Carpentier, American reality and, especially, American plants are and always have been baroque, and it is the task of the American writer to inscribe them.

"LO BARROCO VEGETAL"

Carpentier made an intriguing amendment to subsection 13 of a typed manuscript of *Los pasos perdidos*. In the description of the narrator's first meeting with the Adelantado, and telling of the difficulty of penetrating the closed world of the jungle, the author crossed out the term "lo vegetal barroco" [the vegetal baroque] with nineteen typed lowercase xs.[143] This correction took place at the original moment of typing: it was immediately replaced with the typed phrase "grandes barroquismos telúricos" [immense telluric baroques], which survives in the published version of the novel.[144] Such a change is significant in a discussion of Carpentier's botanical imagination. The phrase "lo vegetal barroco" seems to express perfectly Carpentier's twin interests in plants and baroque stylistics.[145] So, why did he cross it out?

It is possible that the excision was an attempt to avoid repetition of the adjective "vegetal," which appears in the same paragraph just above in "vasto ciudad vegetal" [vast vegetal city] and just below in "la muralla vegetal" [the vegetal wall].[146] In addition, the adjective "telúrica" [telluric]—which has a more expansive meaning than "vegetal" in that it refers not only to plants but also to the earth more generally—was introduced into the novel by Carpentier a number of times at the editing stage.[147] Nevertheless, the context of this particular deletion is worth pursuing.

The expression "lo vegetal barroco" originally appeared in a passage detailing the difficulty of locating Santa Mónica de los Venados:

> Para penetrar en ese mundo, el Adelantado había tenido que conseguirse las llaves de secretas entradas; sólo él conocía cierto paso entre dos troncos, único en cincuenta leguas, que conducía a una angosta escalinata de lajas por la que podía descenderse al vasto misterio de los grandes barroquismos telúricos. Sólo él sabía dónde estaba la pasarela de bejucos que permitía andar por debajo de la cascada, la poterna de hojarasca, el paso por la caverna de los petroglifos, la ensenada oculta, que conducían a los corredores practicables. Él descifraba el código de las ramas dobladas, de las incisiones en las cortezas, de la rama-no-caída-sino-colocada. (*PP*, 129)[148]

The isolation of this jungle city, which the narrator becomes acutely aware of in the novel's final chapter when his plans to return there are thwarted by a failure of orientation, is driven home by the anaphoric phrase "sólo él" ["he alone" (*LS*, 126)]. Only the Adelantado can interpret the signs in the surrounding vegetation—only he can detect the walkway of lianas, the door in the undergrowth, and crucially, the criss-crossed branches, the branches that have not fallen by chance but have been intentionally positioned, just like the crosses erasing the key phrase "lo vegetal barroco" in Carpentier's manuscript.

It is tempting to regard the deletion—but continued visibility—of this redolent term as an example of *sous rature*, where words or phrases are crossed out to indicate their inadequacy but allowed to remain in place because of the lack of a better alternative expression.[149] Yet this is not a convincing reading of the term "lo vegetal barroco" in Carpentier's work, which remains present only in the manuscript version and which expresses Carpentier's botanically infused stylistics very well. Rather, like the Adelantado's concealment of the location of his newly founded city, Carpentier suppresses the term "lo vegetal barroco" at the very moment of its invention. The phrase is muted not only through Carpentier's repeated overtyping but also through its position in a disordered manuscript littered with additions and deletions. The determined concealment of these words, like the Adelantado's withholding of "las llaves de secretas entradas" (*PP*, 129) ["the keys to its secret entrances" (*LS*, 126)] can be seen as an ultimate baroque gesture on the part of Carpentier that rivals the jungle's ludic capacity for "disfraz, estratagema, juego de apariencias" (*PP*, 169) ["disguise, stratagem, artifice, metamorphosis" (*LS*, 166)]. By deleting the expression, Carpentier arguably elides a phrase that could have become an interpretative key to so much of his thinking and writing about the baroque.

Although this term never made it into Carpentier's published work, the synthesis of the botanical and the baroque it denotes governs much of the author's fictional and nonfictional writing. Carpentier's conception of the vegetal underpinnings of cultural expression in the Americas, whether of art, architecture, or literature, and inversely the proclivity of plants and trees to typify New World baroque traits such as hybridity, metamorphosis, and the marvelous real, all reveal the centrality of the

botanical to the author's work and to the formulation of neo-baroque
aesthetics in Spanish America. In this way, plants are revealed to be pivotal to one of the most significant Latin American aesthetic movements
of the twentieth century, not only as the inspiration for recurrent images
or forms but the very means of their expression.

So far in this discussion the relationship between botanically attentive writing and genre or form has been paramount. The centrality of
plants to Spanish American literature has been considered from the late
colonial period to the present and across a number of genres including
georgic poetry, the novel, and the essay. Although there are significant
differences across the works under study here, in all of them plants function as a means to rework European literary traditions and forms and
in turn to fashion a literary identity that is distinctively Spanish American. In the works of Landívar and Bello, for instance, reflections on the
ills of intensive agricultural practices or on the negative consequences
of deforestation contest the optimistic view of farming promulgated by
the georgic mode and give rise to antiagricultural poems. In the nineteenth-century plantation novel the *langage des fleurs* is subtly undercut
through persistent references to local flora as well as the resignification
of key flowers from the European floriographic tradition. And Carpentier's New World baroque draws on botanical imagery to formulate a
specifically Latin American aesthetic.

Another central theme in Spanish American cultural engagements
with plants is the expression of a belief that trees or flowers are sentient,
communicative beings. Such a view has its origins in pre-Columbian
cosmologies but features in many Creole representations of nature from
the late colonial period onward. In the *Rusticatio Mexicana*, for instance,
animistic beliefs are expressed through the extended anatomical metaphor that renders plants as maimed or bleeding bodies. In the case of
Isaacs's *María*, the vitality of plants is emphasized through their complex
associations with the female protagonist's hair. The life of plants, which

variously manifests itself through anthropomorphic descriptions of flowers and trees, the "plantification" of people, and an engagement with "vegetal thinking"—the way in which plant life "thinks" or "acts"—is fundamental to cultural expression across Spanish America and to our understanding of environmental ethics and aesthetics in the region.

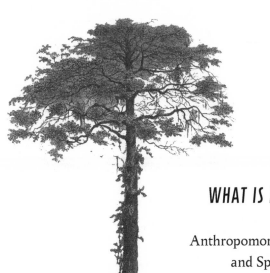

CHAPTER 4

WHAT IS IT LIKE TO BE A TREE?

Anthropomorphism, Phytomorphism,
and Spanish American Culture

The figure of men or women metamorphosing into plants or trees is recurrent in the Western literary tradition from the classical texts of Virgil and Ovid through to the works of Dante, Ariosto, Tasso, Spenser, and Shakespeare. In Ovid's *Metamorphoses* several characters are transformed into a vegetal state, including Daphne who becomes a laurel tree, and Dante and Spenser both include episodes in which people who have been changed into trees cry out in pain when branches are broken from them.[1] In the seventeenth century, the English writer and horticulturist John Evelyn published a book on forestry in which he observed, succinctly, "*Homo* is but *arbor inversa*."[2] At first glance, the trope of arborization as adopted by Ovid and others seems to persist in a number of Spanish American works of the twentieth century, with instances ranging from Lam's plant-people hybrids to the long dead Nahuatl woman who inhabits an orange tree in Gioconda Belli's novel *La mujer habitada* (*The Inhabited Woman*), published in 1988.[3] Nevertheless, in Spanish American culture the figure of phytomorphism is fundamentally different from the deployment of the trope within European literature. An exploration of instances of plants turning into people and people turning into plants across a number of twentieth- and early twenty-first-century literary and filmic texts and visual art will show that, in Spanish American culture, anthropomorphism and phytomorphism are often tied to indigenous animist beliefs, which consider plants not to be separate from humans but to be part of a broad continuum of life.

Such a view originates in pre-Columbian cosmologies and persists in the thinking of many indigenous groups across Latin America today. In his study of Tukano culture, Gerardo Reichel-Dolmatoff notes how, for native Amazonians, "man is in every respect a part of his environment. . . . What we call nature is conceived by [him] as an extension of biological man."[4] Animism, whereby life and personality are ascribed to "animal, vegetable, [and] mineral alike," underpins much Native American thinking about the environment.[5] Whereas Western views of the natural world segment the human from other life forms, animism effaces the differences between, say, plants and people, stressing a mutuality of culture and the possibility of metamorphosis into and out of other states.

The fluidity of identity between humans and nonhumans in Amazonian society is also central to the arguments of Descola's groundbreaking *Beyond Nature and Culture*, where he notes that: "A classic feature of many animist ontologies is the ability to undergo metamorphosis that is recognized to belong to beings with an identical interiority. A human can be embodied in an animal or a plant; an animal can adopt the form of another animal; a plant or an animal can shed its outward clothing and reveal its objectivized soul in the body of a human being." Viveiros de Castro's theory of multinaturalism likewise identifies a belief in a "metaphysical continuity" between humans and nonhumans that underpins the Amazonian worldview and posits an originary core of humanity in all living things, including plants. Kohn's explorations of extra-human life in relation to the Runa of the Upper Amazon continues the work of

Descola and Viveiros de Castro, contributing to "posthuman critiques of the ways in which we have treated humans as exceptional." In this manner, thinking "beyond the human" can help us to develop, in the words of Kohn, "a precise way to analyze how the human is both distinct from and continuous with that which lies beyond it" at a crucial moment in the history of human engagements with nature. Miller's *Plant Kin* deepens again the sense that understanding human relationships with plants can have political and ecological implications. Miller takes up Natasha Myers's playful idea of the "Planthroposcene"—an era in which humans make alliances with plants rather than contribute to their (and hence our own) oblivion—in her understanding of human-plant encounters as "central to planetary health, individual and communal survival, and local and global well-being."[6]

The recent turn to plants in the humanities and sciences has increasingly engaged with and substantiated animistic views of vegetal life. Marder's formulation of the idea of "Plant-Thinking" as a philosophical category emphasizes the ethical dimensions of plants and the interconnections between the human and the vegetal. Hall has likewise insisted upon the need to see plants as autonomous and intelligent beings. Research into plant neurobiology has supported these philosophical arguments by revealing how plants possess signaling systems that are homologous to the nervous systems of animals.[7] Recently scientists have confirmed the presence of "a certain kind of language" among plants, and Peter Wohlleben has shown how forests mirror human society, with trees supporting each other's growth, sharing nutrients, and warning each other about danger.[8] 89 232

Transformations of plants into people and people into plants in Spanish American culture are, therefore, embedded in specifically indigenous American beliefs about the coextensiveness of the human and the nonhuman—beliefs that have recently been rearticulated from within a philosophical and scientific framework. Whereas in the Western literary tradition plants are often highly symbolic (consider, for instance, the floriographic tradition), the interactions between people and plants in Latin American culture must be understood as part of a worldview in which nature and culture have long been regarded as coterminous.[9] Through a plant-centered reading of both canonical and less well-known works of art and literature—Rivera's *La vorágine*, Juan Carlos Galeano's poetry, folktales, and a documentary film, and the performance art of the Cuban American Ana Mendieta—in this chapter I will argue that the figure of phytomorphism in Spanish American literature and culture does not simply repeat literary tropes but, rather, expresses important local beliefs about the relationship between humans and nature.[10] Marder has noted how, within the Western metaphysical tradition, plants have often been relegated to a secondary position and regarded as something to be consumed or manipulated by humans.[11] The persistent dissolution of boundaries between the human and the botanical in the works considered here destabilizes Western ontological distinctions and provides the basis for an ecologically charged defence of vegetal life, where plants are regarded not simply as a resource but as animate beings upon which we depend and to which we owe our consideration.

LA VORÁGINE (1924)

Often classified as a *novela de la selva* or jungle novel, José Eustasio Rivera's *La vorágine*, relates in the first-person singular the story of Arturo Cova, an urban poet who elopes with his lover and, after a series of mishaps, finds himself deep in the disputed no-man's-lands of the Amazon rainforest. This is a work that, since its first publication almost a century ago, has generated countless critical interpretations, from analyses according to Jungian archetype to ecologically inflected readings relating to mapping, the rubber boom, or "plant-horror."[12] I aim to deepen these ecocritical readings of the novel by considering in detail the tropes of people metamorphosing into trees and of trees acting as humans. Trees, I will contend, are central not only to the action of *La vorágine* but to its plant-centered poetics—what Vieira has recently called the novel's "*phytographic* vision of a future golden age of plant life that is simultaneously alluring and frightening."[13]

The forest is the dominant natural feature of the novel. Tapping into the international condemnation of the rubber industry's treatment of indigenous people in the disputed Putumayo district of the Amazon during the first decades of the twentieth century, Rivera sets *La vorágine* primarily in the tropical jungle. The rubber grove is an important locus in the work and the author insistently presents plants and trees as animate. This emphasis is achieved in a number of ways, from the use of rhetorical figures familiar from the Western literary tradition, such as prosopopoeia and anthropomorphism, to more radical instances of plant-human transposition that draw on local imaginaries of the forest as a communicative and intelligent entity.

Anthropomorphism is widespread in *La vorágine*, often bestowing idealized human characteristics on nature, particularly trees, as in Cova's celebrated description of a palm being struck by lightning: "era bello y aterrador el espectáculo de aquella palmera heroica, que agitaba alrededor del hendido tronco las fibras del penacho flamante y moría en su sitio, sin humillarse ni enmudecer" ["it was a beautiful yet awesome sight to see that heroic (palm) tree waving the plumes of its flaming crest around its ripped trunk, dying unrooted, proudly and bravely"].[14] As well as being an established trope of classical literature, anthropomorphism was frequently adopted in Romantic writing—a tradition that is often regarded as an important influence on Rivera's novel.[15] In "Anthropomorphism and Trope in the Lyric," Paul de Man speaks of the power as well as the limitations of the figure, which has significant consequences for a reading of Rivera's novel: "Anthropomorphism freezes the infinite chain of tropological transformations and propositions into one single assertion or essence which, as such, excludes all others."[16] According to this view, anthropomorphism tends to anthropocentrism and risks imposing a human-centered interpretation of nature. In *La vorágine*, however, anthropomorphism is also capable of evincing ecological consciousness.

By projecting human characteristics onto nature (particularly trees), Rivera expresses people's communion with and dependence upon the natural world and anticipates much recent philosophical and scientific reevaluations of vegetal life.[17]

In his classic 1948 article on *La vorágine*, William Bull notes the presence in the work of two kinds of anthropomorphism. The first is Cova's poetic use of the trope in the early part of the novel "simply for stylistic effects."[18] Examples of this are Cova's characterization of the palm tree as heroic or his famous apostrophe to the jungle that opens the second part of *La vorágine*, where he adopts a familial metaphor to convey the close ties of the forest trees: "Tus vegetales forman sobre la tierra la poderosa familia que no se traiciona nunca. El abrazo que no pueden darse tus ramazones lo llevan las enredaderas y los bejucos, y eres solidaria hasta en el dolor de la hoja que cae. Tus multísonas voces forman un solo eco al llorar por los troncos que se desploman" (190).[19]

In line with de Man's concerns, the anthropomorphizing tendencies of this address fail to engage with the jungle plants on their own terms. Cova credits the trees with human capabilities such as speech and physical dexterity, and there is throughout a strong sense not only of the sentience of nature but also of its solidarity, as the creepers vicariously extend the embrace that the tree's branches cannot. In his essay on "Apostrophe" (the mode of poetic address to "unhearing entities" that Cova adopts above), Jonathan Culler suggests that the "apostrophizing poet identifies his universe as a world of sentient forces," conferring subjectivity, feeling, and "animicity" onto inanimate objects. According to this definition, the worldview of the apostrophizing poet has much in common with that of the native Amazonian: the jungle is presented as alive—not just as a growing, transpiring botanical entity but in possession of human social structures and emotions. Nevertheless, Culler goes on to argue that this poetic strategy is nothing short of an act of self-aggrandizement: "a device which the poetic voice uses to establish with an object a relationship which helps to constitute him. . . . One who successfully invokes nature is one to whom nature might, in its turn, speak."[20] As such, Cova's apostrophic address to the living jungle at the opening of part 2 of the novel can be seen as a self-conscious attempt on the part of the protagonist to emphasize his own poetic sensibilities and prowess. In this sense, in the early part of the novel, Rivera's poetics of plants can be situated firmly within a Romantic aesthetics of nature, where the natural world serves to illustrate human emotions and the visionary poetic voice is presented as a privileged intercessor between man and his environment.

The second kind of anthropomorphism that Bull identifies in *La vorágine* relates to what he sees as a genuine belief in the sentience of nature on the part of the poet-protagonist. Although Bull argues that this belief stems from Cova's incipient madness in the later sections of the novel (his inability to distinguish fantasy from reality), Cova's anthropomorphic proclivities can also be situated as part of the broader poetics of animism that increasingly propel the text. Cova and a number of other characters in the novel, who do not show signs of mental illness, often express conviction in the sentience of plants. This is emphasized not only through literary tropes such as apostrophe or prosopopoeia, when the jungle's plants and trees are themselves empowered to speak, but through a persistent arborization of people and anthropomorphism of trees.

In much of the latter half of *La vorágine*, the anthropomorphism of nature works to reveal not a heroic flora but one as downtrodden and ailing as the Amazonian rubber workers condemned to live within it. Clemente Silva, whose surname invokes the "selva" or jungle through which he treks in search of his lost son, describes the damaging process of latex collection in the Amazon—a boom that wiped out tens of thousands of people as well as trees in the first years of the twentieth century: "Por entonces se trabajaba el caucho negro tanto como el siringa, llamado goma borracha por los brasileños; para sacar éste, se hacen incisiones en la corteza, se recoge la leche en petaquillas y se cuaja al humo; la extracción de aquél exigía tumbar el árbol, hacerle lacraduras de cuarta en cuarta, recoger el jugo y depositarlo en hoyos ventilados" (262–63).[21] Although the language is factual, almost technical, in its presentation of the process of rubber extraction, the noun "lacradura" (a Colombian provincialism meaning a sign or aftereffect of an illness) is one example of the widespread use of anatomical discourse in the description of the tapping and felling of trees.[22] While in the Putumayo rubber zone with a French naturalist and explorer, Silva comes across a disfigured tree: "El árbol, castrado antiguamente por los gomeros, era un siringo enorme, cuya corteza quedó llena de cicatrices, gruesas, protuberantes, tumefactas, como lobanillos apretujados" (266) ["The tree, hacked in the past by rubber workers, was a gigantic siringo, the bark of which was a mass of scars, thick, proturberant, swollen, like squeezed tumours" (228)].[23] This rubber tree is both old and of large stature, two qualities that, as Anderson notes, often lead to the veneration of trees in human society. Although in *La vorágine* the tree is not felled, it has been severely damaged by the process of rubber extraction. The simile comparing its rutted bark to a cyst and the references to scars, tumefaction, and castration are part of the generalized medical lexicon that Rogers has identified in the novel.[24]

The personifying discourse is intensified following Silva's realization that this tree was the very one on which, years before, he had inscribed a message to his missing son, Luciano—a message that, against all odds, the son had read and responded to. This discovery precipitates a strong sense of cohesion with plants in Silva, who compares his injuries at the hands of his bosses to those of the mutilated rubber tree:

> —Señor, diga si mi espalda ha sufrido menos que ese árbol.
>
> Y, levantándome la camisa, le enseñé mis carnes laceradas.
>
> Momentos después, el árbol y yo perpetuamos en la Kodak nuestras heridas, que vertieron para igual amo distintos jugos: siringa y sangre. (266–67)[25]

This is not just an example of the kind of anthropomorphism that de Man has expressed suspicion of. Rather, Silva's account of the contusions on the tree and his own body draws out the mutuality of plant-human anatomy as well as their dual experience of mistreatment. In Spanish, as in English, the verb "sangrar" (to bleed) is used routinely to describe the process of tapping rubber. Here and elsewhere in the novel, the fluids of trees and men—rubber and blood—coalesce, blurring, like Silva's use of the first-person plural, the boundary between plants and humans.[26]

In the famous lament that opens the third part of the novel, an unnamed rubber worker describes a fight over tapped latex in which "la leche disputada se salpica de gotas enrojecidas" ["the disputed latex is splashed with red"], concluding, "¿Más qué importa que nuestras venas aumenten la savia del vegetal?" (289) ["But what does it matter if our veins increase the supply of sap?" (261)]. Here the "sangre blanca" (287) ["white blood" (259)] of the forest trees is literally and metaphorically augmented by human blood to meet the world demand for rubber. Once again, the language of the novel is insistently anthropomorphic: the rubber tapper goes on to speak of how he makes martyrs of the trees and fells those "que no lloran" (289) [that do not cry], while collecting the "llanto trágico" (289) ["tears" (261)] of others. Yet, again, this anthropomorphism does not lead to a sense of the singularity of humans but, rather, of the shared physicality of people and plants. The rubber worker inflicts damage on the trees, but he in turn is bled by swarms of mosquitoes and his eyes water because of the pollen: "¡Así el árbol y yo, con tormento vario, somos lacrimatorios ante la muerte" (289) ["Thus both the tree and I, suffering, are tearful in the face of death" (261)].

The lack of stability of ontological categories in this section of the novel, in which the line between plants and people becomes ever more indistinct, culminates in the final line of the soliloquy, when the tapper exclaims: "¡Y lo que hizo mi mano contra los árboles puede hacerlo contra los hombres!" (289) ["And what my hand has done to trees, it can also do to men" (262)]. On the surface, the statement points to the dehumanization of rubber workers in this lawless frontier zone, a familiar interpretative matrix for the spiralling violence of the Putumayo during the rubber boom.[27] Yet a plant-centered reading of the rubber worker's lament also shows that the process of becoming less human is matched by one of becoming more plant-like, as man and tree merge through their shared experience of exploitation.

As Seymour Menton shows, the comparison of sap to blood in this section of La vorágine has a clear literary antecedent in canto 13 of Dante's Inferno when Virgil and Dante walk through a wood where the bodies of those who have committed suicide have been transformed into trees:

> I reached my hand
> A little in front of me and twisted off
>
> One shoot of a mighty thornbush—and it moaned,
> "Why do you break me?" Then after it had grown
> Darker with blood, it began again and mourned,
>
> "Why have you torn me? Have you no pity, then?
> Once we were men, now we are stumps of wood."[28]

This section from Dante is not only evoked by Silva's and the anonymous rubber worker's accounts of bleeding and injured rubber trees but also by a sequence early on in Rivera's novel. Before entering the jungle, Cova has a nightmare in which, armed with a rubber tapper's axe and collecting jar, he pursues his naked lover, Alicia, through a nocturnal forest. He stops before an *Araucaria*, which he mistakenly takes to be a rubber tree, and as he scores the bark he hears a voice saying: "¿Por qué me desangras? . . . Yo soy tu Alicia y me he convertido en una parásita" (112) ["Why do you bleed me? . . . I am your Alicia, now but a parasite!" (51)].[29]

Nevertheless, the persistent intermingling of blood and sap in the novel, although bringing to mind the epic tradition, has more local underpinnings. Lamia Tewfik has discussed the recurrence of images of blood and bleeding in the personification of plants in Anglophone Caribbean poetry—images that he relates to the poets' remembrance of slaughtered ancestors.[30] In *La vorágine* the metaphorical description of the rubber trees' blood likewise recalls the brutal murders of tens of thousands of indigenous people during the rubber boom, as well as the destruction of trees, and the creatures and other life forms they sustained. Despite the knowing parallels with European forerunners, human transfiguration into vegetal form in *La vorágine* is not meant to be read through the lens of epic myth, or as an Amazonian retelling of Ovid. Instead, descriptions of suppurating human and vegetal flesh are part of a powerful ecological statement that effaces the distinction between humans and nonhumans and that unites Amazonian trees and people as mutual victims of capitalism and violence.

Silva's coextensiveness with the jungle is made apparent not only through his surname and the comparison of his mutilated body to a scarred rubber tree but also by his reference to an angry rubber worker's attempt to "destroncar[le]" (263). This is a verb meaning both to mutilate and, when applied to trees, to chop down.[31] Elsewhere in the novel Silva communicates both through and with trees. A tree trunk becomes the intermediary for a conversation between Silva and his errant son when they carve messages to each other onto the bark of an imposing rubber tree. Later Silva relates how he got lost in the jungle and found his way out by "listening" to a palm tree:

> Paróse ante una palmera de cananguche, que, según la leyenda, describe la trayectoria del astro diurno, a la manera del girasol. Nunca había pensado en aquel misterio. Ansiosos minutos estuvo en éxtasis, constatándolo, y creyó observar que el alto follaje iba moviéndose pausadamente, con el ritmo de una cabeza que gastara doce horas justas en inclinarse desde el hombro derecho hasta el contrario. La secreta voz de las cosas le llenó

su alma. ¿Sería cierto que esa palmera, encumbrada en aquel destierro como un índice hacia el azul, estaba indicándole la orientación? Verdad o mentira, él lo oyó decir. ¡Y creyó! (314–15).[32]

As Amanda M. Smith notes of this episode: "Through his experiences of becoming lost and then removed from a rigid category of human separateness, Silva integrates himself into the jungle ecology and gathers navigational information in dialogue with it."[33] Silva's appeal to the tree for guidance is starkly opposed to Cova's earlier apostrophizing to the jungle and corresponds closely to indigenous views of the forest as animate. Descola notes that native Amazonians believe that "it is . . . the corporeal form that differentiates between humans and nonhumans." Unlike in Western culture, Amazonians do not believe there is a radical disjunction between the interiority of people and plants but simply that there are "different kinds of human species."[34] Although the "cananguche" palm (*Mauritia flexuosa*) has the outward appearance of a tree, Silva insistently anthropomorphizes it through reference to human anatomy and capability (references to its head, shoulders, voice, and so on). Silva's listening to nature in this episode, and his earlier recognition of the physical connections between his body and the scarred rubber tree, mark a radical shift in how plants are perceived in the novel.

As a former rubber worker, Silva had once been part of a system that subjugated vegetal life, exploiting it as a mere commodity. The contrast between that view and his sympathy for the trees here can be seen to correspond to what Nurit Bird-David has delineated as a broader schism between "modernist" epistemologies of nature and indigenous practices relating to trees (in this case, among the Nayaka of India):

> If "cutting trees into parts" epitomizes the modernist epistemology, [then] "talking with trees," I argue, epitomizes Nayaka animistic epistemology. "Talking" is short-hand for a two-way responsive relatedness with a tree—rather than "speaking" one-way to it, as if it could listen

and understand. . . . To "talk with a tree"—rather than "cut it down"—is to perceive what *it* does as one acts towards it, being aware concurrently of changes in oneself and the tree. It is expecting response and responding, growing into mutual responsiveness and, furthermore, possibly into mutual responsibility.[35]

In the case of Silva, "talking with trees" saves him from certain death. In the first edition of the novel, Silva's oneness with nature culminates in an arresting visual image: a black-and-white photograph of a rubber worker climbing a tree, which a caption tells us is Clemente Silva. Felipe Martínez-Pinzón has noted the way in which this photograph dissolves the differences between the man and the tree, with the rubber worker appearing as "casi sumergido en la naturaleza" [almost submerged in nature], as the lines between his body and the surrounding vegetation are erased.[36] In this picture the folds of Silva's trousers mirror the rucked textures of tree bark—arboreal contours described in *La vorágine* as "repliegues" (266) ["folds" (229)], a word choice that further accentuates the continuity between the tree trunks and the clothes of the rubber tappers who straddle them. Martínez-Pinzón regards this photograph as one indication in the novel of the breakdown, via modernist poetics, of a hygienicist discourse aimed at distancing man from nature. In *La vorágine* such distinctions certainly do not hold: man is in the midst of nature, and nature in the midst of man, as when Silva laments that, like a worm-eaten tree, he is "¡Engusanado, engusanado y estando vivo!" (246) ["Wormy, wormy, while yet alive" (205)].

Despite Cova's masculinist and colonialist discourses (widely discussed in literary criticism on the novel), even he shows a growing oneness with nature as *La vorágine* progresses. As Jean Franco argues, while in the jungle Cova finds himself "in the grip of a powerful material force. . . . Not only do the trees physically hem him in but the jungle determines his thoughts and sensations."[37] Cova attributes his perception of nature as animate to hallucinations brought on by cerebral fever, which also deprives him of speech and sensation. He hears sand and puddles talking and a mahogany tree entreat a shadow wielding a scythe to hack him to death while Cova rests under its canopy: "Picadlo, picadlo con vuestro hierro, para que experimente lo que es el hacha en la carne viva. ¡Picadlo aunque esté indefenso, pues él también destruyó los árboles y es justo que conozca nuestro martirio!" (229) ["Cut him, cut him with your steel . . . that he may know what it is to have an axe bite into his living flesh. Cut him, even though he is helpless, for he, too, has destroyed trees, and it is only just that he know our sufferings" (186)]. This episode—in which Cova not only hears a tree speaking but also, unable to move his mouth, sends a defiant telepathic message back, "por si el bosque entendía [sus] pensamientos" (229) [as if the forest understood (his) thoughts]—seems to confirm Bull's reading of anthropomorphism in the novel as connected to Cova's growing mental and physical infirmity.[38] It also anticipates a more explicit instance of phytomorphism later in the text when the protagonist loses sensation on one side of his body during an attack of beriberi: "lo demás no era mío, ni la pierna, ni el brazo, ni la muñeca; era algo postizo, horrible, estorboso, a la par ausente y presente, que me producía un fastidio único, como el que puede sentir el árbol que ve pegada en su parte viva una rama seca. . . . me sentía sembrado en el suelo, y, por mi pierna, hinchada, fofa y deforme como las raíces de ciertas palmeras, ascendía una savia caliente, petrificante. Quise moverme y la tierra no me soltaba. ¡Un grito de espanto! ¡Vacilé! ¡Caí!" (374).[39] This is an example of inverse anthropomorphism in the novel. Here Cova not only finds himself rooted to the ground and hence immobile (taking on one of the apparent characteristics of plants that led to their categorization as an inferior life form by the ancient Greeks, among others), but he feels the warm sap of latex running down his leg, once more invoking the connections between latex, blood, and in this instance, semen.[40] The medical interventions of his companion, who calls for him to be bled, does nothing to offset this slip, quite literally, into a vegetative state. This proposed cure would serve only to reinforce

Cova's arborization in the novel since it realizes the mahogany tree's wish for the protagonist to understand firsthand the tortures that he himself has meted out as a rubber tapper. Cova's experience of "becoming a tree" is far from idealized in *La vorágine*. His reference to the gripping earth is reminiscent of an earlier description of a personified nature by his guide, El Pipa, who shares a vision of talking and gesticulating trees after imbibing the Amazonian hallucinogen *yagé*—a moment in the text that Alejandro Mejías-López has described as embodying the "fusión completa entre árbol y hombre" [the complete fusion between tree and man].[41] Pipa reports how, during his hallucination, he saw trees railing against their inability to move and censuring the humans who had tapped and felled them.[42]

Unlike the anthropomorphism of nature in much Romantic writing where the agency ascribed to plants is merely rhetorical, the animistic trees of *La vorágine* represent a real threat to the novel's protagonists.[43] Trees are complicit in the deaths of a number of characters, including— the indeterminate ending of the novel leads us to assume—Cova himself. Cova notes how, while he was trekking through the forest, the trees "iban creciendo a cada segundo, con una apariencia de hombres acuclillados, que se empinaban desperezándose hasta elevar los brazos verdosos por encima de la cabeza" (293) ["the trees were growing taller every second, like men who have been crouching and rise and stretch until their arms are high above their heads" (267)]. Moments later he starts to run in fear and becomes entangled in the undergrowth. Silva relates such views to "el embrujamiento de la montaña" (294) ["the witchery of the jungle" (268)]—a condition through which trees enchant travelers and cause them to get lost in the jungle or to engage in heinous acts.[44] According to Silva's account: "cualquiera de estos árboles se amansaría, tornándose amistoso y hasta risueño, en un parque, en un camino, en una llanura, donde nadie lo sangrara ni lo persiguiera; mas aquí todos son perversos, o agresivos, o hipnotizantes" (294) ["any of these trees would seem tame, friendly, even smiling in a park, along a road, on a plain, where nobody would bleed it or persecute it; yet here they are all perverse, or aggressive, or hypnotising" (268–69)].

The novel abounds in examples of the forest's aggression toward human beings. When Silva is lost in the Amazon, he describes how the vines that Cova imagined as "embracing" each other when he first entered the jungle, "no le dejaban abrir la trocha" ["resist his efforts to blaze a trail"], and when he tries to flee from his menacing companions "un árbol cómplice lo enlazó por las piernas con un bejuco y lo tiró al suelo" (308–9) ["the treacherous lianas of a tree caught his legs and tripped him" (284–85)]. The body of Silva's son, killed by a falling tree, is finally located near the roots of a jacaranda, and the novel's indeterminate final sentence strongly suggests that Cova and his companions have also died at the hands of plants: "¡Los devoró la selva!" (385) [The jungle devoured them].[45]

This image of an anthropophagous forest echoes the phrasing of Silva's anguished lament for his son upon learning of his death: "Lo mató un árbol" (286) ["A tree killed him" (255)]. It also suggests a wilful deviance on the part of plants. One of Silva's overseers speaks of a "malign" tree that exudes an irresistible perfume "a semejanza de las mujeres de mal vivir" ["like women of ill-repute"], which attracts men and leaves their bodies "veteado de rojo, con una comezón desesperante, y van apareciendo lamparones que se supuran y luego cicatrices arrugando la piel" (269–70) ["mottled with red, itching frightfully. Then large red spots appear that fester, and then dry up leaving the skin scarred and wrinkled" (233)]. In this instance, a discourse of botanical unknowability is instrumented to undermine Silva's account of humanitarian abuse in the rubber district: "¡Tiene tantos secretos la botánica, particularmente en estas regiones!" (269) ["Nature (lit. "botany") has so many secrets, especially in these regions" (232)]. His scars, the boss insinuates to a visitor, are a token of sexual deviance rather than mistreatment. As Mejías-López notes, however, the accusations against Silva in the end serve only to strengthen the bonds between men and trees: "Hombre, árbol, selva y mujer son víctimas en una cadena de violaciones por la pluma del capital y los discursos de una modernidad siempre colonial y siempre patriarcal" [Man, tree, jungle, and woman are victims in a chain of violations by the pen of capital and the discourses of a modernity that is always colonial and always patriarchal].⁴⁶

Relationships between humans and plants are complex in the novel—sometimes antagonistic, sometimes sympathetic, but continual and ever evolving. Camilo Jaramillo has recently examined the trope of "plant horror" in *La vorágine*, showing how the topos of the jungle as "green hell" evinces "proto-environmental consciousness about modernity's use of nature."⁴⁷ Meeker and Szabari have also explored the concept of "plant horror" in relation to US cinema. Although arising from a different cultural perspective, their analysis of the function of plant horror, particularly the trope of plants metamorphosing into humans, coincides with my reading of the ecological impulses of the figure of arborization in *La vorágine*:

> Anticipating an ecological discourse that postdates these films, we might say then that they gesture toward the possibility of a new mode of environmental thinking, one in which the separation between natural object and human subject no longer informs our relationships to the world around us.... [T]he plant horror genre provides us with a kind of preview of what Timothy Morton has recently described as "the ecological thought"—a way of acting and thinking that refuses the long-standing distinctions between outside and inside, between "us" and "another," that have so often informed the human approach to nature.⁴⁸

Moving beyond the human-centered anthropomorphism that was prevalent in the Romantic period, Rivera's animistic poetics reconfigures the relationships between people and plants, foreshadowing the environmental discourses expressed by local Amazonian poets and storytellers from the second half of the twentieth century onward. Throughout the novel the rhetorical figures of arborization and anthropomorphism are given new life in an Amazonian context where metamorphosis between plants and people is commonplace in the locals' animist ontologies. Cova's ingestion by the jungle in the final line of the novel is often seen as the apogee of "plant horror" in *La vorágine*. It also marks the culmination of the work's vegetal-inspired aesthetic, where the line between people and plants—between a materialist reading of jungle as commodity and a relational reading that draws out the interconnection between humans and nonhumans—is finally and irreversibly erased.

AMAZONIA (2003), *CUENTOS AMAZÓNICOS* (2007), *THE TREES HAVE A MOTHER* (2008)

In the foreword to the English edition of Juan Carlos Galeano's recent collection of folktales from across the Amazon basin, *Cuentos amazónicos* (*Folktales of the Amazon*), Michael Uzendoski has noted that "[t]ransformation and shape-shifting, rather than fixity, are the basic premises of Amazonian existence."[49] A frequent metamorphosis that takes place in the work of this Colombian-born poet and folklorist, now resident in the United States, is that between people and plants, particularly trees. The opening story of *Cuentos amazónicos* relates how the Amazon River emerged from the trunk of a fallen tree that had germinated on the spot where a young man died.[50] Later tales speak of trees and plants that bleed and of humanoid forest guardians like the *curupira* and the closely related *chullachaqui*, who also plays a leading role in Galeano's film *The Trees Have a Mother*, codirected with Valliere Richard Auzenne. Galeano's poetry is infused with animistic ontologies, where people are able to communicate with animals and plants and where nonhuman nature adopts the speech and behavior of the human world. I contend that figures of anthropomorphism and phytomorphism in Galeano's work mark the continuation of long-established animist tendencies in Latin American culture. His effacing of cultural differences between plants and people draws on pre-Columbian cosmologies as well as on the eco-logical thinking of Creole works such as *La vorágine* so as to reconfigure and rebuild human beings' relationships with the nonhuman world at a moment of profound environmental crisis.

Galeano's collection of poetry, *Amazonia*, was first published in 2003. It draws on a range of Amazonian mythical figures, including the shape-shifting freshwater dolphin reputed to metamorphose into human form in order to seduce women living along the Amazon River.[51] Although such mythical events are treated in a matter-of-fact and often comical manner, with anthropomorphized animals and plants engaging in everyday human activities such as going to the "mercados, bares y cinemas" [markets, bars, and movies], Galeano's poems are nevertheless inflected with a clear ecological undercurrent.[52] The relationship they envisage between humans and nonhumans is governed by the Amazonian belief system that Viveiros de Castro calls "perspectivism," through which animals or plants "see themselves as humans: they perceive themselves as (or become) anthropomorphic beings when they are in their own houses or villages and they experience their own habits and characteristics in the form of culture."[53] In his ascription of human attributes to nonhuman nature, Galeano's adherence to perspectivist beliefs goes well beyond a mere rhetorical reflex. Rather, it insists on viewing plants as sentient and in possession of a culture that is recognizably human. It also produces a strong sense of community between nature and people, which the Peruvian author and commentator Róger Rumrrill regards as central to all Amazonian cultural expression.[54]

What is remarkable about the human-tree hybrids in many of Galeano's poems is their lack of remarkability. In "La espera" (The wait), for example, two trees toast the day ahead by stretching out their branches; in "Música" (Music) trees become angry when a noisy river boat disrupts their sleep; in "Árboles" (Trees) some young trees go out dancing in the city, causing much upset for their elders.[55] Roberto Forns-Broggi notes the lack of artifice or ethnographic distance in Galeano's work, which "incorpora de manera casual y natural una perspectiva fractal de la subjetividad que no se limita a lo humano sino que se entrelaza y convive con lo no humano" [incorporates in a casual and natural fashion a fractal perspective of subjectivity that is not limited to the human but that intertwines and coexists with the nonhuman].[56]

In Galeano's poems, even the most unlikely events are presented in a deadpan manner, as in "Amazon Show," in which two tree magicians who had the power to transform leaves into money "volvieron millonarios a unos árboles muy pobres" ["made a few poor trees into millionaires"].[57] One of the most important articulations of the relationship between plants and people in his poetry is expressed in the poem "Pasto" (Grass), which explores a process of phytomorphism, imagining the overgrowth of people and objects with grass:

> El pasto crece en las casas, en los cuerpos, nuestras
> orejas y bolsillos.
>
> Mientras mi padre lee los periódicos, dos conejitos
> pastan felices en sus brazos.
>
> Los camiones que llevan árboles inmensos para los
> jardines botánicos
> avanzan, islas flotantes, por el pasto.[58]

The increasing indistinguishability of humans and nonhumans, nature and culture, is marked in the poem not only by the physical transformation of people, who sprout grass rather than hair from their heads and ears, but through the figure of a firefly that looks like a pin. The noun "pasto" [grass] and etymological or sonic cognates such as "pastel" [cake] are repeated some nine times in the poem, mirroring the superabundance of grass, which threatens to efface human culture. The tone of the poem seems largely playful—the rabbits are munching happily and mothers take advantage of the dew to brush their children's vegetal tangles—but "Pasto" also expresses ecological concerns. The description of truckloads of giant trees extracted from the jungle for botanical gardens in an intensified image of colonialist plant prospecting that inflates the seed into the mature and uprooted tree is a stark reminder of deforestation in the Amazon. In contrast to this extractive model, the diminutive rabbits engage in a much less harmful process of plant consumption, as they feast on the sprouting grass of their human hosts.

Elsewhere in *Amazonia*, the relationship between people and plants is more openly hostile. In "Cedro" (Cedar), the eponymous tree (presumably the tropical *Cedrela odorata*) "camina huyendo de los hombres y se pone a / llorar todas las noches" ["walks away from the kingdom of men and cries every night"]. The declarative statement in the final line of the poem: "El cedro debería ser más hombre" ["The cedar should be more of a man"] accentuates the ontological fluidity between trees and men and at the same time critiques masculinist discourses (often twinned with environmentally dubious attitudes) that value emotional constraint and physical resilience.[59] Hall notes that one of the central reasons for the destruction of the environment is the Western view of nature as "devoid of the attributes which require human attention—such as mentality, agency, and volition."[60] By imbuing trees with the recognizable human emotions of sadness and fear, Galeano encourages a more ecologically responsible relationship with nature that sees people and plants as part of a continuum and bound by strict ethical codes.

Such codes are central to many of the stories in Galeano's *Cuentos amazónicos*, a repository of folktales from across the Amazon that the author recorded in the field and reworked according to his "poetic sensibilities."[61] In his introduction to the English edition of the stories, Galeano speaks of the distinction between Western conceptions of nature and the view held by Amazonians of the world as "a place where humans are kin to animals and trees." In his discussion of the kinship relationships between plants and people in animist societies, Hall has noted the positive ecological repercussions of this worldview given that "local kinship relationships are accompanied by obligations of responsibility, solidarity, and care." Although, as Hall notes, these obligations do not preclude predatory activities such as using plants for food or felling trees for shelter, as Galeano's work makes clear, violation of the codes can lead to misfortune.[62] "Lupuna," for instance, tells of how, after a period of drought in the Colombian Amazon, a group of loggers decide to beat the trunk of a ceiba tree (locally known as a "Lupuna blanca") to invoke rain in order to replenish the river and allow them to remove their cargo of felled trees from the forest. However, no rain falls, and on the following day the logger who carried out the beating is struck down by severe stomach pains. A visit to a shaman reveals that the logger had not only selected the wrong kind of tree (a "Lupuna colorado," or *Cavanillesia hylogeiton*, that had a spirit protector in its trunk) but also defiled nature by urinating at the tree's base.[63] Although the shaman's timely intervention saves the logger's life, the story illustrates the danger of not respecting nature, especially the tutelary spirits of trees or plants.[64] Another tale collected from the Brazilian Amazon, "Seringa" focuses on the *mae de seringa* (the mother of the rubber tree), represented as a beautiful young woman whose clothes are made from bark and who tends to the domestic chores of a rubber worker when he is absent from his hut. One day he decides to spy on her, and this causes her to flee and the rubber trees that had previously supplied his needs to dry up. The man becomes destitute and leaves the forest in search of work.[65] The anthropomorphism of the "mother of rubber," who in this story (unlike the moving, talking, disco-dancing but still determinedly tree-like vegetation of many of Galeano's poems) adopts human form, is consistent with other renditions of this popular Amazonian myth. During the rubber boom, tappers reported that if they sliced a tree too deeply or widely, the rubber tree's tutelary spirit would appear to them with bloodied arms and legs.[66] As reflected in Galeano's story, the strong sense of kinship between people and plants thus regulates deforestation, just as the overexploitation of game or fish is controlled by a belief in forest spirits such as the *curupira* or *chullachaqui*.[67]

As in *Amazonia*, the lack of ontological distinction between humans and plants is central to many of the stories in *Cuentos amazónicos*. "Plantas boas" ("Boa Plants") opens by relating the vigorous growth of two pot plants owned by a recently married couple: "Con sus hojitas, la planta hembra trepaba desde su matero por el poste cerca de la puerta que daba a la vereda. La planta macho, más grande, se enredaba en la columna de la cocina. Con el tiempo, el hombre y su mujer se despertaban con los ruidos de las hojas moviéndose en la sala. Veían cómo las plantas boas se desenredaban de los postes y se dirigían por el patio grande de tierra hasta la charca donde vivían taricayas, cupisos y el árbol renaco" (*CA*, 63).[68]

From the outset, the plants' growth and habits are described in non-vegetal terms. Although some plants are "dioecious," meaning that they have either male or female reproductive organs, the reference to separate "female" and "male" plants alerts us early on to the anthropomorphizing tendencies of the narrator. In this story the plants move, interact with other animals, and are even able to whistle. Yet it is at the end of the story that their proximity to the animal and, indeed, human is fully realized. The narrator relates how the newlyweds moved from the village to the nearby city of Iquitos, leaving the plants in the care of a new couple. On a return visit to the village, the woman calls at her old house and is concerned to see that her plants have disappeared. When she asks about them, she is told that the husband of the new owner had returned home one night in a rage and had taken a machete to the plants: "les dio tantos machetazos que las paredes de la cocina se salpicaron de sangre" (*CA*, 64) ["he hit them so many times with a machete that the kitchen walls were covered with blood" (*FA*, 96)]. The description of the blood-stained walls is a vivid—in this case disturbing—reminder of the sentience of plants in Amazonian thought. As Joe Moshenska has observed of bleeding trees in the epic tradition: "Blood that appears, that is rendered visible and tangible, is simultaneously redolent of life and presages death: it is a form of sudden appearance that signals an imminent disappearance."[69]

As in *La vorágine*, the cohesion of people and plants is crystallized in Galeano's narrative through the topos of bleeding vegetation. At this moment, the tone of the text shifts from the characteristically ludic presentation of human and nonhuman relations to a distressing reminder of the catastrophic consequences of ecological predation or carelessness. Similar moments arise in *Amazonia*, as when Galeano writes apocalyptically of the complete destruction of the Amazon's forests in "Fábula" ("Fable"):

> Pero en la selva nos dijeron que para traer más luz
> le echáramos más árboles al fogón del sol.

> Un día se nos fue la mano, y le echamos toda la selva
> con sus pájaros, los peces y los ríos.[70]

This tone of impending doom is intensified in Galeano's 2008 documentary film, *The Trees Have a Mother*, which intersperses Amazonian folktales with the story of a mother searching for her son who went missing in dense forest near Iquitos some eight months before.[71] Much of the film is concerned with the persistence of mythical beliefs in the Amazon: the young man's disappearance is attributed by a shaman and many locals to a supernatural forest being with uneven-sized feet—the *chullachaqui*, "amigo de los árboles" (*CA*, 99) ["friend of the trees" (*FA*, 43)] and a Peruvian variant of the *curupira*—who is credited with being responsible for leading hunters deep into the forest until they get lost. Nevertheless, toward the end of the documentary, the focus shifts to environmental damage in the Amazon—unchecked logging, water pollution, overfishing—that according to Galeano's informants threatens to displace even the supernatural denizens of the forest. The *chullachaqui*, Galeano's interviewees report, although still in existence has retreated further into the jungle away from human contact.

Galeano's documentary exemplifies the important role that myth plays in conservation in the Amazon, recuperating the Amazonian animistic imagination at a time of increasing environmental pressure, when the *chullachaqui* and his kin must struggle to preserve the forest against not only solitary hunters but also multinational corporations. In the Amazon, widespread belief in the tutelary spirits of trees as well as "lugares encantados" [enchanted places] (special features or areas such as lagoons, waterfalls, or glades, held sacred by locals) have preserved tracts of land that would otherwise have been obliterated during periods of intense exploitation such as the rubber boom.[72] Yet these mythical beliefs are often strained in the film. The shaman whom the mother visits for information about her son appears distracted and ill-tempered and vacillates between assuring the woman that the boy is well and conceding he is dead. Likewise, the existence of the *chullachaqui* is disputed by many of the film's interviewees—an ambivalence playfully exploited by Galeano who represents the figure on screen as a bowlegged humanoid who, although often blurred or concealed by foliage, is obviously covered in thickly applied green paint.

As elsewhere in Galeano's oeuvre, in the film the relationship between people and plants is significant, accentuated not only through the central figure of the *chullachaqui* but also by persistent references to logging and habitat destruction. Just over halfway through the documentary, a series of commentators speak of the importance of plant "mothers." The first tells of seeing a human apparition amid her *hierbaluisa* (lemon verbena) plants; the second speaks sincerely of the aliveness of trees and plants; a third talks of plant mothers and of their obliteration by loggers who use chainsaws to tear the forest apart. Such animistic views contrast starkly with a later shot in which a log company official speaks of how workers engage in clearing the forest from early morning to nightfall. Shortly after, there is a sequence in which machinery hoists up an enormous tree trunk against a background of nondiegetic, elegiac singing—a shot that pans out to reveal many more trunks, laid out cadaverously along a large boat. As Joni Adamson notes of this documentary, discussions of the lost son "turn into discussions of increasingly complex multicultural, multinational, and multispecies relationships that are being changed by chemical spills, overfishing, water pollution, and poverty."[73]

Unsurprisingly, a number of scholars have credited Galeano's work with expressing "explicit ecological concerns."[74] A 2011 edition of *Amazonia* is included in a 2014 review article on Latin American ecocriticism, and Adamson has argued that Galeano's folktales "illuminat[e] the consequences of global economic development for local humans, animals, and nonhumans."[75] The environmental inflections of Galeano's work correspond, in particular, with what Cynthia Deitering has called the "toxic consciousness" of the late twentieth and early twenty-first centuries.[76] Galeano reveals a world in which Amazonian flora and fauna, as well as people, are fighting for survival. At the end of the documentary, an intertitle notes that a different shaman had recently alleged that the missing son at the center of the film had, in fact, not been abducted by a *chullachaqui* but was working in a cocaine lab deep in the jungle and would return a rich man. This revelation resolves a narrative tension that had built up throughout the film about how a viewer external to the Amazon might interpret local beliefs about the fate of the disappeared man. The more plausible explanation—that his disappearance might be connected to international commodity chains, perhaps a consequence of him stumbling upon some illegal activity in the forest, which the viewer cannot help but feel must have resulted in the man's death—is one of a number of disenchantments in the film. The evident endurance and power of animist beliefs among the documentary's interviewees is matched by the persistent lack of sentimentality regarding such beliefs, which (as exemplified in a scene shot in a market in the Belén district of Iquitos, showing jars containing the remnants of freshwater dolphin genitals, used as aphrodisiacs and love potions) can also cause significant environmental degradation.

This is not to say that Galeano's work aims to undermine or dissipate the folk imagination of the Amazon. To the contrary, Galeano suggests the need for a more intensive reenchantment of nature—for the return of the *chullachaqui* or, at the very least, an ethically sound engagement with the natural world. Galeano's work goes well beyond being a repository of folk belief. Bringing indigenous conceptions of nature into dialogue with contemporary ecological thinking, he provides a powerful voice for the "more-than-human world" of plants, whose aliveness, he shows, is not only the basis of Amazonian mythology but fundamental to the future of humanity.[77]

ANA MENDIETA AND *ÁRBOL DE LA VIDA*

Beyond the Amazon, the human-plant hybrid is also an important motif in the work of the Cuban American artist, Ana Mendieta (1948–1985). Although relatively unknown during her lifetime, over the past two decades Mendieta's work has been the subject of a number of scholarly articles and books, and retrospectives of her work have been exhibited in Europe and the United States.[78] Interpretations of Mendieta's artistic practice tend to revolve around questions of feminist aesthetics and cultural identity, with her trajectory as an exile from Castro's Cuba being held as central to what she called her "earth-body" works, many of which involved the artist's corporeal integration into her environment by the use of natural materials such as mud, flowers, or grass.[79] Discussions of polemical early photographs and films of performances exploring violence (*Rape Scene* [1973], *Moffitt Building Piece* [1973], *Blood Writing* [1974]), gory re-creations of practices relating to Afro-Cuban Santería (*Chicken Movie, Chicken Piece* [1972]), and the ongoing controversy surrounding her tragic death have tended to dominate the critical response to Mendieta's art, sidelining the important role of plants.[80] My aim in reflecting on the botanical underpinnings of Mendieta's work is not only to establish the prominence of plants to the artist's practice but also to show how her humanization of plants and "plantification" of people aligns with and illuminates the phytomorphic tendencies of Latin American culture more broadly.

Mendieta's interest in plants spanned her career, from individual works such as her 1975 film *Flower Person, Flower Body*, to her series *Árbol de la vida* (Tree of Life) for which she staged a number of photographs representing the dissolution of boundaries between the human body and trees. Although it is barely mentioned in the critical literature, in 1982 Mendieta embarked on a series of leaf drawings, printing her character-istic *silueta* shape—the outline of a female form that dominated her filmic and photographic work—using a variety of instruments.[81] Robert Katz notes how for her collaborative book project with Carl Andre, *Pietre Foglie* (1984), Mendieta worked on leaves collected from different plants in the grounds of the American Academy in Rome. Unlike the ephemeral physi-cality of her earth-body works, these leaf drawings left a lasting record of Mendieta's thinking about plants. In them, the coalescence of the human spine and the midrib (the name given to the strengthened vein along the middle of a leaf) stresses the fusion of the botanical and the human, just as elsewhere Mendieta formed curvaceous female figures from *ficus* tree roots (*Tallus Mater*, 1982). At the time of her death in 1985, she was preparing a major outdoor installation with a clear botanical focus. This work was to be called *The Jungle*, which some regard as an explicit tribute to the most famous painting of fellow Cuban artist Wifredo Lam, who was an important influence on Carpentier's botanical thinking also. It was to consist of seven tree trunks emblazoned with images and arranged on a triangular patch of grass in MacArthur Park, Los Angeles.[82]

In many of her works Mendieta displays marked botanical knowledge. Indeed, she often selected plants or trees with a specific appearance or cultural resonance.[83] For her planned installation in MacArthur Park, she intended to use redwood trees, and she favored leaves from the copey (*Clusia rosea*)—a plant native to the Caribbean—for her leaf drawings.[84] Another proposal, unrealized at the time of her death, was to create a goddess-shaped grass spiral in the grounds of Bard College in New York State. For this design Mendieta specifically proposed the use of a grass she called "*Racrostes*," which she noted was known for its "close cropping

growth and fine texture."[85] She was also familiar with the cultural significance of the *Ceiba petandra*.[86] In 1981 she made a *silueta* figure on a large
ceiba tree venerated by the Cuban community in Little Havana, South
Miami, using hair collected from local barbers. The work, entitled *Ceiba
Fetish*, tapped into the Afro-Cuban view of this tree as sacred and elicited
positive responses from the local community who, as Mendieta recalls,
"activated the image and claimed it as their own" by making additional
offerings such as coconuts and chicken wings at the base of the trunk.[87]

Throughout much of her work, Mendieta strove to erase the differences between the vegetal and the human body. Pages from the artist's
sketchbook relating to her *Árbol de la vida* series speak directly of the
"merging" of the human and the arboreal: "sentada en el tronco de un
arbol unite mi cuerpo con barro al arbol [*sic*]" [seated on the trunk of a
tree attach my body to the tree with earth]. An accompanying sketch,
in blue and black ink, shows a curvaceous figure, arms upright, whose
bottom half tails off into a tree trunk.[88] The resulting work, *Árbol de la
vida* (1976), is a close-up color photograph showing Mendieta's diminutive
naked figure, covered in mud from head to toe against a large tree trunk
(see figure 10). Her eyes are closed and she is resting her body against
the contours of the trunk, having deposited some smears of mud around
her outline. As if to compound her vegetal state, her body is sprinkled
with grass. Although clearly visible against the tree, she seems inert
and organic.[89] Her figure is much less obvious in another unpublished
photograph from this same shoot, taken from below and at a distance,
cutting off her lower body and replacing it with the view of the tree's
exposed roots growing out of an embankment.[90] An untitled 1979 work
in the same series shows her mud-smeared body entirely under another,
slighter tree, her outspread hair entangled amid the tree's exposed roots
and her limp body dangling, as if in midair, in front of a plant-covered
river bank.[91]

The *Árbol de la vida* series calls to mind the goddess iconography prevalent among many feminist artists of this period.[92] This is a connection

FIGURE 10. Ana Mendieta, *Tree of Life*, 1976. © The Estate of Ana Mendieta Collection, LLC. Courtesy Galerie Lelong & Co.

compounded by the series's name, given that the "Tree of Life" often takes the form of a goddess—the Great Earth Mother or Tellus Mater—who is also alluded to by the playful title of Mendieta's ficus tree-root sculpture, *Tallus Mater* (Stem mother).[93] Mendieta makes reference to such myths in the characterization of her earth-body works as related to her childhood experience of being uprooted from her Cuban home and family at the age of twelve: "I am overwhelmed by the feeling of having been cast out from the womb (Nature). My art is the way I re-establish the bonds that unite me to the Universe."[94]

A "return to the maternal" may be one important aspect of Mendieta's performance-based works relating to trees, but her insistent erasure of the boundaries between human and vegetal matter also relates to broader tendencies in Latin American culture to regard humans and plants as interconnected.[95] Another photograph from the *Árbol de la vida* series, for instance, reveals an even more radical merging of humans and plants. It shows a dead tree trunk, lying over a shallow river and partly encased in mud. On top, although not immediately perceptible, is a person, also coated in mud, draped over the lines of the log.[96] Viso speaks of the stamina needed to carry out such a work, which literally and metaphorically embedded Mendieta in her environment. This photograph required the artist to lie still for hours on end, breathing through a straw while the mud dried.[97] Other works involving the overlaying of the human form with flowers or grass repeatedly undermine the idea of a separation between people and plants. Like Galeano's "Pasto," which envisages grass sprouting from the human body, works such as *Grass on Woman* (1972), in which Mendieta was photographed face down on a lawn after friends glued grass cuttings to her back and buttocks, normalize processes of phytomorphism, which seem no more radical than, say, the sprouting of a moustache above Mendieta's lips in her 1972 *Facial Hair Transplant*.[98] Mendieta wrote a few years before her death that her art was "grounded in the belief in one universal energy which runs through everything: from insect to man, from man to spectre, from spectre to plant, from plant to galaxy."[99] Although this statement harnesses New Age ideas of planetary interconnectedness, it also rhymes with indigenous American views of nonhuman life as being coextensive with the human and subject to frequent transformations.[100]

One significant metamorphosis for the artist is death, as Mendieta's repeated engagement with burial imagery and raised body-shaped earthworks bears out. In 1973 she staged *Imagen de Yagul* (Image from Yagul) by lying naked in an open Zapotec grave in Yagul, Oaxaca, and having her body festooned with bunches of white flowers, which she asked her then-lover, the American artist Hans Breder, to arrange so "that the flowers should seem to grow from her body."[101] The work—as with many of Mendieta's botanically infused photographs and films— enacts an ancestral return to the earth and epitomizes the idea of life as a cycle, where human remains are reborn through vegetal outshoots. In this way, it recalls another well-known Latin American work—Frida Kahlo's painting *Roots* (1943)—where the artist is represented as sprouting a vine from her gaping torso. Hayden Herrera compares the human figure in Kahlo's painting to a "tree of life," noting how the artist's blood flows outward through the vine "to feed the parched earth."[102] As with Kahlo, the idea that plants, places, and people are closely entwined is central to Mendieta's artistic vision. She characterized the body of work she produced in language that, like Kahlo's *Roots*, fuses the anatomical and the horticultural: "My works are the irrigation veins. . . . Through them, ascend the ancestral sap."[103]

The silent color film *Grass Breathing* (c. 1974), which shows grass lifting and falling as the human torso below it (Mendieta's) inhales and exhales, is the most radical instantiation of her attempts to collapse the distinctions between people and plants.[104] In this film, the sod exhibits one of the most visible signs of human life—respiration—as the human body and the vegetal become one. Marder and Irigaray write at length about breathing in their coauthored book *Through Vegetal Being*. Marder notes that, "[o]n the face of it, everything in vegetal breathing is opposed to ours." Plants turn the carbon dioxide we breathe out into the oxygen we breathe in. Humans (largely) respire, plants transpire. As Prudence Gibson reminds us in her study of the vegetal turn in contemporary art: "Plants breathe out and in, contrary to humans' in and out."[105]

Mendieta's film is not a dramatic embodiment of the popular metaphor that renders places like the Amazon the "lungs of the earth." Far from the leafy tropical forest, this performance takes place on a neatly cut lawn and does little to conceal Mendieta's human presence underneath the turf. Rather, *Grass Breathing* explores the close relationship between the human and the nonhuman, disrupting binaries such as inside/outside, self/other, culture/nature. In *Through Vegetal Being* Irigaray reflects on how the sharing of air has always been central to the communion of people with plants, recalling how plants in and around Paris once provided a nurturing environment in which she could breathe and, therefore, think. According to Irigaray, plants provide the means for life and for more than life: they not only purify the air but allow progression from "vegetative life to spiritual life." Even more revealing for a reading of Mendieta's performance are Irigaray's comments about breathing as a symbol of difference "between the outside and the inside, breathing also reminded me of the difference between the other and myself. Losing our identity to form a whole with the others, be they human or not human, amounts to giving up our own breathing."[106] Coccia in *The Life of Plants* also argues for an understanding of the human relationship to nature as one of "immersion": "It is impossible to distinguish them physically and spatially: for there to be immersion, subject and environment have to *actively penetrate each other.*" Central to this copenetration is breath. As Coccia explains, through photosynthesis, plants allow "each object to mix with the rest of the objects": "The air we breathe is not a purely geological or mineral reality—it is not just out there, it is not, as such, an effect of the earth—but rather the breath of other living beings."[107]

In Mendieta's *Grass Breathing*, both plants and people give up their "own breathing" (in Irigaray's words) and identity. Inhaling and exhaling, the grass takes on the outward appearance of a human, and Mendieta's position under the sod returns her to plants and to nature. Mendieta's work persistently erases the line between plants and people in provocative and playful ways. Advances in plant science have recently suggested that plants are able to learn and make decisions, to feel and communicate, which poses a number of ethical questions about the (Western) utilitarian view of vegetal life. Mendieta's botanical artworks from the 1970s and 1980s not only invoke phytomorphism, an idea entrenched in Spanish American cultural practices throughout the twentieth century, but also anticipate the posthuman turn of the past two decades by undermining the distinction between people and plants and granting vegetal life subjectivity and the right to exist in and for itself.

Bryan L. Moore has identified personification as a significant trope in nature writing: "it represents the relationship between human and nonhuman, challenges anthropocentrism, and extends 'moral considerability to nonhuman beings.'" As Carolyn Merchant similarly argues: "The image of the earth as a living organism . . . serve[s] as a cultural constraint restricting the actions of human beings."[108] The representation of plants as alive in these Spanish American works has been shown to play a transcendent role in the codification of human relationships with nature throughout the twentieth and twenty-first centuries—relationships that as Rivera, Galeano, and Mendieta make clear, should be unhierarchical and unexploitative. Personification in all these works goes well beyond the Romantic impulse to see nature as a mirror of human emotions. The animist underpinnings of Spanish American works are often evinced through the radical metamorphosis of people into plants and plants into people. By invoking indigenous American myths of an undifferentiated past in which all beings were human, they establish ways of thinking and representing plants that require people to respect and nurture the natural world.

In Spanish American culture the breakdown of boundaries between people and plants is radical and often visceral, with blood flowing from trees and grass sprouting from human skin. Like Rivera's enlisting of animist poetics a century ago in *La vorágine*, Galeano's and Mendieta's more recent vegetal-human hybrids do not, in the words of Cynthia Chase, "take the human as given" but, rather, produce works in which the transfiguration of people into plants is fluid and reciprocal.[109] The phytomorphic tendencies of all of these works are underpinned by pre-Columbian beliefs about nonhuman nature, but they also draw on contemporary ecological thinking to show that the reconfiguration of our relationship with plants is not only valid but urgent. Coccia in his plant-centered understanding of life as a "metaphysics of mixture" speaks of human "immersion," with "no material distinction between us and the rest of the world."[110] It is from such a premise that we can begin to forge more sustainable and ethical interactions with plants. In the work of Rivera, Galeano, and Mendieta anthropomorphism, mythology, and ecology converge to imagine a way of being in nature that does not involve human domination over plants but that attends to our resemblances and interdependencies—the vegetal nature of humans and the human nature of plants. Such an approach also characterizes the work of Pablo Neruda, a poet immersed in botany, who consistently draws on plant imaginaries to forge a poetic and political self.

CHAPTER 5

"NO TERMINO EN MÍ MISMO"

"Vegetal-Thinking" in Pablo Neruda

P ablo Neruda was a voracious collector of books on plants. Among the poet's personal library, donated to the University of Chile in 1954, is the beautifully illustrated 1866 French floriographical text *Nouveau langage des fleurs* by Pierre Zaccone; a 1596 Czech translation of Pietro Andrea Mattioli's *Materia Medica*, replete with botanical woodcuts; a nineteenth-century handmade album consisting of fifteen magnificent plates showing landscapes and flower displays created from minute dried plant specimens; and an array of scientific, comic, and practical botanical books.[1] In his speech to mark the donation, the poet offered an explanation for the large number of books about plants: "se preguntarán alguna vez por qué hay tantos libros sobre . . . plantas. La contestación está en mi poesía" [Now and then they will ask themselves why there are so many books about . . . plants. The answer is in my poetry].[2]

Neruda is often regarded as a poet of oceans. Alongside the persistent oceanic imagery of his poetry, his renowned collections of seashells and other nautical equipment, the boat-like architecture and furnishings of his houses, and iconic photographs of the poet rambling about on the shore at Isla Negra on Chile's Pacific coast, have established Neruda's close ties to the marine environment. But he also had a detailed knowledge of botany, and references to plants span his poetry, from the persistent vegetal imagery of *Veinte poemas de amor y una canción desesperada* (*Twenty Love Poems and a Song of Despair*) and *Odas elementales* (*Elementary Odes*), to the more explicitly botanizing *Oda a las flores de Datitla* (Ode to the flowers of Datitla [2002]), a little-known book that, as the subtitle states, consists of verses by Neruda and a "herbarium" by Matilde Urrutia, his third wife, published some thirty years after his death.[3] Yet it is in Neruda's *Canto general*, which Gordon Brotherston calls his "great American work," that the poet's botanical imagination arguably reaches its fullest expression.[4] The language of plants and their constituent elements—roots, stamens, petals, and branches—permeate the entire poem, as does the sense of the vegetal world as animate and closely related to the human.

Plants are fundamental to our understanding of both Neruda's poetic and political imagination. In Spanish American culture plant imaginaries are often twinned with political insurgency. In the georgics of Landívar and Bello, the treatment of plants reveals a recalcitrance toward the modernizing utilitarian views of nature in Latin America in the lead up to and after independence, as well as a renewed interest in pre-Columbian imaginaries. In *Sab* and *María*, the resignification of the European floriographical tradition was instrumental to the Spanish American authors' critique of white, masculinist, and capitalist discourses. And, across Spanish American culture, from the colonial period to the present, a persistent destabilizing of (Western) ontological distinctions between people and plants has helped to formulate ecologically attuned ways of engaging with nature, in line with pre-Columbian conceptions of plants as animate. For Neruda, plants are fundamental to the expression of a poetics of both insurrection and resurrection. Botanical imagery and (what I will call) the poet's "vegetal-thinking" allow Neruda to establish continuities between the suffering of individuals across time and space—from the indigenous people during the Conquest to miners in the Atacama in the 1940s—and to come to an understanding of human history, and human resilience, against the deep time of nonhuman nature.

THE POET AS BOTANIST

From the late colonial period onward, Spanish American writers engaged with plants in profound and transformative ways across a range of landscapes from Central America to the Southern Cone. Even within this company, however, Neruda emerges as singularly well informed about plants and aware of his role as a purveyor of botanical knowledge. In his classic study of the *Canto general*, Frank Reiss observes that "Neruda has . . . a naturalist's interest in naming and classifying all plants."[5] Following Chilean writers such as Alonso de Ercilla, whose *La Araucana* (*The Araucaniad*) Neruda calls a "catalogación forestal" [a cataloguing of woodland], the poet approached the writing of the *Canto general* with a strong sense of vocation: "Nuestras plantas y nuestras flores deben por primera vez ser contadas y cantadas" [Our plants and our flowers must be spoken of and sung about for the first time].[6] In this statement of intent, Neruda merges the roles of poet and botanist. His aim is to enumerate and catalogue his continent's flora and to do so within a poetic framework—to "sing" of plants in the tradition of his literary forefather Walt Whitman.[7]

The circumstances under which Neruda composed much of his *Canto general* are well-known: the poem came to fruition when Neruda went into hiding after he publicly denounced the Chilean president Gabriel González Videla in the late 1940s. Neruda recalled how he had to travel clandestinely within Chile with little or no baggage, but was lucky enough to find useful books in many of the houses where he stayed, including a multivolume encyclopaedia in which he was able to corroborate geographical and botanical information.[8] He also recalled years later how, when he was ascending the Andes finally to escape Chile, he encountered firsthand the variety and scale of Chilean flora: "La selva andina austral está poblada por grandes árboles apartados el uno del otro. Son gigantescos alerces y maitenes, luego tepas y coníferas. Los raulíes asombran por su espesor. Me detuve a medir uno. Era del diámetro de un caballo. Por arriba no se ve el cielo. Por abajo las hojas han caído durante siglos formando un capa de humus donde se hunden los cascos de las cabalgaduras."[9] Like any good botanist, Neruda catalogues and measures one of his specimens, notwithstanding his lack of scientific instruments. He scrutinizes the trees from crown to understory, observing the depth of tree litter that he elsewhere estimates at more than a meter deep, fusing poetic and scientific discourse in a way that would become characteristic of much of his writing on plants.[10]

Neruda's botanical knowledge, from his wide reading and direct studied experience, surfaces frequently in the *Canto general*. In "Vegetaciones" ("Vegetation"), the second poem of the opening canto, the poet adopts a biblical tone in his litany of the advent of plants and animals in the "tierras sin nombres" ["lands without name"].[11] Neruda refers to a range of well-known American trees, including the iconic Chilean *Araucaria araucana* (monkey puzzle), the *ombú*, rubber, and mahogany. Later in the collection, the flora becomes more obscure. In "Avanzando en las tierras de Chile" ("Advancing in the Lands of Chile"), Neruda recalls the Andean trees he encountered as he was fleeing his homeland, in the description of an animate forest resistant to Spanish colonizers:

> El bosque de maitenes cuyos hilos
> verdes cuelgan como temblor de lluvia
> dijo a España: "No sigas." El alerce,
> titán de las fronteras silenciosas,
> dijo en un trueno su palabra. (*CG*, 485)[12]

Here Neruda's choice of trees is both poetically and botanically sound. Figuring the branches of the mayten (*Maytenus boaria*) as threads swaying in the rain, Neruda alludes to the softness of the tree's wood and contrasts it with the great strength of the alerce or *Fitzroya cupressoides*, a conifer native to the Andes, known for its enormous size and longevity.[13] The metaphorical encoding of the trees thus suggests the strength of resistance to colonial invasion from both the weak and the strong. Neruda's knowledge of plants is conveyed again later in the same poem through references to what emerge as a constant in his botanically oriented writings: the minute, microscopic, even nontangible elements of vegetal life such as stamens, pollen, and fragrance—"erizaba el polen / una alfombra de estambres turbulentos"; "Todo estaba enredado de fragancias" (*CG*, 485) ["the pollen raised / a carpet of turbulent stamen"; "Everything was laced with fragrance" (*CGS*, 77–78)]. Here and elsewhere, Neruda attends not only to giant trees but the minutiae of vegetal life, including seeds, lichens, and moss.

In the opening chapter of his memoirs, Neruda recalls his early incursions into the Chilean temperate rainforest—the scent of laurel, the smell of *boldo* (*Peumus boldus*), which is used in herbal infusions, the sensation of cold water droplets from towering ferns, and the crackle of breaking twigs. Neruda re-creates his childhood delight at the sight of a rotting tree trunk: "*Un tronco podrido: qué tesoro! . . . Hongos negros y azules le han dado orejas, rojas plantas parásitas lo han colmado de rubíes, otras plantas perezosas le han prestado sus barbas y brota, veloz, una culebra desde sus entrañas podridas.*"[14] In this description, Neruda blends the poetic and the botanical in ways that are characteristic of his entire poetic oeuvre. The trunk is rendered comically anthropomorphic through the imposition of fungi ears, a plant beard, and entrails of rotten wood, and the brightly colored parasites are likened to a ruby necklace. A similar tendency can be seen at work in the *Canto general*, as when, for instance, Neruda describes the *topa-topa* (*Calceolaria paralia*), a delicate Chilean shrub that produces yellow flowers, as "un rosario de besos amarillos" (*CG*, 486) ["a rosary of yellow kisses" (*CGS*, 78)]. As well as naming individual specimens of trees or flowers—there are frequent references to the *araucaria*, the alerce, roses, and the copihue or Chilean bellflower (*Lapageria rosea*, the national flower of Chile)—in the *Canto general* Neruda lists the different parts of plants. Throughout the poem he includes innumerable references to stamens, branches, leaves, flowers, petals, shoots, twigs, pollen, buds, spines, seeds, and roots (especially roots), often metaphorically. His interest in and knowledge of botany continued to grow in later life, culminating in the scientific exactitude of "Bosque" ("Forest") from *Memorial de Isla Negra (Isla Negra)* (1962–1964), where the poetic persona exults in phytomorphology via obscure references to "los cotiledones hojosos, / los epipétalos hipóginos, / las drupas de íntimo contacto" ["leafy cotyledons, / close-petaled tulips, / drupes bunched together"].[15]

Throughout the *Canto general*, Neruda shows a marked interest in Chilean native flora. Chilean plants he refers to include the *topa-topa*, copihue, and *boldo*, as well as, for instance, *raulí* (*Nothofagus alpina*) (*CG*, 487), a deciduous tree from the Andes whose local name is drawn from the Mapuche language, and *quintral* (*Tristerix corymbosus*) (*CG*, 718), an evergreen parasite.[16] In the *Canto general*, poems 9 and 13 of the "Canto general de Chile" ("*Canto general* of Chile") include whole stanzas on individual named species: "Peumo" (*Cryptocarya alba*), "Quilas" (*Chusquea quila*), "Drimis winterei" (his spelling of *Drimys winteri*), and "Araucaria." Neruda had direct contact with Chilean flora as a child as well as during his legendary expedition over the Andes, and his knowledge also derived from extensive reading. He owned a number of books specifically on Chilean plants, including Amédée François Frézier's *Relation du voyage de la mer du sud aux côtes du Chily et du Perou* (1716) and Claudio Gay's *Historia física y política de Chile* (Physical and political history of Chile), from 1854.[17]

A passage that Neruda cites from the French geologist Pedro José Amado Pissis's *Geografía física de la República de Chile* (Physical geography of the republic of Chile), from 1875, makes reference to the *Drimys winteri* (see figure 11) and copihue, both plants that Neruda returns to time and again. The intersections he sees between the roles of botanist and poet is made clear in his comparison of Pissis to the Chilean poet Juvencio Valle, whom Neruda admires for having "dado a nuestra geografía vegetal una nueva dimensión mitológica" [given to our vegetal geography

Wintera aromatica

F. Bauer del.   Weddell sc.

London, Published for the Authors, Jan. 1830.

a new mythological dimension].[18] For Neruda, the duty of the poet as botanist—or botanist as poet—is to fuse the scientific with the literary or mythological. Both the *Drimys winteri* and the copihue play an important role in Chilean mythology. As Ana Mariella Bacigalupo notes, *Drimys winteri* (also called the *canelo* or *foye* tree) was central to Mapuche identity: "*Foye* trees are sacred trees of life that connect the natural, human, and spirit worlds and allow Mapuche shamans, or *machi*, to participate in the forces that permeate the cosmos. They are symbols of *machi* medicine, and *machi* use the bitter leaves and bark to exorcise evil spirits, as an antibacterial for treating wounds, and to treat colds, rheumatism, stomach infections, and ringworm. *Foye* trees also serve a political purpose. During colonial times Mapuche used them as symbols of peace during parleys and for deceptive purposes in setting up ambushes."[19] Indeed, an 1803 treaty putting an end to centuries of conflict between the Spanish and the Mapuche was signed under this very species of tree.[20] As George Handley notes, at times Neruda's descriptions of the *Drimys winteri* in the *Canto general* are steadfastly unmythologizing. In the poem "Drimis Winterei," the trees are rendered "Plantas sin nombre, hojas / y cuerdas montañosas" (*CG*, 650) ["Nameless plants, leaves / and mountainous tendons" (*CGS*, 225)].[21] But the same cannot be said of his account of the sacrifice of Pedro de Valdivia's heart to a *Drimys winteri* in poem 12 of "Los libertadores" ("The Liberators"):

> Luego, en el pecho entramos una lanza
> y el corazón alado como un ave
> entregamos al árbol araucano.
> Subió un rumor de sangre hasta su copa. (*CG*, 494)[22]

◄ **FIGURE 11.** *Drimys winteri.* From John Stevenson and James Churchill, *Medical Botany; or, Illustrations and Descriptions of the Medicinal Plants of the London, Edinburgh, and Dublin Pharmacopoeias.* Vol. 3, plate 178. London, 1831. Reproduced by kind permission of the Syndics of Cambridge University Library (8340.c.87).

LAPAGERIA ROSEA *Ruiz & Pav.*

Here the tree is figured through the lens of Mapuche myth, carnivo-
rously ingesting the heart of the man who oversaw the conquest of Chile.
Neruda's portrayal of the copihue is also indebted to indigenous cosmogonies, as we can see from a reference to it in his memoirs: *"En la altura,
como gotas arteriales de la selva mágica se cimbran los copihues rojos* (Lapageria
rosea). . . . *El copihue rojo es la flor de la sangre, el copihue blanco es la flor
de la nieve."*[23] Neruda's use of binomial nomenclature notwithstanding,
this description of the Chilean bellflower is firmly rooted in Mapuche
myths of the plant that relate how its color derives from the spilt blood of
ancestors (see figure 12). Although different versions of the copihue myth
exist, one popular rendition of the legend tells of the appearance of two
flowers, one red as blood and the other white as snow, to mark the spot
where lovers Cophi and Hues, who belonged to enemy tribes, were murdered.[24] Neruda's reference to Mapuche mythology reveals how the poet
regarded plants as not only biological entities (all those stamens, leaves,
and branches) but as carriers of history and culture. Plants were fundamental to Neruda's attempts to understand his own poetic development
as well as the vicissitudes of continental American history and politics.

GREEN MAN

Sara Vial records Neruda's impatience with Alejo Carpentier's verbosity
when the author, born in the same year as Neruda, visited him in Valparaíso.[25] Although plants were a vital point of reference for both writers,
there was a gulf between the theorizing, abstracted Cuban and Neruda's earthbound poetics. Jason Wilson notes that Neruda "saw himself
as an organic or telluric poet in direct contact with the natural world,
rather than with poems and books and culture."[26] Wilson is right to

◀ FIGURE 12. *Lapageria rosea*. From Louis Van Houtte, *Flore des serres et des jardins de l'Europe.*
Vol. 5 (1849). Image courtesy of the Biodiversity Heritage Library. Contributed by Missouri
Botanical Garden, Peter H. Raven Library. www.biodiversitylibrary.org, https://www.bio
diversitylibrary.org/item/54913#page/204/mode/1up/.

be suspicious of Neruda's persistent self-styling as an anti-intellectual, but nature, especially organic materials such as wood, were undoubtedly fundamental to his formation as a poet.[27] In his memoirs, Neruda reflects on the organicism of his verse: "*La poesía debe ser orgánica en cada poeta, fluido de su sangre. . . . Tuve siempre una influencia persistente de los grandes árboles, de la salvaje naturaleza del sur de mi país*" [*Poetry should be organic in every poet, be in his blood. . . . For me, the large trees and wild nature of the south of my country always had a persistent influence*].[28] On a number of occasions Neruda expressed his belief in the influence of environment on poetic form. Just as the verses of his former schoolteacher and fellow Nobel Prize winner, Gabriela Mistral, exude for Neruda "algo volcánico, . . . y geológico" [something volcanic, . . . and geologic] so his own poetry must bear the traces of the humid forests of southern Chile where he grew up.[29] Although colonial poets like Landívar had continued to use established metrical forms to convey Latin American reality, Neruda believed only free verse was suited to "los temas Americanos" [American subjects]: "El verso debía tomar todos los contornos de la tierra enmarañada, romperse en archipiélago, elevarse y caer en las llanuras." [The verse ought to follow all the contours of the thicketed land, fracturing into archipelagos, rising up and falling down into plains].[30] Building on this, Neruda chooses a botanical metaphor to convey how the nature of the temperate rainforests where he grew up infused his poems: "Las tierras de la frontera metieron *sus raíces* en mi poesía y nunca han podido salir de ella" ["The frontier regions sank *their roots* into my poetry and these roots have never been able to wrench themselves out"].[31]

Saúl Yurkievich refers to Neruda's love of wood—the living wood of forest trees, the dead rotten wood of fallen trunks, and the fragrant timber used to construct his childhood homes—that emerges as a central point of reference across Neruda's autobiographical writings and poetry.[32] Wood is one of the primary ways through which Neruda signals his close connections to nature. In "Mi Casa" ("The House") in the *Canto general* the poet speaks of growing up in a simple frontier house with its "paredes cuya madera fresca / recién cortada huele aún" (*CG*, 809) ["walls whose fresh, / recently cut wood still smells" (*CGS*, 375)]. In a speech marking his fiftieth birthday, Neruda recalled how on these very walls he had written early verses of poetry, attracted by the texture of the planks of wood: "lisas como el papel, con venas misteriosas" [smooth as paper, with mysterious veins].[33] Later in life, trekking over the Andes into exile, Neruda once again wrote on wood, this time inscribing his initials on the bark of "el último árbol de Chile" [the last tree in Chile].[34] He recalls leaning on whatever natural material came to hand when working on the manuscript of the *Canto general*: "Lo hacía sobre una tabla, un tronco de árbol, una piedra" [I wrote it on a board, a tree trunk, a stone].[35] Neruda's descriptions of writing directly on wooden surfaces emphasize the organicism of his poetry, which he says springs from "un impulso vegetal" [a vegetal impulse], unmediated by culture.[36] His love of wood is evident in the houses he lived in as an adult, perhaps a homage to his childhood frontier homes.[37] The living room in La Chascona in Santiago is built around a large tree trunk, and many of the rooms in his home in Isla Negra have wooden walls, floors, and ceilings, all constructed from Chilean timber.[38] In her memoirs, Matilde Urrutia remembered her husband's zeal for collecting driftwood and fallen branches around their home on the Pacific coast, some of which he later made into furniture or displayed as natural sculptures.[39]

Neruda calls wood "un elemento natural de mi vida" [a natural element of my life] and, in his "Oda a la madera" (Ode to Wood), "mi mejor amiga" [my best friend].[40] A number of critics have singled out the poem "Entrada a la madera ("Entrance into Wood") from *Residencia en la tierra* (*Residence on Earth*) as being key to understanding this element in Neruda's poetry. The poet conveys the textures of wood with obsessive detail, addressing it in the second person:

Veo moverse tus corrientes secas,

veo crecer manos interrumpidas,

oigo tus vegetales oceánicos

crujir de noche y furia sacudidos.[41]

For Manuel Durán and Margery Safir, in this poem "[w]ood is matter; it stands for the whole of Nature, of living nature; it stands for the roots of trees, of plants, for the source of life." Yet the imagery is also profoundly of death. Neruda writes of the vegetation of the tree dying and receding inwards, which resonates with the animist poetics of *La vorágine*, where Rivera confers pity on the immobile and downtrodden rubber trees by drawing out their anthropomorphic qualities. For John Felstiner, Neruda's poem is suggestive of a regression to the maternal, with the words "materia" [material] and "madera" [wood]—etymologically cognate with "madre" [mother]—central to the poet's vision of a return to, and rebirth through, nature.[42]

The language of plants is fundamental to Neruda's construction of a personal and poetic self. Throughout many of his writings, he presents himself as emerging plant-like from the forests of southern Chile. In the final canto of the *Canto general*, "Yo Soy" ("I Am"), Neruda shifts the hitherto continental focus of the poem inward.[43] In "La frontera" ("The Frontier") he evokes in simple terms his early childhood memories:

Lo primero que vi fueron árboles, barrancas

decoradas con flores de salvaje hermosura, . . .

Mi infancia son zapatos mojados, troncos rotos

caídos en la selva, devorados por lianas. (*CG*, 807)[44]

Neruda suppresses any mention of his parents in these opening lines. Consistent with the maternal imagery of "Entrada en la madera," the infant's first vision is not of his mother (*madre*) but trees (*madera*). This poet is—quite literally—a child of nature, a nature that in Romantic fashion is completely undomesticated and overgrown.[45] Neruda depicts his slight, youthful figure—"delgado niño cuya pálida forma / se impregnaba de bosques vacíos" (*CG*, 808) ["a slender child whose pale form / was impregnated with pristine forests" (*CGS*, 374)]—in terms that continue to stress his physical connections to trees, although reversing the initial sense of the forest as his progenitor. Here he is "impregnated" by the woods, the adjective "pálida" ["pale"] suggestive of the "palos" [sticks] from which he materialized and which his slim form evokes. And if for Neruda life begins with plants, it also ends with them, as the poet's haunting account of glimpsing his father's recently buried coffin at his stepmother's funeral acknowledges: "sacamos la urna, pero ya llena de hongos, y sobre ella una palma con flores negras y extinguidas" ["we . . . took out the urn though now it was full of fungus and had on it a palm leaf with black wilted flowers"].[46]

In a talk given in 1954, four years after the publication of the *Canto general*, Neruda invoked the metaphor of the poet as a plant, rooted in a given geographical local: "El poeta no puede ser desarraigado, sino por la fuerza. Aun en esas circunstancias sus raíces deben cruzar el fondo del mar, sus semillas seguir el vuelo del viento, para encarnarse, una vez más, en su tierra" [The poet cannot be uprooted, but by force. Even under these circumstances, the roots will stretch across the depths of the sea, the seeds will be dispersed by the wind, to materialize, once again, in his land].[47] According to this model, a poem is a "seed," which can be separated from its vegetal progenitor (the poet) and take on a life of its own. This is a persistent image across Neruda's writings, where the seed/poem is a potent symbol of hope within a deadening political system. Just as Landívar and Bello appealed to the transformative power of agriculture, in the *Canto general* Neruda, an admirer of Bello's poetry, employs crop growing metaphorically, figuring himself as a farmer in possession of seeds that can sow hope for future generations.[48] In "La vida" ("Life") in the canto "Yo Soy," Neruda enumerates his life's possessions as "semillas, / desarrollos radiantes y dulzura" (*CG*, 831) ["seeds, / radiant growth and sweetness" (*CGS*, 395)]. Elsewhere, the poet compares the poetry of the Spanish baroque writer Francisco de Quevedo to an "árbol grandioso que la tempestad del tiempo no doblega y que, por el contrario, lo hace esparcir alrededor el tesoro de sus semillas insurgentes" [grandiose tree that the storms of time have not bent over but, on the contrary, have scattered all around its store of insurgent seeds].[49]

Neruda's appeal to agricultural imagery is not only reminiscent of Bello's "La agricultura de la zona tórrida" but can be traced back to a now obscure botanical book—the Spanish translation of Harold William Rickett's *The Green Earth* (1943). Rickett was a noted twentieth-century botanist who spent much of his career working as a bibliographer at the New York Botanical Gardens.[50] The book was full of information about how plants grow, feed, and reproduce, aimed principally at the amateur botanist, and seems to have attracted Neruda's interest to an unusual degree. Although the poet did not often annotate his books the fourth chapter, dedicated to plant growth, contains multiple underlinings, especially of facts relating to seeds.[51] The chapter begins in a way that directly anticipates Neruda's later self-styling as a "farmer": "I know a man who is a poet. It is true that he would not know himself by such a title, for he does not write verse; he is a farmer. He is a poet because he knows the joy of creation. A never failing delight is the appearance of living, growing plants in a patch of dirt where, only a few days before, he has placed some dry grains."[52] Although the metaphor is reversed in Rickett's account—farmer as poet, rather than poet as farmer—the confluence between Neruda's imagination of poets as sowers of "insurgent seeds" and Rickett's botanical text is suggestive of Neruda's continued appeal to plants as a means to define his own poetic vocation. The language of plants is central to Neruda's expression of his personal and poetic gestation. It also plays a transcendent role in the *Canto general*, especially in relation to the poet's formulation of what I term "vegetal-thinking" as a means to overcome political oppression.

"VEGETAL-THINKING"

In "Vegetaciones" in the *Canto general* (in which the poet establishes the mythical origins of the continent), America emerges as determinedly vegetal:

> Útero verde, americana
> sabana seminal, bodega espesa,
> una rama nació como una isla,
> una hoja fue forma de la espada.
> una flor fue relámpago y medusa,
> un racimo redondeó su resumen,
> una raíz descendió a las tinieblas. (*CG*, 420)[53]

Here images of irrepressible fecundity are fused with botanical precision. This "América arboleda" (*CG*, 420) ["Arboreal America" (*CGS*, 15)] is not just an amorphous green space but also an assemblage of differentiated botanical parts, stretching above and below the ground. Even in these early stanzas, plants are established as a source of resistance against colonial oppression, with the leaf likened to the form of the sword (later in the *Canto general* it is compared to a lance).[54] In canto 3 of the poem "Los conquistadores" ("The Conquistadors"), Cortés is depicted riding roughshod through the vegetation, "parando su tropa entre orquídeas / y coronaciones de pinos, / atropellando los jazmines" (*CG*, 451) ["halting his army among orchids / and coronations of pines, / trampling the jasmine" (*CGS*, 46)], stirring into animacy plants that in turn address the indigenous people "desde el musgo . . . , desde / las raíces" (*CG*, 451) ["from the moss, / from the roots" (*CGS*, 46)], imploring them not to trust the new arrivals. The first poem of canto 4, "Los libertadores," opens with an intensification of this imagery of vegetal resistance, with trees explicitly aligned with the anticolonial struggle. The first three verses of the poem begin anaphorically—*"Aquí viene el árbol, el árbol"* (*CG*, 478; original italics) [*"Here comes the tree, the tree"* (*CGS*, 71)]—infusing it with the cadences of a political song and complementing the populist imagery of the tree as an *"árbol del pueblo"* [*"tree of the people"*], *"el árbol de los libres"* [*"the tree of the emancipated"*], or *"árbol pan"* (*CG*, 478–79) [*"bread tree"* (*CGS*, 71–72)].[55] Later in "Los libertadores," Araucanian warriors "germinate" from the earth, with Toqui Caupolicán, who led the resistance against the Spanish, imagined as growing from the stump of a *raulí* tree:

> Los invasores vieron el follaje
> moverse en medio de la bruma verde,
> las gruesas ramas y la vestidura
> de innumerables hojas y amenazas,
> el tronco terrenal hacerse pueblo,
> las raíces salir del territorio. (*CG*, 487)[56]

This poem figures the Araucanian chief as a sort of green man with a "rostro forestal" (*CG*, 488) ["woodland face" (*CGS*, 80)], another of the vegetal/human hybrids recurrent in Spanish American cultural expression. Often figured in colonial narratives as a source of great wealth for colonizers, trees and plants in "Los libertadores" emerge as firmly allied with the indigenous people and are used as metaphors for their profusion and tenacity.

A number of critics have recognized the importance of tree imagery in the *Canto general*, particularly in "Los libertatores." Durán and Safir, for instance, note how the tree functions as a symbol of renewal: "By linking the image of the tree to the liberators . . . , Neruda establishes a continual time process in which each leaf is an individual liberator which may die or fall to the ground, but as it does so, it returns to the earth and becomes the seed and nurture for the eventual growth and further strength of the tree." In his reading, Reiss also notes the ways in which the emergence and organization of those engaged in the anticolonial struggle apes the growth of a tree. Both observations reveal a central truth of Neruda's poetics, which is the projection of "vegetal-thinking" onto the natural world.[57]

For my formulation of the term "vegetal-thinking," I draw on Marder's *Plant-Thinking* in which he considers the philosophical and ethical status of plants. Marder has written a number of groundbreaking works that have reconfigured the traditional view of plants in Western philosophy from mere passive objects to entities that have experiences and desires. Central to *Plant-Thinking* is Marder's proposal of a "vegetal anti-meta-physics" that counters the human desire for individual self-preservation: "the plant materially articulates and expresses the beings that surround it; it lets beings be and, from the middle place of growth, performs the kind of dis-closure of the world in all its interconnectedness that Heidegger attributes to human *Dasein*."[58]

In his *Canto general* Neruda anticipates the posthuman celebration of vegetal life in scholars such as Marder, Coccia, and Irigaray, as well as recent advances in plant neurobiology, by proposing the collaborative, communitarian life of plants—particularly trees—as a paradigm for human civilization. For Neruda, plants can teach humans about how to work together, especially in order to overcome political repression. The *Canto general* was completed and published during a difficult political moment for Neruda, but the pessimism of the collection is tempered by reminders from the botanical world of the potential for regeneration and renewal. In the final line of the moving penultimate poem of the *Canto general*, "Mi partido" ("To My Party"), Neruda extols the Communist Party for conferring on him an immortality of sorts: "Me has hecho inde-structible porque contigo no termino en mí mismo" (*CG*, 835) ["You have made me indestructible because with you I do not end in myself" (*CGS*, 399)]. Such a view also explains Neruda's reverence for plants, where the life of the species takes priority over individual existence and where plants are vehicles for rebirth. As Marder notes: "Vegetal afterlife . . . is a non-mystified and material 'resurrection,' an opportunity for mortal remains to break free from the darkness of the earth. Thanks to the plant, fixed in place by its roots, dead plants, animals, and humans are 'unmoored' from their resting places."[59]

Roots are foremost in Neruda's imagination of the fraternal bonds that link humans across place and time, especially Latin Americans: "Pero si descendemos desde la copa y desde la flor, . . . si pasamos desde la hoja al tronco y desde el tronco al origen: allí nos encontramos. Mexicanos y chilenos nos encontraremos en las raíces."[60] In the early 1940s Neruda turned to the metaphor of roots to explain a shift in his own understanding of national identity in the Americas—a shift that led, in fact, to a radical restructuring of the *Canto general*, which had begun as a poem about Chile. Neruda explains that, in the course of writing the poem, he came to the realization that "las raíces de todos los chilenos se extendían debajo de la tierra y salían en otros territorios" [the roots of all Chilean people extended below the ground and came up in other territories].[61] Roots mark a metaphorical ground zero for Neruda—a subterranean confluence where all men, whether mestizo or indigenous, Chilean or Mexican, are equal: "juntos bajo la tierra todos estamos juntos" [joined under the ground we are all together].[62] Their continental reach erases the national boundaries imposed by centuries of colonial and postcolonial rule and validates the pan-American poetics of Neruda's epic *Canto general*.

Neruda himself wrote at some length about the "roots" in his work, admitting how one of his translators had berated him about the ubiquity of the image in his poetry: "demasiada *raíz*, demasiadas *raíces* en tus versos" ["too much *root*, too many *roots* in your poems"].[63] In the same prose piece, "La cazadora de raíces" (The root hunter), Neruda recalls being presented with an enormous oak root, some one hundred kilograms in weight and five hundred years old—an object he immediately felt a bond with, imagining that the root belonged to some distant relative: "un padre vegetal que de alguna manera se hacía presente en mi casa" [A vegetal father that somehow came to be in my house].[64] Such a root would have been an ideal addition to the baroque collections of Carpentier's *El recurso del método*, yet for Neruda the value of the object resided not in its bizarre attributes but, rather, in its suggestion of a shared humanity.

In the same essay Neruda uses human anatomical terms in his descriptions of roots: "Nada más hermoso que esas grandes *manos* abiertas, heridas y quemadas que atravesándose en un sendero del bosque nos dicen el secreto del árbol enterrado, el enigma que sustentaba el follaje, los *músculos* profundos de la dominación vegetal. Trágicas e *hirsutas*, nos muestran una nueva belleza: son esculturas de la profundidad: obras maestras y secretas de la naturaleza."[65] This insistent anatomizing of the tree roots is in line not only with the general proclivity for anthropomorphism in Spanish American literature but with Neruda's own insistence on comparing plants to humans. One instance of this is the poet's repeated puns on the phonic correspondences in Spanish between "hojas" [leaves] and "ojos" [eyes], as in the second poem of canto 1 of the *Canto general*, "Algunas bestias" ("Some Beasts") where the nouns form a half rhyme:

> El jaguar tocaba las hojas
> con su ausencia fosforescente,
> el puma corre en el ramaje
> como el fuego devorador
> mientras arden en él los ojos
> alcohólicos de la selva. (*CG*, 421)[66]

Among Neruda's many books on plants were a number that explored the physiology of roots through detailed cross sections and text.[67] Yet despite his botanical knowledge Neruda tends to draw out the mysterious, impenetrable nature of plant roots. In his discussion of the ancient oak root above, Neruda employs both the noun and the adjective "secret." This insistence on the cryptic aspects of roots is in line with Coccia's view of them as "the most enigmatic forms of the plant world."[68] Coccia outlines the long tradition likening plant roots to the human head, from Plato to contemporary scientists working on plant neurobiology, who situate plant intelligence in the root system.[69] Aristotle expressed this view in *De Anima* when he argued that, "if we are to distinguish and identify organs according to their functions, the roots of plants are analogous to the head in animals."[70] Recently Wohlleben has shown how, within a forest, the "root systems of neighbouring trees inevitably intersect and grow into one another," supported by fungal connections that help transmit information about predators, drought, and other threats.[71]

Neruda anticipates these developments in plant science throughout the *Canto general* by insistently using roots as symbols of interaction and communication. In "Silvestre Revueltas, de México en su muerte (oratorio menor)" ["To Silvestre Revueltas, from Mexico, on His Death (Oratorio Minor)"], Neruda details how the death of the eponymous Mexican musician and personal friend is transmitted far and wide by plants, first by "Las pequeñas raíces" ["the little roots"] who inform the grains, then "Todos los árboles de América ya lo saben / y también las flores heladas de nuestra región ártica" (*CG*, 743) ["Now all America's trees know / and our artic region's frozen flowers too" (*CGS*, 314)]. Through simple diction, Neruda imagines complex and far-reaching vegetal chains of communication. Although the idea of a plant world fully attentive to human matters is somewhat whimsical, recent advances in plant neurobiology show that the modes of vegetal interaction depicted by the poet are not so outlandish. As Karban has argued: "In addition to sensing, plants communicate among tissues on the same individual to coordinate their responses to the environment. They eavesdrop on neighbouring individuals to acquire information about future risks of competition, disease, and herbivores. They communicate with those microbes that allow them to forage more effectively and with animals that facilitate mating and move their seeds to locations where they are likely to thrive."[72]

For Neruda, the power of plant communication does not end there. "A Silvestre Revueltas" goes on to describe how news of the man's death spreads even beyond the plant kingdom: "De ventisquero a lago, de lago a planta, / de planta a fuego, de fuego a humo: / todo lo que arde, canta, florece, baila y revive" (*CG*, 744) ["From glacier to lake, from lake to plant, from plant to fire, from fire to smoke; everything that burns, sings, blossoms, dances and revives" (*CGS*, 314)]. Marder has noted how plants "actively establish relations of contiguity with other plants and with minerals, with sunlight, and with animals, participating in the chains of material interpretation that add up to life itself." Likewise, Coccia speaks of how roots "put into communication the different elements of the pedological biosphere—the underground world they inhabit," as well as other plants.[73] This underground world includes rocks and minerals. Neruda expresses the sense of ontological fluidity between plants and nonplants ("everything is in everything," in Coccia's shorthand) not only through instances of plants communicating with other natural objects but through the vegetal-metal composites that proliferate in the *Canto general*—the "pétalos de piedra" ["stone petals"], "ramajes de cristal salpicado" ["branches of spattered crystal"], and "plateada raíz" (*CG*, 440, 472, 661) ["silvery root" (*CGS*, 35, 64, 235)].[74] In the poem "Minerales" ("Minerals") at the beginning of the *Canto general* Neruda describes the process through which plants are transformed into coal, establishing from the outset of his epic work the key poetic image of vegetal life as foundational for all matter:

> iba la sal destituyendo
> el esplendor de la montañas,
> convirtiendo en traje de cuarzo
> las gotas de lluvia en las hojas
> y transmutando los abetos
> en avenidas de carbón. (*CG*, 428)[75]

As well as symbolizing processes of communication, root metaphors are also fundamental to Neruda's poetics of regeneration in the *Canto general*. In "Aquí viene el árbol," the opening poem of "Los libertadores," for example, the central tree grows in spite of—or even because of—the death and martyrdom of the victims of colonial violence:

> *Aquí viene el árbol, el árbol*
> *cuyas raíces están vivas,*
> *sacó salitre del martirio,*
> *sus raíces comieron sangre*
> *y extrajo lágrimas del suelo (CG, 478; original italics)*[76]

As in the gruesome image of the *canelo* tree ingesting Valdivia's heart later in the same canto, Neruda shows how plants—indeed all forms of life—survive on a cycle of death and renewal. These roots may feed off misery, but in the end they will flourish and grow. As the very final poem of the *Canto general* pronounces, in a full flight of communist rhetoric, the roots of the "árbol rojo" ["red tree"] seek not only "el dolor, sino la fuerza" (*CG*, 836) ["sorrow but strength" (*CGS*, 399)].

Neruda's "vegetal-thinking" also substitutes a human-centered model of temporality with that of the plant world in order to forge a more hopeful view of the future path of human history. Writing in the 1940s, faced with the rise of fascism in Europe and, after 1946, with his own political persecution, Neruda takes a long view of history in the *Canto general*, predicated on the tempo of vegetal growth. This is a view that stayed with Neruda until the end of his life. In the opening poem of the posthumously published collection *Jardín de invierno* (*Winter Garden*), perhaps one of Neruda's most consciously botanical volumes, the poet considers imminent death through the metaphor of fallen leaves turning to dust:

> cuando
> de ser y de no ser vuelven al fondo

despojándose de oro y de verdura

hasta que son raíces otra vez

y otra vez, demoliéndose y naciendo, suben a conocer la primavera.[77]

The echo of *Hamlet* explicitly reveals how, for Neruda, metaphysical questions often find their answers in the world of plants. In the poem the leaves merge with the soil and return to the world of roots, leaving behind their rich and fecund earthly hues of gold and green—but only for a while. Here and elsewhere in the late volume, a change of season heralds a new beginning, when the roots "despiertan en cada primavera" ["awaken to life every spring"].[78] This sense of plant time is also present in "La bondad combatiente" ("Combative Kindness") in the canto "Yo soy" of the *Canto general*, where Neruda reflects on political agitation through the lens of vegetal life. Here the poetic persona imagines himself as a tree, impassively putting down roots, immune to physical and verbal taunts:

Vino a morderme Lunes y le di algunas hojas.

Vino a insultarme Martes y me quedé dormido.

Llegó Miércoles luego con dientes iracundos.

Yo lo dejé pasar construyendo raíces. (*CG*, 825)[79]

Plant time contrasts with the truncated time of the human world, which in this poem is compressed into just four days of a calendar week (Monday to Thursday). Although the behavior of the arboreal narrator seems passive and ineffectual, the poem ends explosively with the war cry: "Morderán sombra y sangre de campanas / bajo las siete leguas de mi canto" (*CG*, 825) ["They'll bite shade and blood from bells / beneath the seven leagues of my song" (*CGS*, 389)]. The reference to seven leagues draws on the folktale trope of seven league boots that magically enable the wearer to cover great distances, thus emphasizing the way in which space might be rendered malleable.[80] The phrase also recalls the seven days invoked in the Genesiacal temporal movement of the poem, which suggests, in turn, the malleability of time. The plural noun "campanas" [bells] is also significant. Wilson describes "campana" as a "powerful word . . . that cuts across all Neruda's writing," and Reiss notes its importance in the *Canto general* in particular, including as a means to evoke the "shape of a plant in nature, either the copihue . . . or the well-known *campanilla*."[81] The connections between the shape of a bell and the flowers of the native Chilean copihue help to illuminate the blood imagery in this poem, since indigenous mythologies of the plant relate its color to the spilt blood of ancestors. The closing lines of the poem therefore instrumentalize Mapuche myths and native flora to produce an image of botanical strength and resistance. Roots—and the plants they sustain—are a source of fortitude and power in Neruda, even in the face of unremitting political oppression.

Through roots, Neruda proposes an understanding of human history against the deep time of nature, where suffering and injustice will, in the end, be ameliorated. Handley has observed this recourse to deep time across a number of Neruda's poems, including in "Bosque" in *Memorial de Isla Negra* (singled out above for its obscure botanical vocabulary). The poem opens with an account of the poet searching, "para enterrar de nuevo / la raíz del árbol difunto" ["for the dead tree's root / to bury it over again"]. In the third stanza the poet describes the process of digging a hole "para raíces resurrectas" ["for roots to resurrect"].[82] In the *Canto general* there is a similar discourse of rebirth and renewal—drawing on the deep time of roots, plants, and soil—in the poem "La tierra se llama Juan" ("The Earth's Name Is Juan"), in which the everyman of the title— Juan the carpenter or Juan the miner—is imagined as coming back to life: "Regresó de la tierra. Ha nacido. / Ha nacido de nuevo como una planta eterna" (*CG*, 681) ["He returned from the earth. He was born. / He was born again like an eternal plant" (*CGS*, 254–55)]. Handley explores the tension of what deep time might mean for Neruda's political commitments: "Nature's deep time and its capacity for perpetual regeneration potentially mean that human injustice is not what it appears to be, that action is not urgent, and that peace is not found in political solutions but in the solace of the wild."[83]

The invocation of a vegetal temporality does not equate to political inertia in Neruda, however, but quite the opposite. The wild is a place of "solace" precisely because it can help us find political solutions, albeit in the long term. In their tenacious ability to feed off poor soil, survive harsh climates, and like the root in "Bosque" apparently come back from the dead, plants can teach us a lot about how to survive and bide our time in an unfavorable world. De Costa stresses the optimism of the *Canto general*, in which the "New World triumphs over the Old, life over death."[84] It is my contention that this optimism is partially achieved through the language of plants. Deep time represents hope in Neruda's work, particularly through botanical images of roots and, indeed, seeds.

Rickett's *The Green Earth* was an important text for Neruda's thinking about plants and there is compelling evidence to show that the poet used the book as a source of information about the way in which seeds grow. The annotations in the book reveal his interest, in particular, in how seeds mature through the division of their nuclei. In Neruda's Spanish copy of the book, a section referring to the seed's "wonderful ability to divide itself into two" is underlined, as is, just below, the statement: "The nucleus first divides itself into two nuclei." Further down on the same page, a sentence describing the growth of plant cells is also underlined as follows: "The result of this rapid *geometric progression* [progresión geométrica] is a body of very small cells, *actively dividing and enlarging* [que se dividen y crecen activamente]."[85]

While Neruda's references to roots emphasize integration and contraction, often across racial or geographical lines, seeds function the other way around. As Rickett's botanical work made clear for the poet, seeds grow through multiplication and expansion. In the words of Marder: "In its singularity, the seed is already a legion: whether spilled or spread, it is both one and many."[86] As a model for human life, seeds suggest the hope of building from small beginnings as well as—like roots—the power of regeneration and resurrection. Rickett's account of the seed in *The Green Earth* resonates in productive ways with the poet's treatment of life and death in the *Canto general*, as when the botanist sets out how the ancients believed that "the planted seed must first die; a miraculous resurrection occurs in the soil, the seed springs to life again and shapes itself in the image of its ancestors."[87] In the poem "El empalado" ("Impaled"), part of Neruda's extended consideration of the Araucanian chief Caupolicán in "Los libertadores," the poet adopts the seed as a symbol of hope in the face of the warrior's death:

> La sangre quemante caía
> de silencio en silencio, abajo,
> hacia donde está la semilla
> esperando la primavera. (*CG*, 489)[88]

As in his late collection *Jardín de invierno*, here Neruda invokes a metaphorical spring as an antidote to suffering and death. In "El empalado" the depth of the seed below the ground is indicated both by the choice of "hacia" [toward], suggesting the circuitous flow of blood, and the repetitive phrase "de silencio en silencio" ["from silence to silence" (*CGS*, 81)]. Coccia has also reflected on what the underground environment of the root, and by extension the seed, must be like: "Light barely reaches them. Here the sounds and noise of our higher world are a deaf, continuous tremor. . . . Water percolates, like any liquid that comes from the world above and, like everything down here, makes efforts to go down toward the center."[89] In his plant-centered poetics, Neruda also places himself in the position of a seed, imagining the subterranean silence and the slow descent of blood. The conditions that this seed finds itself in reminds the reader of those described in the closing address to the dead poet in "Abraham Jesús Brito (poeta popular)" ["Abraham Jesús Brito (People's Poet)"] in the *Canto general*, whom Neruda figures throughout the poem as an errant tree taking root: "Un poco más profundo eres ahora. / Ahora tienes tierra y tienes tiempo." (*CG*, 670) ["You're a little deeper now. / Now you have land and you have time" (*CGS*, 243)]. Safely ensconced under the ground, the seed has both the requisite nutrients and—key to Neruda's "vegetal-thinking"—time in order to successfully resurrect itself.

Neruda's seeds are also always intent on multiplying. In the final poem of the tenth canto, "El fugitivo" ("The Fugitive"), he adopts the maize plant to illustrate the idea of life as a cycle, where corn will emerge "desde las raíces / de mi pueblo, para nacer, / para construir, para cantar, / y para ser otra vez semilla / más numerosa en la tormenta" (*CG*, 716) ["from my people's / roots, to be born, / to build, to sing, / and to be seed again, / more numerous in the storm" (*CGS*, 287)]. In this explicitly political poem, Neruda equates the irrepressible fecundity of the maize plant with the growth of communism (in the penultimate line of the poem he refers to "red hands"). Here Neruda describes the multiplication of the seeds—a proliferation that in the final stanza of the poem is equated with the "pueblo innumerable" (*CG*, 717) ["innumerable people" (*CGS*, 287)] of which the poet is a part. Maize is an important symbolic plant in the Americas, often denoting indigenous strength and culture. For Neruda the maize plant serves the double function as a sign of indigeneity and as a powerful visual conglomeration of seeds. The physiology of seeds, like roots, is fundamental in this instance to how Neruda expresses his Utopian Marxism. As Mark J. Mascia notes: "'germination' takes place only after struggle and implied devastation; utopia is born from dystopia."[90] Although the poem "El fugitivo" was written and published as Neruda was fleeing persecution, in its final lines he looks to the world of plants for a source of hope and discovers it in the enduring image of maize: "*Muerte, martirio, sombra, hielo, / cubren de pronto la semilla. / . . . Pero el maíz vuelve a la tierra. / . . . Desde la muerte renacemos*" (*CG*, 717; original italics) ["*Death, martyrdom, shadow, ice, / suddenly shroud the seed. / . . . But the corn returns to the earth. / From death we're reborn*" (*CGS*, 287)].

Greg Dawes's *Verses against the Darkness: Pablo Neruda's Poetry and Politics* steers a middle ground between two long-established tendencies in Neruda criticism. The first tendency is a liberal formalist tradition that includes the work of De Costa, Durán and Safir, Emir Rodríguez Monegal, and Enrico Mario Santí, who, in Dawes's words, "generally agree that [Neruda] was an extraordinarily gifted poet, but . . . terribly misguided in his politics and personal life." The other critical tendency, Dawes observes, is to "rely on biographical, historical, and philosophical information to explain Neruda's political stances," and includes the work of Marxist critics Alain Sicard and Jaime Concha.[91] Dawes draws on both traditions, bringing close readings of the poems into dialogue with their historical and biographical contexts. My analysis of Neruda's "vegetal-thinking" also supports a more nuanced reading of the *Canto general*, allowing the work to be both philosophically and formally sophisticated and, at the same time, underpinned by Marxist ideology. Although Soviet-inspired botanical images (for instance, the "red tree" of the penultimate verse of the *Canto general*) contributed in no small part to readings of the poem as a work of propaganda, Neruda's persistent recourse to plant vocabulary and metaphors reveals an impressive unity of thought as well as philosophical, political, and poetic complexity across this transcendent work.[92]

As for many of the writers and artists considered in the course of this book, the pursuit of "vegetal-thinking" was twinned with political insurgency in Neruda's work. For Landívar and Bello, plants were integrated into a powerful (post)colonial rejoinder to a classical agrarian tradition. In *Sab* and *María*, European floriographical discourse was invested with new contestatory signification; and Carpentier's New World baroque drew on vegetal imaginaries to express Spanish America's aesthetic Otherness. Likewise, Rivera, Galeano, and Mendieta all appealed to anthropomorphism to destabilize Western ontological distinctions between people and plants and, concomitantly, to undercut notions of human superiority over nonhumans.

Neruda can be placed at the vanguard of this mode of "vegetal-thinking." His determined botanical referencing in the *Canto general*, which extends to his other collections of poetry as well as his critical and autobiographical writings, reveals a poet steeped in not only botanical knowledge but plant-centered ways of thinking and acting that dovetail with his Marxist ideals of human fraternity and unity. Recurrent images of roots and seeds form the substratum of Neruda's vegetal poetics/politics that insists on a long view of history, akin to a kind of geological deep time, where human suffering and dispossession nourish the kernels of future rebellion and rebirth. Neruda also holds up plants as models of fraternalism, with the *Canto general* anticipating Marder's definition of a "vegetal anti-metaphysics" in its emphasis on how plants eschew individualism in favor of collective modes of being.

The metaphor of the poet as a sower of "semillas insurgentes" ["insurgent seeds"] that runs throughout Neruda's writings is powerfully articulated in an anecdote about a childhood encounter.[93] Neruda recalls how, while playing in his back garden as a boy, he peered through a hole in the fence and was presented with a surprising and wonderful gift from another child his age, a little white sheep. Neruda at once set off in search of one of his own treasures to give in return, "una piña de pino, entreabierta, olorosa y balsámica" [a pinecone, half-open, fragrant and balsamic].[94] The cone or *strobilus* of the pine contains its female reproductive organs and seeds, which as a collector of botanical texts the adult Neruda is likely to have known. As the pinecone opens, the seeds are dispersed, so even this half-open cone would still have contained many seeds. Neruda himself extrapolates the wider meaning of this early exchange, seeing it as the beginning of his lifelong commitment to "la fraternidad humana" [human fraternity]:

Conocer la fraternidad de nuestros hermanos es una maravillosa acción de la vida. Conocer el amor de los que amamos es el fuego que alimenta la vida. Pero sentir el cariño de los que no conocemos, de los desconocidos que están velando nuestro sueño y nuestra soledad, nuestros peligros o nuestros desfallecimientos, es una sensación aún más grande y más bella porque extiende nuestro ser y abarca todas las vidas. . . .

Así como dejé allí aquella piña de pino, he dejado en la puerta de muchos desconocidos, de muchos prisioneros, de muchos solitarios, de muchos perseguidos, mis palabras.[95]

Once again, Neruda makes explicit the connections between plants, people, and poetry. His comparison of his poetry to an aromatic pine-cone—a literal instantiation of an overarching botanical metaphor in his work—posits the vegetal as a model for how his committed verse could reach, and transform, the lives of others, advocating a plant-like model of existence that "extiende nuestro ser y abarca todas las vidas" [extends our being and unites all living things].

AFTERWORD

In the late 1970s the Argentine poet Silvina Ocampo collaborated with the photographer Aldo Sessa on a volume of poems and photographs entitled *Árboles de Buenos Aires* (1979) (Trees of Buenos Aires). In it Ocampo and Sessa portray a vegetal world in close proximity to the human. The collection includes photographs of people climbing on and sleeping below trees and there are poems about trees that dance through the night, copulate, and sing as well as arresting photographs that draw out the parallels between human and plant anatomy, showing tree "eyes" and "arms."[1] Fiona J. Mackintosh has discussed Ocampo's debt to classical authors, especially Ovid, in the figuration of processes of metamorphosis between trees and people.[2] Yet, the anthropomorphic qualities of trees throughout *Árboles de Buenos Aires* also speaks of a conception of a multispecies world, in line with so many of the works discussed in this book—images of jungle trees gesticulating and talking in *La vorágine*; Galeano's description of the nocturnal revelries of Amazonian saplings in *Amazonia*; and the comparison of felled trees to amputated human limbs in Carpentier's *El siglo de las luces*. In the poem "Ceibo," Ocampo underscores the ontological fluidity of people and plants via chiastic questions posed to the eponymous *ceibo* (not the towering *Ceiba petandra*, but the *Erythrina crista-galli* or cockspur coral tree, which is a national tree of Argentina) and her collaborator, in turn:

> "Arbol, ¿qué hombre serías
> si no fueras un árbol?"
> le he preguntado a un ceibo.
> "Aldo, ¿qué árbol serías
> si no fueras un hombre?"
> le he preguntado a un hombre. (83)[3]

The parallelism in the phrasing of the questions, as well as the sonic and lexical coincidence between the addressees ("árbol" and Aldo), point to a wider lack of distinction between people and plants, which in this poem, at least, is confirmed by the indifference of both tree and man to their ontological status: "'No me importa ser árbol.' / 'No me importa ser hombre,' / contestaron los dos" (83) ["I don't mind being a tree." / "I don't mind being a man," / they both answered]. This "plantification" of people and personification of trees is one of the preeminent features of Spanish American representations of vegetal-human relations.

Ocampo and Sessa's collaborative depiction of trees in *Árboles de Buenos Aires* draws attention at every turn not only to the kind of plant-human interactions that characterize Spanish American literary and artistic engagements with the vegetal world but also to the divergences between Western philosophical views of plants as simplistic and unintelligent, on the one hand, and indigenous American and (increasingly) scientific views of plants as complex interactive entities, on the other. In order to correct entrenched misunderstandings of plants as lacking in feelings, in the poem "Lapacho" Ocampo playfully rewrites one of the central statements of existential despair by the poet Rubén Darío:

"Dichoso el árbol que es apenas sensitivo"
dijo Darío, yo suprimiría el "apenas"
y diría "dichoso el árbol que es tan sensitivo"
aunque cambiara el metro. (16)[4]

In this way Ocampo and Sessa's collection can be regarded as not only distilling many of the themes in Spanish American engagements with plants but as prefiguring the recent "plant turn" in philosophy, literature, and science. Their respectful depiction of "la vida de los árboles" (12) [the life of trees]—including the recognition of "amistad entre árboles" (39) [friendship among trees]—anticipates, for instance, Wohlleben's work on tree alliances, which shows how pairs of trees grow so as not to impinge on each other's space and "are often so tightly connected at the roots that sometimes they even die together."[5] Far from presenting an anthropocentric view of vegetal life, Ocampo's poems are respectful of the differences between plants and people whilst acknowledging that plants may be capable of "behavior" and "feelings" normally attributed only to humans. As the poet explains in the final poem of the collection, "Apologia": "Yo no quise hablar de los árboles / como si fueran personas, / ni atribuirles mi sensibilidad, / tan superiores los considero" (97) [I didn't want to speak of the trees / as if they were people, / nor attribute to them my sensibilities, / so superior do I consider them].[6] In this poem, Ocampo goes on to articulate a by now familiar desire among Spanish American writers and artists: the wish to "Olvidarme de cómo siento, / de cómo escucho, de cómo veo" (97) [To forget how I feel, / how I listen, how I see] and to adopt a kind of "vegetal-thinking"—as when Mendieta folded herself naked against tree bark or Neruda sought hope in the deep time of seeds.[7] Although at the end of "Apologia" Ocampo relinquishes the attempt to speak as a tree, the preceding poems and photographs in *Árboles de Buenos Aires*, which graphically display the coalescence of bark and skin, burls and eyes, human limbs and tree limbs, powerfully express the cohesion between people and plants and of our past and future interdependencies.

Ocampo and Sessa's collection also appeals to trees to voice anxieties about ecological crisis. "Tormenta" (Storm), which, spread over three pages, takes up more space than any other poem in the book, is presented alongside a double-page collage of eight photographs showing trees in various states of decay: a tree with enormous roots upturned; a tree that has smashed through a car window screen; an uprooted tree stretched across a road. Although much of this poem and many of the accompanying photographs attribute the destruction of trees to the eponymous natural force—common enough in the subtropical maritime city that is the focus of the collection—the tone of "Tormenta" is apocalyptic:

> Los troncos sangran,
> los troncos mueren
> tejiendo jaulas involuntarias
> para los pájaros
> que han quedado huérfanos. . . .
> Si no son hombres los que os han matado
> para hacer edificios o avenidas
> os mataron ciclones o los rayos. (31–33)[8]

The poem is reminiscent of *La vorágine*, where the sap of trees is figured as blood, and of Bello's "La agricultura de la zona tórrida," in which birds are left homeless when land is cleared for plantations. Many of Sessa's photographs provide glimpses of the fabric of the city—the buildings and avenues mentioned by Ocampo, as well as trucks and cars—that have all contributed to the demise of trees. Although there is not yet a sense that the storms might too be a result of human damage (although, we now know that extreme weather is a consequence of climate change), Ocampo's "Tormenta" and Sessa's accompanying photographs make manifest the relationship between capitalism and ecological crisis—of human culpability for the death of these trees—whose fractured "bodies" and bleeding limbs are displayed in agonizing detail.

The explicit connection made throughout Ocampo and Sessa's *Árboles de Buenos Aires* between respect and care for plants and the future health of our planet is at the forefront of many of the works considered here. In one of his *Nuevas odas elementales* (*New Elemental Odes*) from 1955, Neruda writes: "Volví a mi tierra verde / y ya no estaba" [I returned to my green land / and it was no longer there].[9] This is a line that Rivera-Barnes takes as denoting Neruda's growing recognition, from the *Canto general* on, of approaching environmental crisis.[10] In the later collection *Aún* (*Still Another Day*), from 1969, Neruda's beloved southern rainforests are figured as a desolate wasteland. The poet speaks of "los alerces rotos, las araucarias muertas" [broken alerces, dead Araucarias], reversing the optimistic botanical discourse of the *Canto general* in which trees are aligned with regeneration and hope.[11] In his essay "La cazadora de raíces," which was published in the same year as *Aún*, Neruda also reflects at some length on the prospect of a mass vegetal extinction in Chile: "El gran sur forestal se va extinguiendo totalmente, arrasado, quemado y combatido. . . . Tal vez estas raíces chilenas que la cazadora decidió reservar para nosotros serán algún día reliquias, como las mandíbulas de los megaterios."[12] Yet, as Handley argues, Neruda's incipient environmentalism was kept in check by his commitment to Marxism, including "socialist experiments with environmental engineering, feats that he hoped would prove capable of feeding the earth's poor."[13] Among the books in Neruda's personal library was, tellingly, an annotated Spanish translation of a Soviet account of agricultural science by Vadim Safónov, subscribing to principles of Michurinist biology, which regarded plants as entities that must bend to man's will.[14] Such views seem more compatible with the agro-industrial mechanisms that produce the "plant horror" of Schweblin's *Distancia de rescate* than with the plant-centered poetics of Neruda's *Canto general*.

As Neruda's contradictory ecological credentials reveal, "vegetal-thinking" and "environmental thinking" do not always straightforwardly align. Like Neruda, many of the authors studied here are not usually regarded as environmentalists, nor is their work considered environmental literature.[15] Nevertheless, all these works show marked environmental consciousness through the prism of how humans interact with plants. Recurrent descriptions of land clearances in Landívar, Bello, and later Carpentier; concerns over the dominance of monoculture in *Sab* and *María*, and more recently *Distancia de rescate*; extraction of forest products in Rivera, Neruda, and Galeano; and the sustained exploration of the animism of plants: these all show how environmental thinking in relation to flora has a long and important history in Spanish American literature. Almost a century ago, the author of *La vorágine* foresaw the dire consequences of deforestation in the Amazon: "los caucheros que hay en Colombia destruyen anualmente millones de árboles. En los territorios de Venezuela el balatá desapareció. De esta suerte ejercen el fraude contra las generaciones del porvenir."[16] Galeano was born in the Colombian Amazon in 1958 and therefore forms part of the defrauded generation that Rivera speaks of here. In a recent essay Galeano notes how today in Iquitos, one of the cities at the center of Rivera's novel, the "few remaining trees" struggle "to sequester carbon and lower the temperatures."[17] Time and again, in their plant-centered works, Spanish Americans have shown prescience about our present-day environmental crisis. Simon L. Lewis and Mark A. Maslin have recently proposed that the beginning of the so-called Anthropocene coincided with the cross-continental biological and demographic shifts of the conquest of America, including the Columbian exchange.[18] Landívar's unease with accelerated agricultural change in the late colonial period or Bello's at the loss of the cosmically significant ceiba shows that Spanish American writers, even some two hundred years ago, sensed an unprecedented, deleterious, and possibly irrevocable shift in humans' relationships with plants.

In this book I have focused on the myriad ways in which Spanish American writers and artists have drawn on plants to contest dominant social, political, and literary codes, to forge aesthetic movements, and to express personal and national identities. First I focused on how botanical knowledge was employed to rework European traditions and forms—the georgic, floriography, and the baroque—and to fashion a literary identity that was distinctively Spanish American. Then I examined the ways in which writers have depicted plants as animate, communicative beings, thus testing established (Western) dualisms between humans and nonhumans that have traditionally justified the dominance of people over plants. But I have also shown that, through the language of plants, Spanish American writers have engaged with ecological questions, particularly about how to relate to nonhuman others in respectful and nonexploitative ways. Through "vegetal-thinking"—embedded in indigenous views of plants as animate beings and validated by recent scientific studies—Spanish American writers and artists have been able to enter into dialogue with vegetal others and to look to them for models of culture, society, and selfhood. The worlds of people and plants have long been intertwined in Spanish American literature, with botanical discourse fundamental not only to cultural expression—the poetics of plants—but to ecological thinking about our relationship with and obligation to the natural world.

NOTES

INTRODUCTION

1. Paz, *Puertas al campo*, 11–12.
2. Soper, *What Is Nature?*, 155.
3. Moore, *Capitalism*, 2; Latour, *Never Been Modern*, 104 (original italics). See also Haraway, *Simians, Cyborgs, and Women*; Haraway, *When Species Meet*; Tsing, *Mushroom*, vii.
4. A new series by Brill on critical plant studies was launched in 2013 and is edited by Michael Marder. The phrase "plant turn" has been used by Myers, "Conversations on Plant Sensing," 40.
5. See, for instance, Marder, *Plant-Thinking*; Marder, *The Philosopher's Plant*.
6. Hall, *Plants as Persons*, 3. Current estimates place the number of flowering plant species in the world at between three hundred and four hundred thousand, not including "lower plants" such as fungi, mosses, or ferns. See Beerling, *Emerald Planet*, vi.
7. Coccia, *Life of Plants*, 69. See also Irigaray and Marder, *Through Vegetal Being*, esp. ch. 3, "Sharing Universal Breathing," 21–26.
8. Descola, *Beyond Nature and Culture*; Viveiros de Castro, "Cosmological Deixis."
9. Kohn, *How Forests Think*, 1.
10. Miller, *Plant Kin*, 4–5.
11. See de la Cadena, *Earth Beings*; de la Cadena, "Indigenous Cosmopolitics."
12. Karban, "Language of Plant Communication."
13. See, for instance, Gagliano, Mancuso, and Robert, "Towards Understanding Plant Bioacoustics."
14. See Soper, *What Is Nature?*, 82–86, for a discussion of some of the ambiguities of anthropomorphism.
15. See McMeekin, "Representations," 171–72, for a discussion of floral emblems on ceramic spindle whorls. Martel ("El árbol y la piedra," 184–91) talks about representations of the ceiba in the Maya codices.
16. See, for instance, Kissam and Schmidt, *Flower and Song*; Damrosch, "Aesthetics of Conquest," 104.
17. Westerfelhaus, "She Speaks to Us," 112.
18. Morehart, "Ritual Time," 153. See León-Portilla, *Bernardino de Sahagún: First Anthropologist*.
19. Morehart, "Ritual Time," 153.
20. Ascani and Smith, "Psychotropic Herbal and Natural Medicines," 119.

21. Morehart, "Ritual Time," 153.

22. See Russell and Rahman, *Master Plant*; Kiple (*Movable Feast*, 113–14) speaks of the significance of amaranth, which was an important food crop and used ceremonially by the Aztecs.

23. Staller, *Maize Cobs*, 59; Wake, "Maize Theatre," 164; Miller, *Plant Kin*, 197–98. Brotherston (*Image of the New World*, 118) discusses the importance of maize in Maya iconography.

24. See Carrasco, "Cortés and the Sacred Ceiba," 400–401. For a reference to the iroko, see Cabrera, *El monte*, 150.

25. Botanical descriptions and drawings by non–Latin Americans are considered in accounts such as Gerbi, *Nature in the New World*; Stepan, *Picturing Tropical Nature*; Bleichmar, *Visual Voyages*.

26. Crosby, *Columbian Exchange*. Schiebinger (*Plants and Empire*, 83) has used the term "biocontact zones," after Mary Louise Pratt, to refer to the "exchange of plants and their cultural uses" between Europeans and non-Europeans, including in the Americas.

27. Alcocer (*Time Travel*, 126) refers to Fuente's use of this symbol.

28. Smith, *Enchanted Amazon*, 131–33.

29. The definition of the term "Neotropical realm" is from Allaby, *Environmental Science*, 85. The estimate of plant species in the Amazon is drawn from Simms and Reid, *Up in Smoke?*, 33.

30. Heffes, *Políticas de la destrucción*, 15–68.

31. Rivera-Barnes and Hoeg, *Reading and Writing*; Kane, *Natural World*; Barbas-Rhoden, *Ecological Imaginations*.

32. DeVries, *History of Ecology*; Anderson and Bora, *Ecological Crisis*. Jaramillo, "Green Hells," and Vieira, "*Phytographia*," adopt an ecocritical position with a focus on plants.

33. See DeVries, *History of Ecology*, 137–60, 161–62, 230–32; Rivera-Barnes, "Pablo Neruda's Latin American Landscape," 150–55; Williams, "Nature," 75. Wylie, "Anthropomorphism and Arboricide," in Anderson and Bora, *Ecological Crisis*, forms the basis for my discussion of plants in chapters 1 and 4 of this book.

34. In addition to the studies mentioned above, Alcocer, *Narrative Mutations*, and Alcocer, *Time Travel*, both contain thought-provoking discussions of plants in Latin American culture. For instance, Alcocer (*Narrative Mutations*, 81) describes how, within Caribbean literature, plants and trees have often been used to "metaphorize heredity by conflating or dissolving the categories of plants and people," and supplying vegetal metaphors for culture.

35. Buchmann (*Reason for Flowers*, 221–34) outlines some of the main flower imagery in the Western literary tradition.

36. Mahood, *Poet as Botanist*, 3.

37. Seaton, *Language of Flowers*; Rosenthal, *Race Mixture*, ch. 4; Meeker and Szabari, "From the Century"; Bataille, "Language of Flowers"; Scarry, "Imagining Flowers"; Taussig, "Language of Flowers."

38. Gagliano, Ryan, and Vieira, "Introduction," xvi.

39. Gagliano, Ryan, and Vieira, *Language of Plants*; Laist, *Plants and Literature*; Gibson,

Plant Contract. Other recent works published in the area of critical plant studies include Janzen, *Media, Modernity*; Keetley and Tenga, *Plant Horror*; Ryan, *Green Sense*, which focuses on the flora of Southwest Australia; Gibson and Brits, *Covert Plants.*

40. Gagliano, Ryan, and Vieira, "Introduction," vii.

41. The role of the garden in Rubén Darío has been considered by Martínez Domingo, *Los espacios poéticos*, 5 and DeGrave, "Ecoliterature," 91–92.

CHAPTER 1. "¡SALVE, FECUNDA ZONA!"

1. *OED Online*, s.v. "agriculture," accessed July 22, 2017, https://www.oed.com/; Schiebinger and Swan, "Introduction," 1; Crosby, *Columbian Exchange*, 66, 67.

2. Ortiz, *Contrapunteo cubano*, 254–61. See also Kosiba, "Cultivating Empire," 236–38; Whitehead, "Crises and Transformations," 891; Bakewell and Holler, *History of Latin America*, 243.

3. Outside the Hispanic tradition, other celebrations of agriculture in the "New World" include John Grainger's *The Sugar Cane* (1764), which the author called a "West-Indian georgic." See Gilmore, *Poetics of Empire*, 90. The intersections between agriculture and literature in the United States have recently been explored by Dolan, *Beyond the Fruited Plain.*

4. Neruda, *Obras completas* 1:636; Neruda, *Canto general*, trans. Schmitt, 211.

5. Laird, *Epic of America*, 3.

6. See also Dale, "Parícutin," 523. Echenberg (*Humboldt's Mexico*, 137) notes how Humboldt corrected some of Landívar's observations about the volcano.

7. Higgins, *Criollo Archive*, 113.

8. Putzeys Álvarez, "Lo vegetal," 37 (see 60–61 for a list of the different tree and flower species included in the poem).

9. Higgins, *Criollo Archive*, 167.

10. Higgins, *Criollo Archive*, 156; Browning, "Natural History," 14. Browning cites a number of contemporary sources to show that there was concern in Guatemala in the late eighteenth century about the lack of agrarian independence in the country and the need to develop agriculture and commerce. See Browning, "Natural History," 19–23.

11. Bello did not, however, share Bolívar's revolutionary zeal for the complete overthrow of the imperial order. Jaksić, *Andrés Bello*, is a comprehensive intellectual biography of Bello, which clearly sets out the poet and statesman's loyalty to the colonial regime. Cussen (*Bello and Bolívar*, 88) cites a statement that he argues was written by Bello: "We are convinced that the South Americans cannot be good republicans."

12. Henríquez Ureña, *Ensayos*, 37. Bello's poems—as Altschul (*Geographies of Philological Knowledge*, 167) has noted—have been "enshrined by literary historiography as foundational." Miranda ("Andrés Bello," 153), Gomes ("*Silvas Americanas*," 181), and Meyer-Minnemann ("Poesía de fundación"), as well as Henríquez Ureña, have all drawn attention to the importance of Bello's poems for literary independence.

13. Apart from some draft verses, only "La agricultura de la zona tórrida" was completed. See Cussen, *Bello and Bolívar*, 117–18.

14. Favret, *War at a Distance*, 133. Cussen (*Bello and Bolívar*, 118) speaks of the poem's

"georgic tone." Cussen (*Bello and Bolívar*, ch. 1) considers Bello's classical education and early poetic influences. He notes that Bello translated Book 5 of the *Aeneid* when he was fifteen (3).

15. Virgil, *Eclogues, Georgics*, 168–69 (*Georgics*, II.458–59); Low, *Georgic Revolution*, 8.

16. Bello, *Obras completas: poesías*, 1:74; Bello, *Selected Writings*, 37. Page references for the Spanish will henceforth appear parenthetically in the text, as *OCP* with volume and page; short English translations will be included parenthetically in the text as *SW* with page. Longer English translations will appear in the notes.

17. [You who look to the soil . . . / for the substances that feed men, / first observe the atmospheric conditions / and climate of the terrain: . . . / and what / the habits of peasants of old were / and what native plants it nourishes.] Original Spanish cited in Cussen, *Bello and Bolívar*, 41.

18. DeVries, *History of Ecology*, 34.

19. Landívar, *Rusticatio Mexicana*, 142. For ease of reading, all quotes from this text are in English and come from the prose translation by Graydon W. Regenos included in Laird's edition. The original Latin is included only when discussing significant words or lines in the original. Page references will henceforth appear parenthetically in the text as *RM* with page number. Any quotes in Latin will give the book and line number.

20. The variety of flowers in Landívar recalls Bernardo de Balbuena's 1604 epic poem, *La grandeza mexicana* (Mexican grandeur), which in canto 4 includes a catalogue of indigenous and, as Reiss ("American Baroque," 405) has noted, nonindigenous flora.

21. Granziera, "Concept of the Garden," 185.

22. Hesiod, *Theogony*, 40.

23. Putzeys Álvarez, "Lo vegetal," 45.

24. For example, in the opening stanzas of book 1 of the poem, Landívar talks of the "fields" ["campos"] and "gardens" (*RM*, 124) ["hortos" (1.8, 9)] of his native land.

25. Putzeys Álvarez, "Lo vegetal," 62–63, has collated all instances of the color green in the poem.

26. Laird (*Epic of America*, 59) discusses the theme of exile in the poem.

27. Virgil, *Eclogues, Georgics*, 148 (*Georgics*, II. 173).

28. Maize and cocoa were native to South America; sugarcane and bananas were not. See Crosby, *Columbian Exchange*, ch. 3.

29. "You weave the summer's wreath of golden grain, / and offer grapes to the bubbling pail. . . . / You give sweet sugarcane, whose pure sap / makes the world disdain the honeycomb. . . . / Living red teems on your cactus plants" (*SW*, 29).

30. Foster, *Handbook*, 167.

31. For a discussion of the dissemination and beliefs surrounding the passionflower, see López Terrada, "Hérnandez and Spanish Painting," 163.

32. Meyer-Minnemann ("Poesía de fundación," 79, 81) notes how the abundance of the tropics in Bello's poem is also evocative of the classical Golden Age. Cussen, *Bello and Bolívar*, 123.

33. Higgins (*Criollo Archive*, 179) argues that the section on beavers is an "allegorical narrative about the organization of American societies as productive and rational entities."

Kerson ("Republic of Beavers," 25) has shown that the portrayal of the society of the beavers in Landívar's epic is indebted to classical utopias such as Plato's *Republic* and Thomas More's *Utopia*.

34. Browning, "Natural History," 25.

35. Higgins, *Criollo Archive*, 233.

36. See Landívar, *RM*, 191. For a history of sugar's arrival in the Americas, see Abbott, *Sugar*, 21-27.

37. Hughes, *End of Work*, 5. Hutchins also notes that labor was "an essential component of the edenic experience." Hutchins, *Inventing Eden*, 24. See also my discussion of these issues in Wylie, "Politics of Vegetating," 182-84.

38. Virgil, *Eclogues, Georgics*, 108-9 (*Georgics*, I.145-46).

39. Landívar refers to how workers are attacked by a "fly . . . with a fierce proboscis" (*RM*, 161), just as Virgil mentions fierce swarms of gadflies in book 3 of the *Georgics*; Virgil, *Eclogues, Georgics*, 186-87 (*Georgics*, III.147-49).

40. Wake, "Maize Theatre," 160.

41. See, for instance, Cussen, *Bello and Bolívar*, 126; Hoeg, "Andrés Bello," 63-64.

42. "Go and enjoy the farmer's life, his lovely peace, / Untroubled by bitterness and envy. . . . / Go breathe the mountain air, that gives / lost vigor to the tired body, and retards / fretful old age, and tinges pink / the face of beauty" (*SW*, 33).

43. Note that I do not draw on the published English translation for these terms, as it does not convey the concern with disease in the original Spanish.

44. "Let the axe break the matted trees / and fire burn the forest; in its barren splendor / let a long gash be cut. / Give shelter in the valleys / to thirsty sugarcane; . . . / Make coffee trees adorn the slopes; . . . / Let gardens flourish, orchards laugh with joy." (*SW*, 33-34).

45. Kaempfer, "Economías de redención," 286, describes this as a "destrucción transformadora" [transformative destruction], necessary for the founding of a postcolonial nation. "Huerta" can be translated as "orchard, cultivated plot, vegetable patch, kitchen garden or parkland grounds next to a riverbank." See Samson, "Outdoor Pursuits," 133. Lottman ("Gardens of Teresa de Ávila," 330) argues that the opposition between the terms *huerta* and *vergel* is equivalent to that between "labor and leisure, between the kitchen garden or practical orchard and the luxurious pleasure garden dedicated to the senses."

46. Earlier in the poem, Landívar boasts how the beauty of his homeland, Guatemala, surpasses the wonders of the ancient world (*RM*, 148).

47. Martí, "Nuestra América," 165.

48. Crosby, *Columbian Exchange*, 70.

49. Sage, *Warfare in Ancient Greece*, 25.

50. Laird, *Epic of America*, 271n4; Ovid, *Metamorphoses*, 147-48.

51. See a discussion of this etymology in Chamberlain, "On the Words for 'Fear,'" 304.

52. Miller, *Environmental History*, 79.

53. Catallus, *Student's Catallus*, 158; Horace, *Carminum Liber*, 6.

54. Rosaldo, *Culture and Truth*, 69.

55. See also Brumble, *Classical Myths*, 195.

56. Landívar, *RM*, 234; Virgil, *Aeneid VII–XII*, 286–87 (XI.721–24).

57. Bleichmar, *Visual Voyages*, 67.

58. Examples of these images are included by Bleichmar, *Visual Voyages*, 68–75.

59. Kerson, "Heroic Mode," 160.

60. Las Casas, *Brevísima relación*, 13; Las Casas, *Short Account*, 11.

61. Landívar describes the cochineal insect as "gifted with a gentle nature, abhoring murder among its fellows, abhoring civil disorder" (*RM*, 150). Las Casas, for instance, says that the murdered king of Española was "muy obediente y virtuoso y naturalmente pacífico y devoto a los reyes de Castilla" (*Brevísima relación*, 19) ["dutiful and virtuous, a man of placid temperament much devoted to the King and Queen of Spain" (*Short Account*, 19)].

62. Las Casas describes how "fueron infinitas las gentes que yo vide quemar vivas y despedazar y atormentar por diversas y nuevas maneras de muertes y tormentos" (*Brevísima relación*, 22) ["I saw with my own eyes how the Spaniards burned countless local inhabitants alive or hacked them to pieces, or devised novel ways of torturing them to death" (*Short Account*, 23)].

63. Hoeg, "Andrés Bello," 59.

64. "The ancient tree / for long the challenge of the laboring crowd, / groans, and trembles from a hundred axes, / topples at last, and its tall summit falls. / The wild beast flees; the doleful bird / leaves its sweet nest, its fledgling brood, / seeking a wood unknown to humankind. / What do I see? a tall and crackling flame / spills over the dry ruins of the conquered forest." (*SW*, 34).

65. Virgil, *Eclogues, Georgics*, 150–51 (*Georgics*, II.207–11).

66. Regier, *Fracture and Fragmentation*, 53.

67. See Dávila Durand, "Lo que se debe hacer," 85.

68. The *ceibo* is a common name for the ceiba. See Salazar, Soihet, and Méndez, *Manejo de semillas*, 61. The fact that Bello is referring to a ceiba, not a *ceibo*, is confirmed not only by the description of the tree's large stature but by other references to both of these trees in Bello's poem. In an author's note to the poem, Bello (*OCP*, 71n221) refers to the role of the "bucare" (*Ceibo erythrina*) as a good source of shade for young cacao plants. In contrast, an unpublished fragment of the *silva* includes a description of a group of imposing trees including ceibas and laurels, which "ramas a ramas / pugnando por gozar de las felices / auras y de la luz, hacen la guerra" [branch to branch / struggling to reach / light and sun, they battle]. This fragment has a number of parallels with the section of the poem describing the "ceibo anciano," not least the reference to a "tronco anciano" [ancient trunk]. See Bello, *Obras completas: Borradores de poesía*, 2:46.

69. García-Goyco, "Mapa de Cuauhtinchan No. 2," 363; Anderson, *Big Old Trees*, 105–7.

70. Hartman, "Ceiba Tree," 16–18. I witnessed the presence of these sacrifices—mostly remains of birds but also of a pig's head—on a visit to the park in December 2017. These sacrifices and the god Changó are discussed at greater length in Niell, *Urban Space as Heritage*, 238–39.

71. Anderson (*Big Old Trees*, 5) argues that "trees are intimately tied to notions of the sacred."

72. The word "conquered" is used in the English translation, though not in the original. See Bello, *SW*, 34.

73. Roberts, *Comprehensive Etymological Dictionary*, 1:198; *Diccionario de la lengua española*, s.v. "desterrar."

74. Alcocer, *Narrative Mutations*, 88.

75. Cabrera, *El monte*, 149.

76. Cabrera, *El monte*, 191–92. [An obscure fear prevents the peasant from raising his axe against the sacred trunk. . . . Only a reckless or irresponsible person would agree to cut down the ceiba, which materialized, more than symbolized, in their eyes, the terrible omnipotence of God. . . . Ceibas take revenge. Ceibas do not forgive. . . . "I prefer to live in misery, to leave my children without food, to have us die of hunger before I would chop down a ceiba" is the unvarying exclamation of the rural man when one tries to remove the "tree of the Virgin Mary," of the most holy one, of Oddúdua or Aggayú, the tree of spirits.]

77. Hartman, "Ceiba Tree," 25.

78. Putzeys Álvarez, "Lo vegetal," 53.

79. 2 Cor. 4:6. All quotations from the Bible are from the King James version.

80. Bello, *OCP*, 1:47. ["Ceibas, acacias, myrtles now entwine, / and reeds and vines and grasses too. / From branch to branch, they all / perpetual warfare make, struggling to reach / the light and sun." (*SW*, 11)].

81. Hoeg, "Andrés Bello," 64.

82. Collins, *"Soledades,"* 54. For a discussion of the *silva*, see González Echevarría, "Colonial Lyric," 191; Clarke, "Silva," 1306.

83. Gomes, *"Silvas Americanas,"* 189; Carreño, "Of 'Orders' and 'Disorders,'" 228.

84. Beverley, *Góngora's "Soledades,"* 37.

85. "Let not unseasonable rains / ruin the tender crops; let not the pitiless tooth / of gnawing insects devour them. / Let not the savage storm destroy, / or the tree's maternal sap / dry up in summer's long and heated thirst." (*SW*, 35).

86. Frazer, *Golden Bough*, 451. Pogue Harrison (*Gardens*, 27) reflects that "Prayers, rain dances, implorations—perhaps even the concept of God himself—have their source in this inability of the gardener to remain impassive vis-à-vis the larger, uncontrollable forces that bear upon or determine the outcome of his efforts."

87. Carson, *Silent Spring*, 21.

88. Schweblin, *Distancia de rescate*, 22; Schweblin, *Fever Dream*, 16. Page references to the Spanish (*DR*) and English translation (*FD*) will be given parenthetically in the text following quotations.

89. Oliveira and Hecht, "Sacred Groves," 255, also 251.

90. See Schweblin, *Distancia de rescate*, 68, 83, 84.

91. Keetley, "Introduction," 1.

92. Cited in Bravo, "Pablo Messiez."

93. Locatelli and De Falco, "Regulation of Pesticides," 39. Information about the increase in pesticide use is drawn from a report by the NGO, Red Universitaria de Ambiente y Salud, "Use of Toxic Agrochemicals."

94. Sontag, *Illness as Metaphor*. "Elixirs of Death" is the title of ch. 3 of Carson, *Silent Spring*.

95. The health of the soy plants in *Distancia de rescate* conforms to a point made by Meeker and Szabari ("From the Century," 36) about how horror is often generated by the super-productive nature of plants.

CHAPTER 2. PLANTS AND PLANTATIONS

1. Crosby, *Columbian Exchange*, 211. According to DeVries, *History of Ecology*, 162, the impact of monoculture crop production across Latin America was "in equal measure cultural and ecological."

2. Ward ("Nature and Civilization," 97) for instance, has noted that "Women in *Sab* are not so different from female characters in Isaacs' *María*," particularly through their shared "proximity to nature." Sommer, *Foundational Fictions*, includes chapters on both the novels.

3. The question of Jewishness in *María* has been the subject of various articles, including Faverón Patriau, "Judaísmo y desarraigo," and Paulk, "Foundational Fictions." Although the religious heritage of Enrique Otway is not made explicit in the novel, a number of critics of *Sab* argue that he is of Jewish descent. See, for instance, Cruz, "Sab," 68.

4. Seaton, "Considering the Lilies," 255.

5. Rosenthal, in *Race Mixture*, uses the resonant term "floral counterdiscourse" in relation to Lydia Maria Child's abolitionist novel *Romance of the Republic* (ch. 4) as well as, in passing, to *Sab* (95). I draw on this useful concept throughout this chapter.

6. Geisweidt ("Horticulture of the Head," 7) has argued that "Hair offer[ed] the early moderns a material referent for their shared experience of life cycles with plants." During the same period, botanists were able to view plant hairs under the microscope for the first time. See Geisweidt, "Horticulture of the Head," 9.

7. See, for instance, Albin, Corbin, and Marrero-Fente, "Gertrudis the Great," where they stress Avellaneda's qualities as a literary pioneer.

8. Harter, *Gertrudis Gómez de Avellaneda*, 19. Davies ("Introduction," 2) notes that "although published in Madrid, *Sab* is a Cuban novel."

9. Schlau, "Strangers in a Strange Land," 501. For a discussion of Romanticism in the novel see, for example, Harter, *Gertrudis Gómez de Avellaneda*, 126; Servera, "Introducción," 55. Both Harter and Servera note the influence of Bernardin de Saint Pierre. Schlau ("Strangers in a Strange Land," 498) refers to the presence of Chateaubriand; Rosenthal (*Race Mixture*, 75) talks of the influence of Heredia on Avellaneda.

10. Critics have not always agreed on the meaning of the novel. For instance, Jackson ("Fact from Fiction," 83–89) and Schlau ("Strangers in a Strange Land") both stress the novel's abolitionist stance, whereas Branche ("Ennobling Savagery?") discredits its antislavery message. Pastor (*El discurso*), Guerra ("Estrategias femeninas"), and Kirkpatrick (*Las Románticas*, 158) all draw attention to *Sab*'s feminism.

11. Goody, *Culture of Flowers*, 235–37. Examples of this tradition include Wirt, *Flora's Dictionary*, and Jazmín, *El lenguaje de las flores*.

12. Gómez de Avellaneda, *Sab*, 82; Gómez de Avellaneda, Sab *and Autobiography*, 59.

All further page references to the Spanish will be given parenthetically in the text. Shorter English translations are included after the Spanish in the text; longer translations will be given in the notes.

13. Sartillot, *Herbarium*, 9. The only other character in the novel to be compared to a rose is Enrique, whose cheeks are described as having a "bello color de rosa" (*Sab*, 159) ["handsome rosy hue" (Sab *and* Autobiography, 117)].

14. Seaton, *Language of Flowers*, 17. Sartillot (*Herbarium*, 10–11) notes that, in general, "flowers are traditionally associated with beauty, innocence, virginity, indifference, and passivity."

15. "That mercantile and profit-oriented atmosphere, those unceasing preoccupations with interests of a material nature withered the lovely illusions of her youthful heart. Poor, delicate flower! Beautiful, useless, you were born to perfume gardens, gently caressed by Heaven's breezes!" Sab *and* Autobiography, 135.

16. The reference to wilting also invokes the use of flower imagery in Garcilaso de la Vega's Sonnet 23: "Marchitará la rosa el viento helado, / todo lo mudará la edad ligera / por no hacer mudanza en su costumbre" ["the rose will wither in the icy blast / and fickle time will alter everything, / if only to be constant in its habit" (Vega, *Selected Poems*, 41–43)]. I am grateful to Dr Caroline Egan, University of Cambridge, for this reference.

17. Harter, *Gertrudis Gómez de Avellaneda*, 77.

18. Gómez de Avellaneda, *La hija de las flores*, 290–91; Rivera, "El lenguaje de las flores," 15.

19. Gómez de Avellaneda, "La primavera," *Obras de La Avellaneda*, 1:83. [To the tree you give back flowers, / fragrance and color. . . . / But you do not give back lost flowers to man! / But you do not revive dead illusions!]

20. Gómez de Avellaneda, "Cuartetos, al Excmo. Sr. Don Pedro Sabater," *Obras de La Avellaneda*, 1:210.

21. "It was a small enclosure protected from the hot south wind by a triple row of tall reeds of a handsome dark green known as *pitos*, which, when gently ruffled by the breeze, produced a soft and melancholy murmur, like that of a gently purling brook. The garden was a perfect square, the other three sides of which were formed by arches of rushes covered by showy festoons of vines and garden balsam, where buzzing hummingbirds as brilliant as emeralds and topazes sipped from red and gold blossoms.

In this small enclosure, Sab had assembled all of Carlota's most beloved flowers. An *astronomía* displayed sumptuous clusters of deep purple blossoms. There were lilies and roses, *clavellinas* and jasmine, the modest violet and the proud sunflower, enamored of the eye of heaven, the changeable pink *malva*, wood sorrel with its pearly blossoms and the *pasionaria*, whose magnificent calyx bears the sacred marks of the Redeemer's passion. In the center of the garden, there was a little pond in which Sab had collected some small, brightly colored fish; encircling the pond was a bench shaded by the broad green leaves of the banana trees." Sab *and* Autobiography, 56.

22. Davies, "Gift in Sab," 49.

23. DeLoughrey, "Globalizing the Routes," n.p.

24. Rosenthal, *Race Mixture*, 95. Ibarra ("Gómez de Avellaneda's *Sab*," 387) refers to transculturation.

25. Gómez de Avellaneda, *La hija de las flores*, 379–80.

26. Bennett (*Lilies of the Hearth*, 74) notes that roses and lilies are the only flowers mentioned in the Song of Solomon. See Seaton, *Language of Flowers*, who includes in her appendix "A Combined Vocabulary" that gives the meaning of different flowers in five popular nineteenth-century books of floriography. This includes the violet (196–97) and the sunflower (194–95).

27. Grigson, *Englishman's Flora*, 108.

28. Davies, "Gift in Sab," 49.

29. Gómez de Avellaneda, *La hija de las flores*, 288. See also Rosenzweig, *Worshipping Aphrodite*, 29. Violets are (according to Grigson, *Englishman's Flora*, 70) a "flower of Aphrodite and also of her son Priapus, the deity of gardens and generation."

30. The prominence of the square, alongside other geometric designs, is discussed in relation to St Augustine and his medieval reception in Turner, *Garden History*, 175. A painting from Ancient Egypt from circa 1400 BC housed at the British Museum shows an ornamental fishpond. See Thacker, *History of Gardens*, 13.

31. Ibarra, "Gómez de Avellaneda's *Sab*," 387; Thieme, *Postcolonial Literary Geographies*, 54.

32. See Taiz and Taiz, *Flora Unveiled*, 280.

33. Ezek. 28:13. See also *The Epic of Gilgamesh*, 100: "There was the garden of the gods; all round him stood bushes bearing gems . . . there was fruit of carnelian with the vine hanging from it, beautiful to look at; lapis lazuli leaves hung thick with fruit, sweet to see. For thorns and thistles there were haematite and rare stones, agate, and pearls from out of the sea."

34. Ibarra, "Gómez de Avellaneda's *Sab*," 387. Sommer (*Foundational Fictions*, 120) calls the garden a "miniature Eden."

35. Méndez Rodenas, "Picturing Cuba," 164, 156. Stepan (*Picturing Tropical Nature*, 43–48) discusses Romantic depictions of the tropics. Araujo (*Brazil through French Eyes*, 36) has recently used the term "tropical Romanticism" to denote moments in which Brazil is portrayed as "a seductive land with a luxuriant natural environment."

36. I discuss the contrast between inside and outside perspectives in Avellaneda's work in Wylie, "Of the Margins and the Center," 298.

37. Rivera-Barnes, "I Do Not Weep," 70, 68; Ward, "Gertrudis Gómez de Avellaneda's *Sab*," 99.

38. "Here those children of nature lived in happiness and innocence: this virgin soil did not need to be watered with the sweat of slaves to be productive; everywhere it gave shade and fruit, water and flowers, and its entrails had not been rent asunder so that its hidden treasures could be torn out by greedy hands. Oh, Enrique! I lament not having been born then when you, an Indian like me, would have built me a palm hut where we would have enjoyed a life of love, innocence, and freedom." *Sab and* Autobiography, 73–74.

39. Bello, *Obras completas: poesía*, 1:67; Bello, *Selected Writings*, 29.

40. Harter, *Gertrudis Gómez de Avellaneda*, 28; Chateaubriand, *Atala*, 43. Carlota refers twice to living more simply with Enrique. Earlier in the novel, she renounces the institution

of slavery and says to Enrique: "Daremos libertad a todos nuestros negros. ¿Qué importa ser menos ricos? ¿Seremos por eso menos dichosos? Una choza con Enrique es bastante para mí, y para él no habrá riqueza preferible a mi gratitud y amor" (80) ["We will give all our blacks their freedom. What does it matter to be less wealthy? Will we be any less happy because of it? A hut with Enrique is enough for me, and for him there will be no greater riches than my gratitude and my love" (Sab *and* Autobiography, 57)].

41. Rivera-Barnes, "I Do Not Weep," 69.

42. See Gómez de Avellaneda, *Sab*, 78.

43. "The tree under which he stood fell, seared by lightning. His horse, which bolted from under the trees shaking as they were lashed by the wind, snapped the reins by means of which his distraught rider was vainly attempting to control him. Striking his head against the branches and severely jolted by the terrified animal, Enrique lost his seat and crashed to the ground, bloodied and unconscious, in the deepest part of the forest." Sab *and* Autobiography, 50.

44. See Gómez de Avellaneda, *Sab*, 90, 80, 138.

45. See Anderson, *Big Old Trees*.

46. Anderson, *Big Old Trees*, 127, see also 115–16.

47. Leving Jacobson, "Nation, Violence, Memory," 174.

48. The narrator notes of Martina that "ninguno de los rasgos de su fisonomía parecía corresponder a su pretendido origen" (*Sab*, 108) ["none of her facial features appeared to match her alleged origin" (Sab *and* Autobiography, 78)].

49. "The ancient tree on the mountain, when it is dry and without sap feeds only *curujeyes* and year after year passes without affecting it. It resists hurricanes and rains, the rigors of sun and the dryness of drought while the tree that is still green suffers the ravages of time and little by little loses its flowers, its leaves, and its branches. But I have here . . . three handsome trees in the prime of their youth, with all the freshness of spring, and four little saplings who are growing exuberantly." Sab *and* Autobiography, 78.

50. Sab also refers to Carlota's "talle de palma" (*Sab*, 132) ["palmlike bearing" (Sab *and* Autobiography, 97)], the only other time she is compared to a tree in the novel. This is, however, a mere cliché (in the same sentence he compares her skin to a lily and her neck to that of a swan). The Mexican poet Antonio Plaza (1832–1882) also uses the phrase "talle de palma" in the love poem "Amor a mártir." Plaza, *Albúm del corazón*, 137.

51. Sommer (*Foundational Fictions*, 121–22) says that the reader admires Teresa for "the reserve and emotional control that cannot be confused with the shyness or coyness that a patriarchal language might require of women." Schlau ("Strangers in a Strange Land," 500) regards Teresa as the "true heroine of *Sab*." Note that the phrase "alma apática" was omitted from Scott's translation of this section of the novel; see Gómez de Avellaneda, Sab *and* Autobiography, 35.

52. "When the hurricane launches its chariot of fire across the land, the *ceiba* tree remains upright, its victorious crown illuminated by the halo which its enemy bestows on it, while the bush, which has vainly attempted to survive in the same way, is left only to attest to the force which has destroyed it. The sun comes out, and the *ceiba* greets it by

saying "Here I am," while the bush exhibits only scattered leaves and broken branches." *Sab and* Autobiography, 140.

53. See Hartman, "Ceiba Tree," 22, 24. Hartman defines "orisha" as "metaphysical beings that act as mediators between humans and the Supreme Trinity" (22).

54. See Gómez de Avellaneda, *Sab*, 146, 151.

55. Harter, *Gertrudis Gómez de Avellaneda*, 128; Schlau, "Strangers in a Strange Land," 496; Rivera-Barnes, "I Do Not Weep," 71.

56. A connection might be made between Teresa's choice of the convent and botanical discourse in *Sab* by way of John Ruskin's description of a bulb as a "cloister": "A baby crocus has literally its own little dome—domus, or Duomo—within which in early spring it lives a delicate convent life of its own." Ruskin, *Proserpina*, 40.

57. Garfield, *Poder y sexualidad*, 66.

58. Benítez-Rojo, "Sugar and the Environment," 40. Monzote (*From Rainforest to Cane Field*, 1) notes that in 1815 the king of Spain granted property owners in Cuba the right to cut down trees on their own land, leading to unchecked deforestation.

59. [Abundant and beneficial showers in districts with large forests, which in the dry season make up for the lack of water, will stop, condemning plants and animals to extinction from the months of November to March; and in hot periods, there will no longer be the enlivening breeze of the woods nor the soothing scent of wild flowers. In short, where trees are destroyed, a scene of solitude and death will supplant the merry spectacle of a young and wild nature.] De la Sagra, *Historia económico-política*, 84. McCook (*States of Nature*, 18–19) briefly discusses the work of de la Sagra.

60. Monzote, *From Rainforest to Cane Field*, 1; Benítez-Rojo, "Sugar and the Environment," 40.

61. Manuel Moreno Fraginals, *Cuba/España*; qtd. in Benítez-Rojo, "Sugar and the Environment," 41.

62. Rosaldo, *Culture and Truth*, 69–70.

63. Indeed, even after emancipation, conditions did not improve greatly for sugar workers. As Mintz (*Sweetness and Power*, 70) notes, after slavery was abolished, across the Caribbean "the planter classes sought to re-create preemancipation conditions—to replace the discipline of slavery with the discipline of hunger."

64. This section is derived in part from Wylie, "Floriography, Sexuality and the Horticulture of Hair."

65. See Masson de Gómez, "Las flores como símbolos." Flower symbolism is also briefly mentioned by McGrady, *Jorge Isaacs*, 151nn25, 26. Hart (*Companion to Spanish-American Literature*, 65) regards flowers and the bird of ill omen as the two most significant symbols in the novel.

66. Isaacs, *María*, 326. All further page references to this edition will be included parenthetically in the text. English translations from the novel are largely my own. I do consult the only existing English translation of *María* (Rollo Ogden's 1890 version), but this is widely acknowledged as unreliable. See, for instance, McGrady, *Jorge Isaacs*, 6. Short English translations are included after the Spanish, and longer translations are included in the notes.

67. See Seaton, "Nineteenth-century metalanguage," 80–84.

68. Bennett, *Lilies of the Hearth*, 74. The rose of Sharon is further discussed in Ward, *Contemplation upon Flowers*, 313.

69. An example of her comparison to a lily is the reference to "su garganta de tez de azucena" (132) [her lily white neck]. These analogies were well-worn in European literature and are a source of humor in *A Midsummer Night's Dream*, for instance, when, as part of the Rude Mechanicals' performance in Act 3, Flute, as Thisby, declares: "*Most radiant Pyramus, most lily white of hue / Of colour like the red rose on triumphant briar*" (original italics); Shakespeare, *Midsummer Night's Dream*, 3.1.87–88.

70. Isaacs, *María*, 286; Taiz and Taiz, *Flora Unveiled*, 329.

71. See Bataille, "Language of Flowers," 12–14. The significance of the rose in Bataille's essay has been discussed by Boldt-Irons, "Introduction," 4. Sartillot (*Herbarium*, 17) notes the slipperiness of floral imagery in French literature, where flowers can be emblems of either beauty or evil, as in Baudelaire.

72. Song of Solomon 4:12; Augspach, *Garden as Woman's Space*, 14.

73. Critics are keen to stress the parallels between Isaacs's family estate, tantalizingly called El Paraíso (Paradise) and the unnamed hacienda of the novel. See, for instance, McGrady, *Jorge Isaacs*, 14.

74. Augspach, *Garden as Woman's Space*, 7.

75. Glantz, "Húmeda identidad," discusses moisture in the novel.

76. This quotation is included in the first three editions of the novel, but it is excised in the fourth (the 1922 edition by Camacho Roldán and Tamayo), on which McGrady's edition is based. It is included in the notes in Isaacs, *María*, 351n.

77. Scarry, "Imagining Flowers," 102.

78. The popular name for the seeds is given in Gamble, "Presence of the Divine," 125. Granziera notes that Francisco Hernández, who compiled an important natural history of New Spain, records the aphrodisiac qualities of *ololiuqui*. Granziera also makes the connection between the plant and Macuilxochitl. Granziera, "Concept of the Garden," 188, 187.

79. Efraín, familiar with the European Romantics and important Romantic antecedents such as Shakespeare (referred to in Isaacs, *María*, 130), venerates wild nature, and many of the landscape descriptions of the novel are modulated through the discourse of the sublime.

80. McGrady, in "Las fuentes de *María*," gives an account of the criticism on Isaacs's use of the writings of Bernardin de Saint-Pierre and Chateaubriand. *Atala*, first published in 1801, was republished as part of *The Genius of Christianity* in 1802.

81. The first book is by Stéphanie-Félicité du Crest de Saint-Aubin and the second by François Guillaume Ducray-Duminil, as noted by McGrady in Isaacs, *María*, 181nn2, 3. *Veladas de la Quinta* contains a comic sketch in which a character repudiates expensive cultivated flowers, especially tulips and hyacinths. Saint-Aubin, *Veladas de la Quinta*, 287–89.

82. Goethe, *Sorrows of Young Werther*, 111.

83. Chateaubriand, *Genius of Christianity*, 239, 288–89. For a discussion of flowers in Milton, see Edwards, *Milton and the Natural World*, esp. part 3, "Transplanting the Garden."

84. Chateaubriand, *Genius of Christianity*, 509–10. The line is reminiscent of 1 Pet. 1:24: "For all flesh *is* as grass, and all the glory of man as the flower of grass. The grass withereth, and the flower thereof falleth away."

85. Sommer, *Foundational Fictions*, 199.

86. Bataille, "Language of Flowers," 12. See, for instance, Peleg, *Orientalism*, 18. María's Jewish heritage makes the analogy with oriental baths more significant. As Sommer (*Foundational Fictions*, 192) argues, for nineteenth-century readers of the novel, Jewishness "signals, among other things, an irrepressible sexuality."

87. See, for instance, King, *Scent*, 89.

88. Ackerman, *Natural History of the Senses*, 13.

89. Boccaccio, *Decameron*, 326–30.

90. Rich, *Cursing the Basil*, 61.

91. ["Good day, María" I said, hurrying to take the flowers from her.

She, turning pale at once, responded shyly to my greeting, and the carnation fell from her mouth. She handed me the flowers, letting some fall at her feet, which she gathered up and put within my reach, blushing again.

"Would you be willing," I said on receiving the last ones "to exchange all of these for the carnation that you had between your lips?"

"I stood on it," she replied, lowering her head to search for it.

"Even trod upon, I would give you all these for that one."

She remained in the same position without answering me.

"Do you allow me to pick it up?"

She bent over just then to pick it up and handed it over without looking at me.]

92. Dryden, *Poems of John Dryden*, 659. Later in the novel the lovers engage in a similar act by both kissing Juan on the lips. McGrady notes this in Isaacs, *María*, 151n1.

93. See Goody, *Culture of Flowers*, 296–97. Lucie-Smith (*Flora*, 141) notes that in sixteenth- and seventeenth-century marriage portraits, the man is often depicted holding a carnation "as a sign of his betrothal."

94. Shakespeare, *Romeo and Juliet*, 2.4.53–57; Dugan, *Ephemeral History of Perfume*, 67.

95. Freud, *Interpretation of Dreams*, 495–96.

96. Freud, *Interpretation of Dreams*, 496.

97. See also Taiz and Taiz, *Flora Unveiled*, 378–403.

98. Corominas and Pascual, *Diccionario crítico etimológico*, 2:98. Note also the double suggestion of the carnation in the words "encarnado" and "clavados" in a description of María blushing: "Las mejillas de María se tiñeron . . . del más suave encarnado. Sus ojos estaban clavados en el suelo" (144) [María's cheeks took on . . . the most delicate shade of red. Her eyes were nailed to the ground]. Sartillot (*Herbarium*, 23) discusses the connections between the carnation and flesh in this passage from Freud.

99. McGrady notes that María's hair color varies in the novel. See Isaacs, *María*, 197n1.

100. Rifelj, *Coiffures*, 199. Hair also features in *Sab* by way of the miniature portrait of Carlota, encased in a bracelet of hair, which Teresa gives to the slave.

101. See Geisweidt, "Horticulture of the Head," 10–13.

102. Ysbrand van Diemerbroeck, *Anatomy of Human Bodies* (1689), cited in Geisweidt, "Horticulture of the Head," 14.

103. Geisweidt, "Horticulture of the Head," 14; Sullivan, *Sleep, Romance*, 4. Hall, in *Plants as Persons*, ch. 5, discusses indigenous American conceptions of plant life.

104. Viveiros de Castro, "Cosmological Deixis," 479.

105. Maffie, *Aztec Philosophy*, 267. Taube (*Major Gods*, 128) describes Tlaltecuhtli as a "female earth goddess," although sometimes the figure is considered male.

106. Ofek, *Representations of Hair*, 14. Glantz argues that María's Jewish heritage makes the cutting off of a lock of hair for Efraín doubly scandalous, since Judaism prohibits all but a husband from seeing or touching a woman's hair. Glantz, "De la amorosa inclinación," 319.

107. Maffie, *Aztec Philosophy*, 267–68.

108. Glantz ("De la amorosa inclinación," 321–22) discusses the connection between María's hair and the bird of ill omen.

109. See Stirling, *Representing Epilepsy*, 56; Temkin, *Falling Sickness*, 22.

110. Stirling, *Representing Epilepsy*, 58.

111. Sommer (*Foundational Fictions*, 197) discusses how María's epilepsy is presented as a form of hysteria, which, according to the conventions of the time, was thought to be treatable by both the restriction and the supplementation of female sexuality.

112. The gauzy head covering can also be related to Scarry's points about the translucence of flowers. Scarry, "Imagining Flowers," 102.

113. Skinner ("Functions of Landscape," 17) notes that the "few moments in which Efraín is unable to enact total control over the landscape are related to the other great failure in the novel, María's illness and death." Llarull ("Long and Winding Road," 93) notes that the presentation of Efraín's return trip through the jungle disturbs the "oversimplified view" of nature elsewhere in the novel.

114. As Buchmann notes (*Reason for Flowers*, 108), there is a long-standing superstition that "good flowers spring from the grave of a good person," thus explaining Laertes's hope in *Hamlet* that "violets spring" from the "fair and unpolluted flesh" of his sister Ophelia. Shakespeare, *Hamlet*, 5.1.233. Poppies widely symbolize death, particularly opium poppies or *Papaver somniferum*. See Buchmann, *Reason for Flowers*, 109.

115. Rodríguez, *House / Garden / Nation*, 128.

116. Beckman, "Jorge Isaacs' *María*," 540; Mutis and Pettinaroli, "Visions of Nature," 424. See also Musselwhite, "Colombia of *María*," 43, for an exploration of the shift in the novel from what he calls a "quasi-feudal colonial order to a bourgeois market economy."

117. Anderson and Reales ("Extracting Nature," 374) propose an alternative reading of the ending, considering Efraín's departure from the family plantation as the beginning of a process of "affective estrangement . . . necessary for the capitalization of environment."

CHAPTER 3. "NACIDO DE ÁRBOLES"

1. Carpentier, "Problemática," 41. ["Our art has always been Baroque, from our splendid pre-Columbian sculpture and our *códices*, to our best contemporary novels, passing

through our continent's colonial cathedrals and monasteries. . . . Let us not fear the Baroque in our style, in our vision of contexts, in our vision of a human figure entwined in the word and the world, placed in the incredible angelic concert of a certain chapel (white, gold, vegetation, convolutions, unheard-of counterpoints, the defeat of Pythagoras) that may be seen in the city of Puebla, Mexico; or in a disconcerting, enigmatic tree of life, blossoming with images and symbols in Oaxaca. Let us not fear the Baroque, our art, born from trees, timber, altarpieces, and altars" (Carpentier, "Questions," 262)].

2. Reiss ("American Baroque," 412) discusses some of the baroque devices used by Carpentier, including "proliferating lists, constant repetitions, hyperbole, violent colors and contrast, utopian pastoral." Note, for instance, the inclusion of the Greek word *ctónico* ["earthly"] in "Problemática," which, Márquez Rodríguez (*Lo barroco*, 223) notes, is a neologism of Carpentier's.

3. Zamora, *Inordinate Eye*, 120. Wakefield (*Carpentier's Baroque Fiction*, 1) also regards the baroque as a "weapon of postcolonial pride and innovation."

4. D'Ors, *Lo barroco*, 90. I consulted Carpentier's copy of d'Ors's *Lo barroco* at the Fundación Alejo Carpentier in Havana.

5. Kaup (*Neobaroque*, 13) explains that, whist ideologically conservative in its original form, the Baroque has always been "profoundly modern aesthetically."

6. Carpentier, "Problemática," 41; Carpentier, "Questions," 262.

7. *Diccionario de la lengua española*, s.v. "florido." Carpentier often uses the verb "florecer" (to flourish) in relation to the baroque. See for example, Carpentier, "Lo barroco," 174. D'Ors (*Lo barroco*, 25) includes a passing discussion of the architectural term "Gótico florido" ["florid gothic"].

8. Carpentier, "Lo barroco," 182; Carpentier, "Baroque," 100.

9. Carpentier, "De lo real maravilloso," 113; Carpentier, "On the Marvelous Real," 85.

10. Moraña ("Baroque," 259) speaks in passing of Carpentier's "telluric" baroque.

11. D'Ors, *Lo barroco*, 118–19. Later, Carpentier in his own copy highlights a section related to the category "Barocchus officinalis." D'Ors, *Lo barroco*, 127.

12. "Just as the tulip bulbs we brought from Holland produced within a few years a changed flower in our Florentine garden—as a result of different treatment, soil, and sun—so the many elements of the Baroque and Rococo which were brought over from Europe went through a fascinating transformation." Kelemen, *Baroque and Rococo*, x. Salgado ("Hybridity," 321–22) discusses the influence of Kelemen on Carpentier.

13. Lezama Lima, "La curiosidad barroca," 80; Lezama Lima, "Baroque Curiosity," 213; Cortázar, *La vuelta al día*, 140.

14. Harss and Dohmann, *Los nuestros*, 72; Celorio, *Ensayo de Contraconquista*, 78.

15. González Echevarría, *Alejo Carpentier*, 224. Carpentier argues that the great task of his generation of Latin American writers is to move away from the traditional evocation of nature that characterized the *novela de la tierra* and write about cities. Carpentier, "Problemática," 22.

16. See Shaw, *Alejo Carpentier*, 1.

17. Márquez Rodríguez, *Lo barroco*, 226.

18. Architectural motifs have been important in general to the formulation of the New World baroque. One of the founding novels of the tradition, Lezama Lima's *Paradiso*, was characterized by Octavio Paz as "un mundo de arquitecturas en continua metamorfosis" ["a world of architectures in continuous metamorphosis"], qtd. in Zamora, *Inordinate Eye*, 337n68.

19. Wakefield (*Carpentier's Baroque Fiction*, 103) notes the coalescence of the trope of *engaño* with architectural imagery in the description of a rock face/cathedral in *Los pasos perdidos*.

20. Carpentier, "Lo barroco," 188–89. "Our world is Baroque because of its architecture—this goes without saying—the unruly complexities of its nature and its vegetation, the many colors that surround us, the telluric pulse of the phenomena that we still feel." Carpentier, "Baroque," 105.

21. Wakefield, *Carpentier's Baroque Fiction*, 115. Carpentier expresses this view in, for instance, Carpentier and Solares, "Nunca he utilizado," 231–32.

22. Carpentier and Solares, "Nunca he utilizado," 231.

23. A posthumous edition with new photographs by the Cuban Roberto Martínez Grandal was published in 1982 by Editorial Letras Cubanas.

24. Carpentier, "La ciudad de las columnas," 62; in Carpentier ("City of Columns," 245) the translation is "that began to germinate and grow." Future page references to the Spanish (Cdlc) will be given parenthetically in the text. Shorter translations from the English version (CC) will be included in the text and longer translations will appear in the notes.

25. Note that the published English translation translates the final line as "wind and rain."

26. Sarduy, *Barroco*, 61–62; Sarduy, "Baroque Cosmology," 296–97.

27. Carpentier, "Lo barroco," 172; Carpentier, "Baroque," 94.

28. In *Los pasos perdidos*, published some ten years before this essay, the narrator noted how in the jungle "Troncos eran las columnas que aquí hacía sombra" ["The pillars here were treetrunks"]. Carpentier, *Los pasos perdidos*, 180; Carpentier, *The Lost Steps*, 176. Future page references to the Spanish (*PP*) will be given parenthetically in the text. Shorter translations from the English edition (*LS*) will be included in the text and longer translations will appear in the notes.

29. Carpentier, *El acoso*, 84; Carpentier, *The Chase*, 64.

30. Carpentier, *El acoso*, 134; Carpentier, *The Chase*, 102.

31. Dauksta, "From Post to Pillar," 111.

32. Hersey, *Lost Meaning*, 14.

33. Frazer, in *Golden Bough*, discusses sacred trees; see, for instance, ch. 9, "The Worship of Trees." Carpentier's copy of this book is in Spanish, *La rama dorada: magia y religión* (México: Fondo de Cultura Económica, 1961), and is held at the Fundación Alejo Carpentier, Havana. The pamphlets and books on church architecture that formed part of Carpentier's personal library are also held by the Fundación Alejo Carpentier.

34. Carpentier's copy of Cook's book is in the Fundación Alejo Carpentier. Cook, *L'Arbre de vie*, 12–15.

35. For an account of this myth, see Frankfort, *Kinship and the Gods*, 178.

36. Shaw (*Alejo Carpentier*, 17) argues that "contact with surrealism marked a turning point in [Carpentier's] literary development."

37. In fact, Carpentier does not quote the original correctly. It should read: "La nature est un temple où de vivants piliers / Laissent parfois sortir de confuses paroles." See Baudelaire, *Complete Verse*, 1:61. For a discussion of Baudelaire in relation to surrealism see for instance, Raymond, *From Baudelaire to Surrealism*.

38. Baudelaire, *Complete Verse*, 1:61.

39. Papapetros, *On the Animation of the Inorganic*, 206.

40. Carpentier refers to Mondrian's paintings of trees in *La consagración de la primavera*, 249.

41. See Hersey, *Lost Meaning*, 14.

42. Carpentier, qtd. in Rowlandson, *Reading Lezama's Paradiso*, 43.

43. Carpentier, *La ciudad de las columnas*, n.p. This is the first image of section 3.

44. Carpentier, *Guerra del tiempo*, 46; Carpentier, *War of Time*, 106.

45. Carpentier provides a definition of the baroque from the *Diccionario de la Real Academia*, which refers to the predominance of the volute: "Estilo de ornamentación caracterizado por la profusión de volutas" ["Style of ornamentation characterized by the profusion of volutes"]. Carpentier, "Lo barroco," 168; Carpentier, "Baroque," 90.

46. See the entry "Volute" in Darvill, *Dictionary of Archaeology*, 457. For the comparison to ferns, see, for instance, Newman (*History of British Ferns*, viii) who observes the growth of a fern from "its first button-like appearance at the head of the rhizome, through its circinate youth,—so like the classic volute."

47. Carpentier, *El siglo de las luces*, 12; Carpentier, *Explosion in a Cathedral*, 12. Future page references to the Spanish (*SL*) will be given parenthetically in the text. Shorter translations from the English edition (*EC*) will be included in the text and longer translations will appear in the notes.

48. Carpentier, "Visión de Ámerica," 117.

49. Carpentier, *El siglo de las luces*, 268.

50. Zamora, *Inordinate Eye*, 129–41, provides an excellent account of de Nomé's connections to the baroque.

51. Manuscript F.2.1.4, "El siglo de las luces" (CM 67), Fundación Alejo Carpentier. The fact that Carpentier had attached the painting to the text suggests he had frequent recourse to it while he was writing or at least correcting his manuscript. It is unclear how he learned of this painting, and he was unlikely to have seen it firsthand, but presumably had seen a better (color) print. I viewed the original painting in the Fitzwilliam Museum, Cambridge, England.

52. I am grateful to Professor Alison Sinclair for her observations on the parallels between the explosion of de Nomé's painting and José Ortega y Gasset's 1911 description of entering a Gothic cathedral: "dentro de una catedral gótica habita siempre un torbellino" [inside a Gothic cathedral there is always a whirlwind]; Ortega y Gasset, "Arte de este mundo," 76. It is unclear whether Carpentier had come across this description, but he was certainly influenced by Ortega y Gasset. See González Echevarría, *Alejo Carpentier*, 52–54.

53. See Goya, *Paintings*, fig. 18.

54. The unlikely physical trajectory of the painting in *El siglo de las luces*, from Havana to Europe, is noted by Carpentier when he speaks of his surprise upon learning, after

having decided to include this painting in the novel, that another of de Nomé's paintings (*The Martyrdom of Saint Ursula*) was actually held in the National Gallery in Havana. Chao, *Conversaciones*, 128.

55. Shaw, *Alejo Carpentier*, 85.

56. "If the cathedral was the Age, then a formidable explosion had indeed overthrown its most solid walls, and perhaps buried the very men who had built the infernal machine beneath an avalanche of debris. If the cathedral was the Christian Church, then Esteban noticed that a row of sturdy pillars remained intact, opposite those which were shattering and falling in this apocalyptic painting, as if to prophesy resilience, endurance and a reconstruction, after the days of destruction and of stars foretelling disasters had passed. "'You always liked looking at that picture,' said Sofía, 'I think it's absurd and nasty.'" (*EC*, 253).

57. The use of paintings in the novel has been discussed in detail by Wall, "Visual Dimension."

58. Goya, *Paintings*, fig. 55. Indeed, it is even conceivable that the series of prints could have been called *Estragos de la Guerra*. See Matilla, *Goya*, 296.

59. Wall, "Visual Dimension," 149.

60. González Echevarría (*Celestina's Brood*, 177) has compared the pulling up of the plants in Remigio's garden in *El siglo de las luces* "to the notion of an explosion in a cathedral, for the *monte* is a temple." This is also suggestive for my reading of the painting as part of Carpentier's vegetal baroque.

61. I do not draw on the published English translation of Carpentier's novel in this instance as it strays too far from the original.

62. *Diccionario de la lengua española*, s.v. "fuste."

63. "Beyond the city walls, beyond the orchards even, out where hundreds of palm trees were lying in the inundations caused by swollen streams, like the shafts of ancient columns torn down by an earthquake. Yet, despite the magnitude of the disaster, people were accustomed to this periodic scourge, which they considered as an inevitable convulsion of the tropics, and they began to work like ants to seal up, repair and level out" (*EC*, 59).

64. Lezama Lima, "La curiosidad barroca," 104. "American leaves with Greek trefoils, the Inca half-moon with the acanthus foliage of Corinthian capstones." Lezama Lima, "Baroque Curiosity," 236.

65. Kaup, *Neobaroque*, 254.

66. Carpentier, "Lo barroco," 182; Carpentier, "Baroque," 100.

67. For his discussion of Lam, see Carpentier, "De lo real maravilloso," 113. The quotation is from an unpublished manuscript by Carpentier, "Wifredo Lam," n.p. Fundación Alejo Carpentier.

68. Sims, *Wifredo Lam*, 42.

69. Images of these paintings are included in Sims, *Wifredo Lam*, 44–46.

70. "Hybrid" is defined as the "offspring of two animals or plants of a different species": *OED Online*, s.v. "hybrid, n. and adj," accessed February 22, 2018, https://www.oed.com.

71. This painting sounds a little like Giuseppe Arcimboldo's fanciful mannerist

botanical-human hybrid, *Vertumnus.* González Echevarría (*Alejo Carpentier,* 233–34), citing a study by Ramón García Castro, notes that Esteban's art preferences, including a painting of an "hombre armario" (*SL,* 19) ["cupboard-man" (*EC,* 18)], register as anachronistic since they suggest pictures such as Dalí's *The Anthropomorphic Cabinet.*

72. "Climbing a tree is an intimate experience which can perhaps never be conveyed. A man who embraces the tall breasts of a tree-trunk is realising a sort of nuptial act, deflowering a secret world, never before seen by man. His glance suddenly takes in all the beauties and imperfections of the Tree. He discovers the two tender branches, which part like a woman's thighs and conceal at their juncture a handful of green moss" (*EC,* 161–62).

73. Sharman, *Tradition and Modernity,* 169.

74. "As the clearing extended its limits farther and farther, age-old trees fell, their foliage as full of birds, monkeys, insects and reptiles as the symbolical trees of the alchemists. Smoke rose from these fallen giants, as they were consumed by fire which penetrated to their entrails before it had finished burning through the bark; and oxen moved between the teeming fields and the newly-erected sawmill, dragging the huge wooden corpses, still full of sap and juices, and with fresh shoots growing out of their wounds; the enormous roots bumped along the ground, clutching at the earth, to be dismembered under the axe, their arms, as they flew off, still trying to catch hold of something" (*EC,* 324).

75. See Manuscript F.2.1.4, "El siglo de las luces" (CM 67), Fundación Alejo Carpentier.

76. The squeamishness of touching these more-than-human hybrids recalls Esteban's horror when he learns of the dissemination of books made from human flesh at the height of the French Revolution. Carpentier, *El siglo de las luces,* 131.

77. Kristeva, *Powers of Horror,* 1–2.

78. Douglas, *Purity and Danger,* 145.

79. Coccia, *Life of Plants,* 13.

80. "Everything here seemed something else, thus creating a world of appearances that concealed reality, casting doubt on many truths. The vines seemed snakes, the snakes vines. . . . The chameleons were twigs, lapis lazuli, lead brightly striped in yellow" (*LS,* 165–66).

81. The term "hyperreal" is a favored postmodern concept. See, for instance, Baudrillard, *Simulacra,* 12–14.

82. Pollan, *Botany of Desire,* 70.

83. D'Ors, *Lo barroco,* 101 (emphasis in original).

84. González Echevarría, *Celestina's Brood,* 185.

85. Carpentier, "Lo barroco," 173; Carpentier, "Baroque," 93.

86. Zamora (*Inordinate Eye,* 141) draws on Raúl Silva Cáceres's analysis of the importance of de Nomé's painting in this account of metonymic displacement.

87. Carpentier, "Lo barroco," 174; Carpentier, "Baroque," 94.

88. Deleuze, *The Fold,* 3. This analogy is also discussed by Zamora, *Inordinate Eye,* 142.

89. Carpentier, *Los pasos perdidos,* 170; Carpentier, *The Lost Steps,* 167.

90. Carpentier, "Problemática," 21 (original italics). I provide the English translation, since this part of the essay has not, to my knowledge, been translated into English.

91. Carpentier, "Problemática," 21. Lezama Lima also speaks of "el sorprendente

'gabinete de física'" ["the surprising 'physicist's cabinet'"]. Lezama Lima, "La curiosidad barroca," 85; Lezama Lima, "Baroque Curiosity," 217.

92. "Bizarre" was a favored Baroque term. See Wellek, "Concept of Baroque," 95. For an account of the history of the wunderkammer, see Impey and MacGregor, *Origins of Museums.*

93. Agamben, "Cabinet of Wonder," 30.

94. Carpentier, "Problemática," 21.

95. See Rogers, "Carpentier."

96. Carpentier, "La Exposición Internacional," 418.

97. See Rogers, "Carpentier," 243. Carpentier's birth certificate shows that he was born in Lausanne in Switzerland. The reasons for this invented origin have been discussed by a number of critics, including González Echevarría, "La nacionalidad," and Pérez Firmat, "Ese Idioma."

98. Rogers, "Carpentier," 245.

99. Ferrari, "Las palabras y las cosas," 233.

100. Carpentier, *Guerra del tiempo,* 93.

101. See ch. 4, "Lo barroco Americano," in Márquez Rodríguez, *Lo barroco.*

102. Carpentier, *Recurso del método,* 328. "Baroque roots or roots that are austere in their smoothness; complicated, intricate or nobly geometrical; at times dancing, at times static, or totemic, or sexual, something between an animal and a theorem, a play of knots, a play of asymmetry, now alive, now fossilized. . . . Roots torn up from remote soil, dragged along, cast up, and again transported by rivers in spate; roots sculptured by the water, hurled about, knocked over, polished, burnished, silvered, denuded of their silver, until from so many journeys, falls, collisions with rocks, battles with other pieces of wood on the move, they have finally lost their vegetable morphology, become separated from the tree-mother, the genealogical tree, and acquired breast-like roundnesses, polyhedric arms, boars' heads or idols' faces, teeth, claws, tentacles, penises and crowns." Carpentier, *Reasons of State,* 257. In *El siglo de las luces,* there is also a reference to "un Gabinete de Curiosidades" (literally "Curiosity Cabinet," but rendered as "regular curiosity shop" in the published English translation of the novel), which includes "raíces de formas zoológicas" (*SL,* 159) ["roots shaped like animals" (*EC,* 147)].

103. Carpentier wrote a short essay on the use of adjectives; see Carpentier, "El adjetivo y sus arrugas," 7–9.

104. This aspect is lost in the published English translation, "hurled about, knocked over," and "silvered, denuded of their silver." Carpentier, *Reasons of State,* 257.

105. Carpentier, *El recurso del método,* 330; Carpentier, *Reasons of State,* 259.

106. Bataille, "Language of Flowers," 13.

107. Taussig, "Language of Flowers," 112. See also Zarcone, "Myth of the Mandrake."

108. See Taussig, "Language of Flowers," 113. Shakespeare uses the simile "shrieks like mandrakes torn out of the earth" in *Romeo and Juliet,* IV.4.47. For further discussion of the image of the mandrake in Shakespeare, see Thomas and Faircloth, *Shakespeare's Plants,* 219–20.

109. Carpentier's own copy was a first edition (La Habana: Ediciones C. R, 1954),

personally signed by Cabrera and dedicated to Carpentier; it is now held by the Fundación Alejo Carpentier.

110. Frazer's talk was entitled "Jacob and the Mandrakes." It was later published as chapter 7 of Frazer, *Folk-Lore*, 2:372–97. The mandrake's associations with sex and fertility are also discussed at length in Simoons, *Plants of Life*, 107–11.

111. Eliade, *Zalmoxis*, 204 (the whole of chapter 7 is on the mandrake). Tusa, in "Detective Story," discusses the influence of Eliade on Carpentier.

112. When reflecting on a visit to the Botanical Garden of Coimbra d'Ors speaks, in particular, of the soundscape of botanical gardens: "No hay paisaje acústico de emoción más característicamente barroca" [There is no acoustic landscape of a more characteristically baroque tone]. D'Ors, *Lo barroco*, 31.

113. Carpentier, *El reino de este mundo*, 29–30; Carpentier, *The Kingdom of This World*, 16.

114. González Echevarría, *Celestina's Brood*, 176.

115. González Echevarría (*Celestina's Brood*, 267n8) also notes the influence of Cabrera in Carpentier's choice of medicinal herbs.

116. See Cabrera, *El monte*, 497. Carpentier folded down the corner of the page including the entry for *ortiguilla* in his copy of *El monte*.

117. See, for instance, Márquez Rodríguez, *Lo barroco*, 34n112.

118. Zamora, *Inordinate Eye*, 146.

119. Following his discussion of hybridity in this essay, Carpentier notes: "Con tales elementos en presencia aportándole cada cual su barroquismo, entroncamos directamente con lo que he llamado lo 'real maravilloso'" ["With such variety, each contributing its version of the baroque, we intersect with what I have called 'the marvellous real'"]. See Carpentier, "Lo barroco," 183; Carpentier, "Baroque," 101. Carpentier draws on botanical language in his statement of the coming together of these two important styles via the verb "entroncar," the etymology of which is drawn from the Latin "truncus," meaning tree trunk. See Corominas, *Diccionario crítico etimológico*, 6:602, s.v. "tronco."

120. Tomasi, "Gardens of Knowledge," 92.

121. On a number of occasions the contemporary Cuban artist Jorge Duporté acknowledged the importance of the ceiba to Carpentier's work. Jorge Duporté specializes in botanical art and draws inspiration for many of his paintings from Carpentier's literary descriptions of plants. See Duporté, *Hacía una cultura*, or the exhibition catalogue *La flora de este reino*, the name of which is a pun on Carpentier's *El reino de este mundo*.

122. See Schele and Freidel, *Forest of Kings*, 66–67.

123. Carpentier, *La consagración de la primavera*, 249 (my translation).

124. Carpentier refers to the *Chilam Balam* in both *Los pasos perdidos* (in the epigraph to ch. 3, for example) and his nonfictional work, including in "Lo barroco," 179.

125. Hurtado, "La seiba," typewritten manuscript, Fundación Alejo Carpentier, n.p. [And the Great Mother Ceiba rose up among / the memories of the earth's destruction.... / And with her branches and her roots / summoned the master.]

126. Qtd. in Anderson, *Big Old Trees*, 100.

127. Landa, *Relación de las cosas de Yucatán*, 60.

128. Shaw, *Alejo Carpentier*, 4–5, discusses Carpentier's contributions to this movement.

129. Cabrera, *El monte*, ch. 7.

130. Carpentier and Santana, "Los pasos encontrados," 191.

131. This was the case when I was in Havana in late 2017.

132. Carpentier, "Problemática," 38–39 (original italics). "But the word *ceiba* (an American tree that Afro-Cubans call 'the mother of all trees') does not suffice to give people of other latitudes an appreciation of the resemblance of that colossal tree to a rostral column: upright, austere, and solitary, of sacred lineage, like an apparition from other times, whose horizontal, almost parallel branches, offer a handful of leaves to the winds, as unreachable as they are incapable of rustling. There it is, on the top of a hillside, alone, silent, motionless, uninhabited by birds, piercing the earth with its enormous scaly roots. Hundreds of meters away (because the ceiba is not a tree of camaraderie or company) grow some papaya trees, herbaceous plants that emerged from the first bogs of creation, their bland bodies covered with gray medallions, their leaves open like beggars' hands, their udder-fruits hanging from their necks. Those trees exist. They are American trees that, by right and presence, form part of the American novel. But they are not fortunate enough to be called pine or palm or walnut or chestnut or birch." Carpentier, "Questions," 260.

133. Puri and Castillo, "Conjectures," 17.

134. Carpentier, *La consagración de la primavera*, 250.

135. Carpentier, *La consagración de la primavera*, 249.

136. Davies and Jokiniemi, *Dictionary of Architecture*, 85. "[L]a Ceiba . . . se hacía más obelisco, más columna rostral, más monumento y elevación sobre las luces del crepúsculo" (*ES*, 175) ["the *ceiba* . . . was becoming more like an obelisk, more columnar, more monumental, as it towered against the dusky sky" (*EC*, 162)]. Note that in Sturrock's translation he does not include the adjective "rostral," which appears in the original Spanish.

137. Carpentier, "Problemática," 39; Carpentier, "Questions," 260. *OED Online*, s.v. "Rostral, adj. and n," accessed February 22, 2018, https://www.oed.com.

138. Oviedo also provided an illustration of the tree. For an enumeration of his references to the ceiba, see Carrillo, "From Mt. Ventoux," 65–66.

139. Carpentier, *El siglo de las luces*, 190; Carpentier, *Explosion in a Cathedral*, 178.

140. Indeed, in most cases, it has not been possible to corroborate the existence of these plants, but given Carpentier's recondite tendencies, they may well exist. The "piñón-botija" (pitcher-pine-kernel), for instance, is another name for the toxic *Jatropha curcas*, a type of spurge or *Euphorbiaceae*. See Janick and Paull, *Encyclopaedia of Fruit*, 371.

141. Carpentier, "Lo barroco," 190; Carpentier, "Baroque," 106.

142. Carpentier, "Problemática," 40; Carpentier, "Questions," 261.

143. Manuscript F.2.1.3, "Los pasos perdidos" (CM 66.2), Fundación Alejo Carpentier.

144. The article "los" was later inserted in pencil.

145. I had already selected the phrase as the chapter title before I came across this erasure.

146. The phrase "vasto ciudad vegetal" is corrected in pencil in the manuscript to "vasto país vegetal" [vast vegetal country], which is how it remained in the published version of

the novel. See Carpentier, *Los pasos perdidos*, 129. In the published English translation of the novel the phrase is translated as "vast vegetable kingdom" (*LS*, 126).

147. For instance, in the manuscript version of subsection 23, Carpentier corrected the original typed term "sidereal" (astral) with "telúrica." Manuscript F.2.1.3, "Los pasos perdidos" (CM 65–67), Fundación Alejo Carpentier.

148. "To penetrate this world, the Adelantado had had to find the keys to its secret entrances: he alone knew of a pass between two trees, the only one within a circumference of fifty leagues, leading to a narrow stairway of stones by which it was possible to descend to the vast mystery of immense telluric baroques. He alone knew of the withe footbridge under the cascade, the postern gate of brush, the entrance to the cave of the prehistoric stone carvings, the hidden trail that led to practicable passes. He could read the code of broken twigs, incisions on treetrunks, the branch not fallen but placed" (*LS*, 126).

149. The practice, normally called "under erasure," was first used by Martin Heidegger and later developed by Jacques Derrida. See the excellent account of this term in Saldívar, "Speculative Realism," 527–28.

CHAPTER 4. WHAT IS IT LIKE TO BE A TREE?

1. In Spenser, *Faerie Queene*, bk. 1, canto 2, st. 28–45, the Red Cross Knight encounters two lovers, Fradubio and Fraelissa, who have been transformed into trees by the sorceress Duessa. Fradubio bleeds when a bough is cut from his trunk. There is a similar episode in Dante's *Inferno* (see below). For a brief account of the literary trope of bleeding and speaking trees, see Kennedy, "Fradubio," 318.

2. Evelyn, *Sylva*, 1:31.

3. Belli, *La mujer habitada*. Alcocer discusses the figure of the human-tree hybrid in *La mujer habitada* in Alcocer, *Time Travel*, esp. ch. 3. He notes: "it becomes increasingly obvious that the novel is establishing an elaborate metaphor involving sometimes very subtle similarities between people and plants" (131). Wishnia (*Twentieth-Century Ecuadorian Narrative*, esp. ch. 2) has studied the figure of screaming trees and other marks of what he sees as precursors of magic realism in pre-1950s works from Ecuador. The Argentine writer Silvina Ocampo writes of a man being entwined in creepers in the story "Hombres animales enredaderas" (Men animals vines) (Ocampo, *Los días de la noche*).

4. Reichel-Dolmatoff, *Forest Within*, 8–9.

5. Reichel-Dolmatoff, *Forest Within*, 8–9; Bird-David, "'Animism' Revisited," S69.

6. Descola, *Beyond Nature and Culture*, 135; Viveiros de Castro, "Cosmological Deixis," 479; Kohn, *How Forests Think*, 7, 9; Miller, *Plant Kin*, 4. For the definition of the "Planthroposcene," see Myers, "From the Anthropocene," 299.

7. Marder, *Plant-Thinking* (see also his tracing of the influence of plants in the Western philosophical tradition, in Marder, *Philosopher's Plant*); Hall, "Plant Autonomy." For signaling systems, see for instance, Baluška, Mancuso, and Volkmann, *Communication in Plants*.

8. Nealon, *Plant Theory*, 11; Wohlleben, *Hidden Life of Trees*. Monica Gagliano has also worked extensively on the language of plants. See Gagliano, "Flowering of Plant Bioacoustics."

9. A similar reflex has been noted in Anglophone Caribbean literature, where, according to Tewfik ("Indian Veneration of Trees," 93): "Bridging the gap between place and self, nature and culture takes shape . . . in the form of attributing human qualities to trees and plants." See also Seaton, *Language of Flowers*.

10. My discussion of *La vorágine* and the film, *The Trees Have a Mother*, dir. Galeano and Auzenne, builds on the arguments of Wylie, "Anthropomorphism and Arboricide."

11. Marder, "Plant-Soul," 86.

12. See, for instance, Menton, "*La vorágine*"; French, *Nature*, ch. 3; Jaramillo, "Green Hells," 99-101; Martínez-Pinzón, "La voz de los árboles"; Wylie, *Colonial Tropes*.

13. Vieira, "*Phytographia*," 229 (original italics). At the end of this essay, Vieira briefly discusses the idea of "plant writing" in *La vorágine*.

14. Rivera, *La vorágine*, 170; Rivera, *The Vortex*, 121. Future page references to the Spanish will be given parenthetically in the text. Shorter translations from the English edition will be included in the text and longer translations will appear in the notes.

15. See, for instance, Olivera, "El romanticismo"; see also, Wylie, *Colonial Tropes*, 101-2.

16. De Man, *Rhetoric of Romanticism*, 241.

17. Castellano has discussed anthropomorphism in relation to ecological thinking in the British Romantic poet John Clare. She accedes to de Man's concerns about the possibility of anthropomorphism being human-centered, but she argues that anthropomorphism in Clare "affirms that the shared essence between humans and animals . . . amounts to a substantialization . . . of an organic community of marginalized life." Castellano, *Ecology of British Romantic Conservatism*, 146.

18. Bull, "Nature and Anthropomorphism," 316.

19. "Your vegetation is a family that never betrays itself. The embrace your boughs cannot give is carried by creepers and lianas. You share even in the pain of the leaf that falls. Your multisonous voices rise like a chorus bewailing the giants [lit. trunks] that crash to earth" (*The Vortex*, 143-44).

20. Waters, "Apostrophe," 61; Culler, *Pursuit of Signs*, 139, 142.

21. "Black rubber was then as much sought as the *siringa*, called 'drunken rubber' by the Brazilians; to get the latter, as you know, incisions are made in the bark, the latex is gathered in cups, and then smoked. Black rubber, on the other hand, was collected by cutting down the tree. Incisions were then made around the trunk at about a handbreadth apart, the sap was collected and then put into ventilated holes" (*The Vortex*, 223).

22. Uribe Uribe, *Diccionario abreviado*, 242.

23. The French naturalist in *La vorágine* has been likened to real-life traveler Eugene Robuchon, who disappeared in this notorious region in 1906. See Rivera, *La vorágine*, 265n87; Goodman, *Devil and Mr. Casement*, 45-48.

24. Anderson, *Big Old Trees*, 7; Rogers, *Jungle Fever*, 91-117.

25. "'Señor, tell me if my back has suffered less than that tree.' And raising my shirt, I showed him my lacerated flesh. A moment later the tree and I perpetuated our wounds in the camera, wounds that for the same master shed different juices: rubber and blood" (*The Vortex*, 229).

26. The coalescence of trees and people in this episode has also been discussed by Mejías-López, "Textualidad y sexualidad," 368–69.

27. See, for instance, Casement, *1911 Documents*, 311.

28. Alighieri, *Inferno*, 131. See also Menton, "*La vorágine*," 432.

29. Menton ("*La vorágine*," 432) quotes the passage from the *Inferno* in Spanish to draw attention to the similarities between it and this dream sequence.

30. Tewfik, "Indian Veneration of Trees," 93.

31. *Diccionario de la lengua española*, 21st ed. (1992), s.v. "destroncar."

32. "He stopped before a cananguche palm, and to his mind came the tradition that tells how this species follows the sun, like a sunflower. Never had he given the matter any thought before. He spent anxious moments watching, and he thought he saw the lofty foliage slowly bending, with the rhythm of a head that took exactly twelve hours to move from the right shoulder over to the left. The secret voice filled his soul. Was it possible that this palm, planted in the wilderness like an index pointing to the blue, was showing him his route? True or false, he heard it speak. And he believed!" (*The Vortex*, 292).

33. Smith, "Mapping the Amazon," n.p.

34. Descola, *Beyond Nature and Culture*, 131, 133.

35. Bird-David, "'Animism' Revisited." She defines "Modernist" epistemologies as the ideas and practices of European and American culture from the seventeenth century to the present (S68).

36. Martínez-Pinzón, "La voz de los árboles," 178–79.

37. Franco, "Image and Experience," 107.

38. I translated this line since it is omitted from James's English translation.

39. "The rest of me was not mine, neither my leg, nor my arm, nor my wrist. They were something false, horrible, bothersome, present and absent at one time, producing an annoyance such as a tree must feel on having a dead bough clinging to its living trunk. . . . I felt myself rooted to the earth; and up to my leg, swollen, spongy, deformed like the tubers of palms, I felt a hot, petrifying sap creeping. I wanted to move, but my leg wouldn't let me go. A cry of fear. I swayed. I fell" (*The Vortex*, 366).

40. Mejías-López ("Textualidad y sexualidad," 382) argues that, within the imaginary of the novel, where sexual aggression and natural exploitation merge, rubber, semen, blood, and tears function as "fluidos intercambiables" [interchangeable fluids].

41. Mejías-López, "Textualidad y sexualidad," 382.

42. See Rivera, *La vorágine*, 213.

43. Marder ("Plant-Soul," 85) notes that, "despite its apparent immobility, the plant exhibits three out of four types of movement enumerated by Aristotle in *De Anima*, in that it can move by changing its state, growing, and decaying."

44. For instance, Silva describes an act of fratricide after two brothers get lost in the jungle. This "embrujamiento" is a trope in the *novela de la selva*, a tradition of writing on the Amazon from the 1920s to the mid-1950s, of which *La vorágine* is the supreme example. In Rómulo Gallegos's *Canaima* (1935), the protagonist Marcos Vargas also appears to go mad in the jungle, and at one point seems to turn into a tree.

45. I provide the translation for the final line of the novel, since the published English version, "The jungle has swallowed them" (*The Vortex*, 379), is not entirely accurate.

46. Mejías-López, "Textualidad y sexualidad," 370.

47. Jaramillo, "Green Hells," 95.

48. Meeker and Szabari, "From the Century," 53.

49. Uzendoski, "Foreword," x.

50. The story is entitled "Moniya amena." Galeano, *Cuentos amazónicos*, 19-20. Further page references to this collection (*CA*) are included parenthetically in the text and will be followed either in the text or in notes by an English translation from Galeano, *Folktales of the Amazon* (*FA*).

51. Slater (*Dance of the Dolphin*, 94-100) has discussed the role of the *boto* in Amazonian tales of enchantment.

52. Galeano, "Árboles," *Amazonia*, 73. An abridged bilingual edition of the collection was published in 2012 (Galeano, *Amazonia*, trans. Kimbrell and Morgan) and I draw on this where possible for English translations of the poems. I would like to thank Juan Carlos Galeano for supplying additional translations (also by James Kimbrell and Rebecca Morgan) of the remaining, as yet unpublished, English versions of poems, which I use where indicated.

53. Viveiros de Castro, "Cosmological Deixis," 470.

54. Rumrrill, *Reportaje a la Amazonía*, 67.

55. Galeano, *Amazonia*, 74 ("La espera"), 43 ("Música"), 73 ("Árboles").

56. Forns-Broggi, *Nudos como estrellas*, 460.

57. Galeano, *Amazonia*, 36; Galeano, *Amazonia*, trans. Kimbrell and Morgan, 29.

58. Galeano, *Amazonia*, 65. "Grass grows on houses, on our bodies, our ears, and pockets. / While my father reads the newspaper, two rabbits graze happily on his arms. / The trucks bringing giant trees for the botanical gardens / advance, like floating islands, through the grass." This English version is an unpublished translation by Kimbrell and Morgan.

59. Galeano, *Amazonia*, 75. The English version is from an unpublished translation by Kimbrell and Morgan. Tosh, *Manliness and Masculinities*, emphasizes colonialism as a specifically male enterprise.

60. Hall, *Plants as Persons*, 1.

61. Uzendoski, "Foreword," ix.

62. Galeano, *Folktales*, xx; Hall, *Plants as Persons*, 100, 111. In the documentary film that was coproduced and codirected by Galeano and Auzenne, *The Trees Have a Mother*, for instance, one commentator explains how it is fine to make use of plants but unacceptable to simply destroy them.

63. According to the botanical glossary included in Galeano, *Cuentos amazónicos*, 150.

64. Galeano, "Lupuna," *Cuentos amazónicos*, 83-84.

65. Galeano, *Cuentos amazónicos*, 79-80.

66. See Smith, *Enchanted Amazon*, 131-33.

67. For a discussion of the *Curupira*, see Smith, *Enchanted Amazon*, 133; Wagley, *Amazon Town*, 235-36.

68. "With thin, tiny leaves, the female plant climbed from her pot to a beam near

the door that led to the street. The male plant, which was bigger and had robust leaves, wrapped around a kitchen column. As time passed, the couple began to be awakened at night by the smooth sound of leaves moving. They saw the plants taking the form of two boa constrictor snakes and slowly unwinding themselves from the columns and heading toward the yard. There, they got into the pond, which contained some *charapa* and *cupiso* turtles and a renaco tree" (*FA*, 95).

69. Moshenska, "Screaming Bleeding Trees," 94.

70. Galeano, *Amazonia*, 40. "But in the jungle they told us that to bring more light / we should throw more trees into the sun's furnace / One day, our hand slipped and tossed in the entire jungle / with its birds, fish, and rivers." Galeano, *Amazonia*, trans. Kimbrell and Morgan, 33.

71. Galeano and Auzenne, *The Trees Have a Mother*.

72. See Smith, *Enchanted Amazon*, 57.

73. Adamson, "Environmental Justice," 180.

74. Larochelle, "Writing under the Shadow," 201.

75. Adamson, "Environmental Justice," 173. See also Yepes, "Derroteros de la ecocrítica."

76. Regarding this term, see Deitering, "Postnatural Novel."

77. The phrase "more-than-human" is used by Abram, *Spell of the Sensuous*.

78. This includes, for instance, the monographs Blocker, *Where Is Ana Mendieta?* and Viso, *Unseen Mendieta*. Exhibitions include "Traces" at the Hayward Gallery, London, in 2013 and at the Museum der Moderne, Salzburg, in 2014.

79. Blocker (*Where Is Ana Mendieta?* 77) speaks of interpretations of Mendieta's earth works as "digging in the dirt to find something she had lost, digging to plant her own roots."

80. Mendieta died in 1985 after falling from the thirty-fourth-floor New York apartment of her husband, Carl Andre, a well-known minimalist sculptor and poet. Andre was arrested but later acquitted of all charges relating to her death. See Katz, *Naked by the Window*.

81. Breen ("Sin título," 63) discusses these leaf drawings. Blocker (*Where Is Ana Mendieta?* 133) reflects on seeing a leaf drawing in the Galerie Lelong in New York.

82. Katz, *Naked by the Window*, 162. Katz also notes how Mendieta was known for stealing plants from people's gardens when she was a student in Iowa City (138). Viso (*Unseen Mendieta*, 283) refers to the influence of Lam.

83. In an interview conducted by Judith Wilson that was to be used as a basis for an article on the artist, Mendieta can be heard showing the interviewer examples of botanical samples and images she had collected, including moss that she had transplanted from the side of a cliff and a tree trunk struck by lightning. Mendieta and Wilson, "Ana Mendieta Plants Her Garden."

84. Breen, "Sin título," 63.

85. Viso photographically reproduces this proposal in *Unseen Mendieta*, 293. This is an instance where Mendieta's botanical knowledge seems to have been imperfect. I have not been able to discover a grass by this name and can only assume she was thinking of *Briza eragrostis*.

86. Mendieta said of this installation: "*The Santeros use a tree that in Spanish is called* Ceiba *and in English is called a cotton silkwood tree. It has very long roots that stick out. In Miami there is*

a tree like that which the Santeros have claimed, and the people do things to that tree when a healer tells them that they have to make a sacrifice." Cabañas, "Ana Mendieta," 15 (original italics).

87. Cabañas, "Ana Mendieta," 15.

88. These pages are reproduced in Viso, *Unseen Mendieta*, 121.

89. Photograph included in Bryan-Wilson, Heathfield, and Rosenthal, *Ana Mendieta*, 101.

90. Photograph reproduced in Viso, *Unseen Mendieta*, 124.

91. See Viso, *Unseen Mendieta*, 148–49.

92. Blocker (*Where Is Ana Mendieta?* 59–61) and Viso (*Unseen Mendieta*, 110) have both discussed goddess imagery in the artist's work.

93. For a discussion of the iconography of the Earth Mother, see Cook, *Tree of Life*, 12–15.

94. Statement made in 1983, qtd. in Viso, *Unseen Mendieta*, 297.

95. Gonzenbach, "Bleeding Borders," 37.

96. A double-page image of this is included in Bryan-Wilson, Heathfield, and Rosenthal, *Ana Mendieta*, 104–5.

97. See Viso, *Unseen Mendieta*, 111.

98. The process of how *Grass on Woman* was created is described by Viso, *Unseen Mendieta*, 77.

99. Qtd. in Katz, *Naked by the Window*, 123. The source was an unpublished artist statement, Ana Mendieta Papers, Galerie Lelong, New York.

100. MacKian (*Everyday Spirituality*, 109) talks of how the concept of "universal energy" is an alternative to reincarnation for some New Age thinkers.

101. *Imagen de Yagul* is reproduced in Viso, *Unseen Mendieta*, 78. See Katz, *Naked by the Window*, 145, for an account of its staging. The year given by Breder in this recollection is 1976, but *Imagen de Yagul* dates from 1973.

102. Herrera, *Frida Kahlo*, 91. Marder ("Place of Plants," 188) discusses Mathilde Roussel's recent exhibition *Lives of Grass* (2010), which has some interesting parallels with Mendieta's use of vegetal materials.

103. Katz, *Naked by the Window*, 123.

104. Mendieta, *Grass Breathing*, c. 1974, Super 8mm. film, silent, colour, 3 min. I was able to view this film on a disc appended to Breen, "Sin título."

105. Irigaray and Marder, *Through Vegetal Being*, 131; Gibson, *Plant Contract*, 125.

106. Irigaray and Marder, *Through Vegetal Being*, 22, 23.

107. Coccia, *Life of Plants*, 37 (original italics), 52, 47.

108. Moore, *Ecology and Literature*, 10 (the internal quote draws on a phrase by Michael Zimmerman); Merchant, *Death of Nature*, 3.

109. Chase, *Decomposing Figures*, 83.

110. Coccia, *Life of Plants*, 32.

CHAPTER 5. "NO TERMINO EN MÍ MISMO"

1. Over five thousand books of Neruda's are held at the Archivo Central Andrés Bello, University of Chile, which I consulted in August 2018. The handmade album is entitled the "*Álbum pintoresco herbario*" (Picturesque album of plants) and was as yet uncatalogued

when I examined it. See Paul Maisonneuve, *Traité élémentaire de botanique* (1894) for the scientific; J. J. Grandville, *Les Fleurs animées* (1847) and Eugène Nus, *L'Empire des légumes: mémoires de Cucurbitus* (1861), for the comic; and J. Horace McFarland, R. Marion Hatton, and Daniel J. Foley, *Garden Bulbs in Color* (1941) as an example of the practical botanical books.

2. Neruda, "[El Rector ha tenido palabras magníficas]," in *Obras completas* 4:948 (this work will henceforth be cited as *OC* with volume number). Unless otherwise indicated, all translations are mine.

3. Neruda's relationship to nature, and his environmental thinking, have been discussed by Handley, *New World Poetics*, and Rivera-Barnes, "Pablo Neruda's Latin American Landscape." However, neither critic focuses in particular on his interest in plants. See Feinstein, *Pablo Neruda*, 291, for more information about *Oda a las flores de Datitla*. Monguió ("Kingdom of This Earth," 15) says: "Nothing is more material than the love of *Twenty Love Poems*, nothing closer to vegetative, germinative, animal nature, a nature onto which the poet is entwined like a vine, planted like wheat or a pine tree."

4. Brotherston, *Latin American Poetry*, 42.

5. Reiss, *Word and the Stone*, 26–27.

6. Neruda, "Mariano Latorre, Pedro Prado y mi propia sombra," in *OC* 4:1087; Neruda, "A la paz por la poesía," in *OC* 4:890.

7. The intersections between Whitman's *Leaves of Grass* and Neruda's *Canto general* are well established. See, for instance, Rodríguez Monegal, *El viajero inmóvil*, 247–49; Durán and Safir, *Earth Tones*, 103; Brotherston, *Latin American Poetry*; Nolan, *Poet-Chief*; and Handley, *New World Poetics*. Neruda owned multiple copies of Whitman's poem, which formed part of his donation to the University of Chile in 1954.

8. Neruda, "Algo sobre mi poesía y mi vida," in *Obras completas* 4:934; also noted in Feinstein, *Pablo Neruda*, 219.

9. Neruda, *Confieso que he vivido*, 210. "The southern Andean forest is populated by huge trees set apart from one another: giant larches [alerces] and mayten trees, as well as tepa and coniferous trees. The raulí trees have an amazing girth. I stopped to measure one. It had the diameter of a horse. The sky overhead can't be seen. Below, leaves have been falling for centuries, forming a layer of humus the hoofs of the mounts sink down into." Neruda, *Memoirs*, 181.

10. Neruda, "Viaje por las costas del mundo," in *OC* 4:506.

11. Neruda, *Canto general*, in *OC* 1:418; Neruda, *Canto general*, trans. Schmitt, 14. Future page references to the *Canto general* in Spanish will be given parenthetically in the text following the acronym *CG*. Shorter translations from the English version (*CGS*) will be included in the text and longer translations will appear in the notes.

12. "The forest of maytens whose green / threads weep like a tremor of rain / told Spain: 'Stop here.' The southland cypress [alerce], / titan of the silent borderlands, / spoke in a thundering voice." Neruda, *CGS*, 77.

13. Bahre (*Destruction of the Natural Vegetation*, 63) contains a discussion of the mayten.

14. Neruda, *Confieso que he vivido*, 17. "*A decaying tree trunk: what a treasure! . . . Black and*

blue mushrooms have given it ears, red parasite plants have covered it with rubies, other lazy plants have let it borrow their beards, and a snake springs out of the rotted body." Neruda, *Memoirs*, 5 (original italics).

15. Neruda, "Bosque," in *Obras completas* 2:1269; Neruda, *Poetry*, 709.

16. Hall and Witte, *Maderas*, 54.

17. Other books he owned on the subject include Federico Johow's *Estudios sobre la flora de las islas de Juan Fernández* (Study of the flora of the Juan Fernández Islands), from 1896; Carlos Muñoz Pizarro's *Sinopsis de la flora chilena* (Synopsis of Chilean flora), from 1959; and *Flores silvestres de Chile* (Wildflowers of Chile), from 1966. I consulted these books at the Fundacíon Neruda, La Chascona, Santiago, in August 2018.

18. Neruda, "Viaje por las costas del mundo," in *OC* 4:507. A contemporary reviewer of Valle's work called him a "poeta vegetal" [vegetal poet]; see Aldunate Phillips, "Juvencio Valle."

19. Bacigalupo, *Shamans of the Foye Tree*, 1.

20. Herrera-Sobek, *Celebrating Latino Folklore*, 1:300.

21. Handley, *New World Poetics*, 262.

22. "Then we drove a spear into his chest / and offered the heart, winged / like a bird, to the Araucanian tree. / A whisper of blood ran up to its crown." Neruda, *CGS*, 85–86.

23. Neruda, *Confieso que he vivido*, 18. "*High up, red copihues* (Lapageria rosea) . . . *dangle like drops from the magic forest's arteries. . . . The red copihue is the blood flower, the white copihue is the snow flower.*" Neruda, *Memoirs*, 6 (original italics).

24. See Beuchat and Valdivieso, *Cuentos*, 54. Another version of the myth relates how the copihue grew in the spot where two Mapuche warriors fought to the death. See Matus and Novoa, *Enciclopedia regional*, 168. Mallon ("Bearing Witness," 347) takes the image of the blood-red copihue as a symbol for the "historical suffering of the Mapuche people in their relationship with the Chilean nation-state."

25. Vial, *Neruda en Valparaíso*, 184.

26. Wilson, *Companion to Pablo Neruda*, 8.

27. Wilson, *Companion to Pablo Neruda*, 2–13. This image is also something that Darío Oses has dispelled in "Pablo Neruda."

28. Neruda, *Confieso que he vivido*, 290 (original italics). This passage was introduced in the revised 2017 edition and is not included in the published English translation.

29. Neruda, "Viaje por las costas del mundo," in *OC* 4:508.

30. Neruda, "Algo sobre mi poesía y mi vida," in *OC* 4:933.

31. Neruda, *Confieso que he vivido*, 220; Neruda, *Memoirs*, 191 (my italics).

32. Yurkievich, "Introducción general," 22.

33. Neruda, "Infancia y poesía," in *OC* 4:920.

34. Neruda, "Viaje de vuelta," in *OC* 4:858.

35. Cited in Santí, "Introducción," 54.

36. Neruda, "Viaje por las costas del mundo," in *OC* 4:506.

37. This includes a house he bought in France, which, as his friend Jorge Edwards recalled, was "pura madera, madera de aserradero y para un aserradero" [pure wood, wood from a sawmill, for a sawmill]. Edwards, *Adiós, Poeta*, 289.

38. See Morgado, "Stone upon Stone," 42.

39. See Urrutia, *My Life*, 243–44.

40. Neruda, "Infancia y poesía," *OC* 4:920; Neruda, "Oda a la madera," *OC* 2:152.

41. Neruda, "Entrada a la madera," *OC* 1:325. "I see your dry currents moving, / broken-off hands I see growing, / I hear your oceanic plants / creaking, by night and fury shaken." The translation into English is from Felstiner, *Translating Neruda*, 97.

42. Durán and Safir, *Earth Tones*, 17–18; Felstiner, *Translating Neruda*, 99.

43. De Costa (*Poetry of Pablo Neruda*, 112) notes how, as the poem progresses, the reader "is drawn closer to the principal narrative voice, who, beginning the poem in an authoritative biblical tone of prophecy, ends it in an intimate conversational style."

44. "I first saw trees, ravines / adorned with flowers of wild beauty, . . . / My childhood is wet shoes, broken trunks / fallen in the forest, devoured by vines." Neruda, *CGS*, 373.

45. Jaime Concha insists, however, that Neruda's relationship with nature is not Romantic but realist. See Concha, *Neruda*, 36.

46. Neruda, "La copa de sangre," *OC* 4:418. The English translation is from Felstiner, *Translating Neruda*, 123.

47. Neruda, "[El Rector ha tenido palabras magníficas]," in *OC* 4:945.

48. Rodríguez Monegal (*El viajero inmóvil*, 237–38) argues that Bello's *Silvas* had a profound influence on Neruda's *Canto general*, and that Bello's unfinished poetic project "fue llevada a cabo en 1950 por un poeta chileno que ni siquiera sabía que era su discípulo" [was concluded in 1950 by a Chilean poet who didn't even know that he was his disciple]. Neruda (*Confieso que he vivido*, 356) does, in fact, refer to his admiration for Bello: "Bello no fue un brillante poeta . . . pero su obra literaria, en especial sus poesías, estaban llenas de amor por la tierra americana, por nuestras montañas y nuestros ríos" [Bello was not a brilliant poet . . . but his literary oeuvre, especially his poems, are full of love for the American landscape, for our mountains and our rivers]. This passage was introduced in the revised 2017 edition and is not included in the published English translation.

49. Neruda, "Viaje al corazón de Quevedo," *OC* 4:454. It is intriguing to note that in 1923, following the publication of Neruda's *Crepusculario* (*Book of Twilight*), the Chilean poet Pedro Prado adopted a metaphor comparing Neruda to "a tree that grows slowly, firm and tall" in his prediction of the great future of the young poet. See Feinstein, *Pablo Neruda*, 39. Years later, another Chilean poet appealed to the image of a tree for less complimentary ends. At a commemoration of the thirtieth anniversary of the poet's death in 2003, Gonzalo Rojas called Neruda a great poet but also "a tree, and a tree needs a lot of pruning." Qtd. in Feinstein, *Pablo Neruda*, 314.

50. For an account of Rickett's life and work, see Howard, "Harold William Rickett."

51. The fourth chapter is entitled "Of the Growth of Plants." This book was part of Neruda's donation to the University of Chile, which I consulted at the Archivo Central Andrés Bello. Darío Oses, Neruda scholar and director of the library at the Fundación Pablo Neruda, confirmed to me in conversation that the poet rarely annotated his books (August 7, 2018). Rickett's book was published in Spanish in 1946, and Neruda donated his books to the University of Chile in 1954—that is, four years either side of the first publication of the *Canto general*.

52. Rickett, *The Green Earth*, 77.

53. "Green uterus, seminal / American savannah, dense storehouse, / a branch was born like an island, / a leaf was shaped like a sword, / a flower was lightning and medusa, / a cluster rounded off its résumé, / a root descended into the darkness." Neruda, *CGS*, 16.

54. See Neruda, *CG*, 468.

55. As Reiss (*Word and the Stone*, 9) has noted, trees in the *Canto general* are often synonymous with the pueblo. Wilson (*Companion to Pablo Neruda*, 196) includes bread among what he calls Neruda's "tiresome Communist Party images."

56. "The invaders saw foliage / moving amid the green mist, / heavy branches clothed / in countless leaves and threats, / the terrestrial trunk becoming people, / the territory's roots emerging." Neruda, *CGS*, 79.

57. Durán and Safir, *Earth Tones*, 97–98; Reiss, *Word and the Stone*, 9.

58. Marder, *Plant-Thinking*, 66.

59. Marder, *Plant-Thinking*, 67.

60. Neruda, "Discurso en el anfiteatro Bolívar," *OC* 4:472–73. [But if we move down from the crown of the tree and from the flower, . . . if we pass down from the leaf to the trunk and from the trunk to the origin: there we find each other. Mexicans and Chileans we will find each among the roots].

61. The poem originated as the "Canto general de Chile," canto 7 of the *Canto general*. Neruda, "Algo sobre mi poesía y mi vida," *OC* 4:931.

62. Neruda, "Viaje por las costas del mundo," *OC* 4:521.

63. Neruda, "La cazadora de raíces," in *OC* 5:206 (original italics). This recollection is also partly included in his memoirs and I use the published translation here: Neruda, *Confieso que he vivido*, 220; Neruda, *Memoirs*, 191.

64. Neruda, "La cazadora de raíces," in *OC* 5:207.

65. Neruda, "La cazadora de raíces," in *OC* 5:207 (my italics). This description is also included in Neruda, *Confieso que he vivido*, 220. ["Nothing more beautiful than those huge, open *hands*, wounded or burned, that tell us, when we come across them on a forest path, the secret of the buried tree, the mystery that nourished the leaves, the deep-reaching *muscles* of the vegetable kingdom. Tragic and *shaggy*, they show us a new beauty: they are sculptures molded by the depths of the earth: nature's secret masterpieces" (Neruda, *Memoirs*, 191–92).] I use the published English translation here.

66. "The jaguar touches the leaves / with its phosphorescent absence, / the puma bolts through the foliage / like a raging fire, / while in him burn / the jungle's alcoholic eyes." Neruda, *CGS*, 17. In an essay on Shakespeare, Neruda makes explicit the connections between "hojas" and "ojos" in a comparison of great writers to trees: "Entonces, estos bardos acumulan hojas, pero entre estas hojas hay trinos, bajo estas hojas hay raíces. Son hojas de grandes árboles. Son hojas y son ojos" [Then, these bards amass leaves, but among these leaves there are warblings, below these leaves there are roots. They are leaves of big trees. They are leaves and they are eyes]. Neruda, "Inaugurando el año de Shakespeare," in *OC* 4:1197. Ocampo (*Árboles de Buenos Aires*, 19) also adopts this wordplay in her poem "Lapacho."

67. For instance, see Dantín Cereceda, *La vida de las plantas*, one of the books that Neruda donated to the University of Chile.

68. Coccia, *Life of Plants*, 77.

69. See Coccia, *Life of Plants*, 78–80; also, for instance, Baluška, Mancuso, Volkmann, and Barlow, "'Root-Brain' Hypothesis."

70. Cited in Coccia, *Life of Plants*, 79.

71. Wohlleben, *Hidden Life of Trees*, 10.

72. Karban, "Language of Plant Communication," 3.

73. Marder, *Philosopher's Plant*, 183; Coccia, *Life of Plants*, 87.

74. Coccia, *Life of Plants*, 67.

75. "Salt kept stripping / the mountains' splendour, / transforming raindrops on the leaves / into a suit of quartz / and transmuting spruces / into avenues of coal." Neruda, *CGS*, 23.

76. *"Here comes the tree, the tree / whose roots are alive, / it fed on martyrdom's nitrate, / its roots consumed blood, / and it extracted tears from the soil."* Neruda, *CGS*, 71–72.

77. Neruda, "El egoísta," *OC* 3:811 ["when / they return to the depths of being and not being / and abandon the gold and the greenery, / until they are roots again, / and again, torn down and being born, / they rise up to know the spring" (Neruda, *Poetry*, 869)].

78. Neruda, "Con Quevedo, en primavera," *OC* 3:817; Neruda, *Poetry*, 874.

79. "Monday came to bite me and I fed it some leaves. / Tuesday came to insult me and I kept on sleeping. / Then Wednesday arrived with irate teeth. / Building roots, I let it pass by." Neruda, *CGS*, 389.

80. Neruda referred to wearing seven league boots when describing how much of Chile he covered in the 1940s. See Olivares Briones, *Pablo Neruda*, 725.

81. Wilson, *Companion to Pablo Neruda*, 101; Reiss, *Word and the Stone*, 48.

82. Neruda, "Bosque," *OC* 2:1268, 1269; Neruda, *Poetry*, 708, 709.

83. Handley, *New World Poetics*, 212–13.

84. De Costa, *Pablo Neruda*, 119.

85. See Rickett, *The Green Earth*, 79; Rickett, *La tierra es verde*, 83.

86. Marder, "Vegetal Anti-metaphysics," 487.

87. Rickett, *The Green Earth*, 77; Rickett, *La tierra es verde*, 82. This page also contained a number of underlinings, although not this sentence.

88. "The burning blood fell / from silence to silence, / down under, where the seed / is waiting for springtime." Neruda, *CGS*, 81.

89. Coccia, *Life of Plants*, 86.

90. Mascia, "Pablo Neruda," 74.

91. Dawes, *Verses against the Darkness*, 24, 25.

92. This was the view of Rodríguez Monegal, *El viajero inmóvil*, 236.

93. Neruda, "Viaje al corazón de Quevedo," *OC* 4:454.

94. Neruda, "Infancia y poesía," *OC* 4:927.

95. Neruda, "Infancia y poesía," *OC* 4:928. [To experience the fraternity of our brothers is a marvelous thing in life. To experience the love of those whom we love is the fire that

feeds life. But to feel the affection of those whom we don't know, of the unknown people that watch over us when we are asleep or alone, in times of danger or dejection, is an even greater and more beautiful sensation because it extends our being and unites all living things. . . .

Thus, in the same way that I left the pinecone back then, I've left my words at the doors of many unknown people, of many prisoners, of many who are alone or persecuted.]

AFTERWORD

1. Ocampo and Sessa, *Árboles de Buenos Aires*. The poem "La morada de los árboles" (The dwelling of the trees) describes trees dancing and copulating (Ocampo and Sessa, *Árboles de Buenos Aires*, 9–12); "Siesta" includes a description of how the trees sing to sleeping gardeners (26); a photograph showing a tree knot resembling an eye accompanies the poem "Una mirada" (A glance, 88–89); and a photograph of the finger-like tree roots of an *ombú* are pictured alongside the poem "Ombumano" (Ombú-hand, 50–51). All further page references to *Árboles de Buenos Aires* will be given parenthetically in the text.

2. Mackintosh, "Classical Reference," 148.

3. ["Tree, what man would you be / if you were not a tree?" / I asked a *ceibo*. / "Aldo, what tree would you be / if you were not a man?" / I asked a man.]

4. ["Happy the tree that scarcely feels" / said Darío, I would delete the "scarcely" / and would say "happy the tree that feels so much" / even though it would change the meter.]

5. Wohlleben, *Hidden Life of Trees*, 5.

6. This is the published English translation of this poem; Ocampo, *Silvina Ocampo*, 140.

7. Ocampo, *Silvina Ocampo*, 140.

8. [Trunks bleed, / trunks die / weaving involuntary cages / for birds / that have been orphaned. . . . / If men hadn't killed you / to construct buildings or avenues / cyclones or lightning would have.]

9. Neruda, "Oda a la erosión en la provincia de Malleco," in *OC* 2:307.

10. Rivera-Barnes, "Pablo Neruda's Latin American Landscape," 146.

11. Neruda, "II," in *OC* 3:526.

12. Neruda, "La cazadora de raíces," *OC* 5:208. [The great forested south is being totally obliterated, razed, burned and attacked. . . . Perhaps these Chilean roots that the hunter held back for us will some day be relics, like the jawbones of megatheriums.]

13. Handley, *New World Poetics*, 180.

14. Safónov, *La tierra en flor*. I consulted this book at the Archivo Central Andrés Bello, University of Chile.

15. Some of these authors and works are referred to in recent ecocritical considerations of Latin American literature. For instance, DeVries (*History of Ecology*, 33) speaks of Bello's "seminal expression of a key tenet of current environmental thought, the preference of the country over the city." Llarull ("Long and Winding Road," 92–96), Anderson and Reales ("Extracting Nature," 370–75), and Mutis and Pettinaroli ("Visions of Nature," 422–25) all offer reflections on the environmental dimensions of *María*. *La vorágine* has also been discussed in relation to environmental issues. See, DeVries, *History of Ecology*, 137–60; French,

Nature, ch. 3; Jaramillo, "Green Hells," 99–101; Smith, "Mapping the Amazon," n.p.; Wylie, *Colombia's Forgotten Frontier*, ch. 5; Vieira, *"Phytographia,"* 228–30.

16. Rivera, *La vorágine*, 298. ["Every year the rubber workers in Colombia destroy millions of trees, while in Venezuela the *balatá* rubber tree has disappeared. In this way, they defraud the coming generations" (Rivera, *The Vortex*, 272).]

17. Mejía Prado, Galeano, and Abecasis, "Amazonia," 257.

18. Lewis and Maslin, "Defining the Anthropocene," 174.

BIBLIOGRAPHY

MANUSCRIPTS

Carpentier, Alejo. Manuscript F.2.1.3. "Los pasos perdidos." Fundación Alejo Carpentier, Havana, Cuba.

Carpentier, Alejo. Manuscript F.2.1.4. "El siglo de las luces." Fundación Alejo Carpentier, Havana, Cuba.

Carpentier, Alejo. "Wifredo Lam." Fundación Alejo Carpentier, Havana, Cuba.

Hurtado, Oscar. "La seiba." Fundación Alejo Carpentier, Havana, Cuba.

PRIMARY AND SECONDARY SOURCES

Abbott, Elizabeth. *Sugar: A Bittersweet History.* London: Duckworth, 2009.

Abram, David. *The Spell of the Sensuous: Perception and Language in a More-Than-Human World.* New York: Vintage Books, 1996.

Ackerman, Diane. *A Natural History of the Senses.* New York: Random House, 1990.

Adamson, Joni. "Environmental Justice, Cosmopolitics, and Climate Change." In *The Cambridge Companion to Literature and the Environment,* edited by Louise Westling, 169–83. Cambridge: Cambridge University Press, 2014.

Agamben, Giorgio. "The Cabinet of Wonder." In *The Man without Content,* translated by Georgia Albert, 28–39. Stanford: Stanford University Press, 1999.

Albin, María C., Megan Corbin, and Raúl Marrero-Fente. "Gertrudis the Great: First Abolitionist and Feminist in the Americas and Spain." *Hispanic Issues On Line* 18 (2017): 1–66. Special issue on "Gender and the Politics of Literature: Gertrudis Gómez de Avellaneda," edited by María C. Albin, Megan Corbin, and Raúl Marrero-Fente.

Alcocer, Rudyard J. *Narrative Mutations: Discourses of Heredity in Caribbean Literature.* New York: Routledge, 2005.

Alcocer, Rudyard J. *Time Travel in the Latin American and Caribbean Imagination.* New York: Palgrave Macmillan, 2011.

Aldunate Phillips, Arturo. "Juvencio Valle: Un poeta vegetal." *Revista hispanica moderna* 4, no. 2 (1938): 105–10.

Alighieri, Dante. *The Inferno.* Translated by Robert Pinsky. London: Dent, 1996.

Allaby, Michael. *Basics of Environmental Science.* 2nd ed. London: Routledge, 1996.

Alonso, Manuel. *El Gíbaro: cuadro de costumbres de la isla de Puerto Rico.* Barcelona: Juan Oliveres, 1849.

Altschul, Nadia R. *Geographies of Philological Knowledge: Postcoloniality and the Transatlantic National Epic*. Chicago: University of Chicago Press, 2012.

Anderson, Kit. *Nature, Culture, and Big Old Trees: Live Oaks and Ceibas in the Landscapes of Louisiana and Guatemala*. Austin: University of Texas Press, 2003.

Anderson, Mark and Zélia M. Bora, eds. *Ecological Crisis and Cultural Representation in Latin America: Ecocritical Perspectives on Art, Film, and Literature*. Lanham: Lexington Books, 2016.

Anderson, Mark D., and Marcela Reales. "Extracting Nature: Toward an Ecology of Colombian Narrative." In *A History of Colombian Literature*, edited by Raymond Leslie Williams, 363–405. Cambridge: Cambridge University Press, 2016.

[Anonymous]. *The Epic of Gilgamesh*. Translated by N. K. Sandars. London: Penguin, 1972.

Araujo, Ana Lucia. *Brazil through French Eyes: A Nineteenth-Century Artist in the Tropics*. Albuquerque: University of New Mexico Press, 2015.

Ascani, German, and Michael W. Smith. "The Use of Psychotropic Herbal and Natural Medicines in Latina/o and Mestiza/o Populations." In *Latina/o Healing Practices: Mestizo and Indigenous Perspectives*, edited by Brian W. McNeill and Joseph M. Cervantes, 83–138. London: Routledge, 2010.

Augspach, Elizabeth A. *The Garden as Woman's Space in Twelfth- and Thirteenth-Century Literature*. Lewiston, NY: Edwin Mellon Press, 2004.

Bacigalupo, Ana Mariella. *Shamans of the Foye Tree: Gender, Power, and Healing among Chilean Mapuche*. Austin: University of Texas Press, 2007.

Bahre, Conrad J. *Destruction of the Natural Vegetation of North-West Chile*. Berkeley: University of California Press, 1979.

Bakewell, Peter, and Jacqueline Holler. *A History of Latin America to 1825*. 3rd ed. Malden, MA: Wiley-Blackwell, 2010.

Baluška, František, Stefano Mancuso, and Dieter Volkmann, eds. *Communication in Plants: Neuronal Aspects of Plant Life*. Berlin: Springer-Verlag, 2006.

Baluška, František, Stefano Mancuso, Dieter Volkmann, and Peter W. Barlow. "The 'Root-Brain' Hypothesis of Charles and Francis Darwin: Revival after More Than 125 Years." *Plant Signaling and Behavior* 4, no. 12 (2009): 1121–27.

Barbas-Rhoden, Laura. *Ecological Imaginations in Latin American Fiction*. Gainesville: University Press of Florida, 2011.

Bataille, Georges. "The Language of Flowers." In *Visions of Excess: Selected Writings, 1927–1930*, translated and edited by Allan Stoekl, 10–14. Minneapolis: University of Minnesota Press, 1985.

Baudelaire, Charles. *The Complete Verse*. Edited and translated by Francis Scarfe. 2 vols. London: Anvil Press, 1986.

Baudrillard, Jean. *Simulacra and Simulation*. Translated by Sheila Faria Glaser. Ann Arbor: University of Michigan Press, 1994.

Beckman, Ericka. "Jorge Isaacs' *María* and the Space-Time of Global Capitalism." *Studies in English Literature, 1500–1900* 56, no. 3 (2016): 539–59.

Beerling, David. *The Emerald Planet: How Plants Changed Earth's History*. Oxford: Oxford University Press, 2007.

Belli, Giaconda. *La mujer habitada*. Tafalla: Txalparta, 2004.

Bello, Andrés. *Obras completas*. Vol. 1, *Poesías*. Prologue by Fernando Paz Castillo. Caracas: Ediciones Ministerio de Educación, 1952.

Bello, Andrés. *Obras completas*. Vol. 2, *Borradores de poesía*. Prologue by Pedro P. Barnola. Caracas: Ediciones Ministerio de Educación, 1962.

Bello, Andrés. *The Selected Writings of Andrés Bello*. Translated by F. M. López-Morillas. Edited by I. Jaksić. Oxford: Oxford University Press, 1997.

Benítez-Rojo, Antonio. "Sugar and the Environment in Cuba." In *Caribbean Literature and the Environment: Between Nature and Culture*, edited by Elizabeth M. DeLoughrey, Renée K. Gosson, and George Handley, 33–50. Charlottesville: University of Virginia Press, 2005.

Bennett, Jennifer. *Lilies of the Hearth: The Historical Relationship between Women and Plants*. Ontario: Camden House, 1991.

Beuchat, Cecilia, and Carolina Valdivieso. *Cuentos sobre el origen del hombre y el mundo*. 2nd ed. Santiago: Ediciones Universidad Católica de Chile, 2001.

Beverley, John. *Aspects of Góngora's "Soledades."* Purdue University Monographs in Romance Languages 1. Amsterdam: John Benjamins, 1980.

Bird-David, Nurit. "'Animism' Revisited: Personhood, Environment, and Relational Epistemology." *Current Anthropology* 40, no. S1 (1999): S67–91.

Bleichmar, Daniela. *Visual Voyages: Images of Latin American Nature from Columbus to Darwin*. New Haven: Yale University Press, 2017.

Blocker, Jane. *Where Is Ana Mendieta? Identity, Performativity and Exile*. Durham: Duke University Press, 1999.

Boccaccio, Giovanni. *The Decameron*. Translated by G. H. William. 2nd ed. London: Penguin, 1995.

Boldt-Irons, Leslie Anne. "Introduction." In *On Bataille: Critical Essays*, edited by Leslie Anne Boldt-Irons, 1–38. Albany: SUNY, 1995.

Branche, Jerome. "Ennobling Savagery? Sentimentalism and the Subaltern in Sab." *African-Hispanic Review* 17 (1998): 12–23.

Bravo, Julio. "Pablo Messiez lleva al teatro la inquietante novela de Samanta Schweblin *Distancia de rescate*." *ABC*, March 17, 2016. https://www.abc.es/cultura/teatros/abci-pablo-messiez-lleva-teatro-inquietante-novela-samanta-schweblin-distancia-rescate-201603171715_noticia.html/.

Breen, Rebecca. "Sin título: Contemporary Women Artists from Latin America and Testimonio (Ana Mendieta, Doris Salcedo, Teresa Margolles)." PhD diss., University of Cambridge, 2012.

Brotherston, Gordon. *Image of the New World: The American Continent Portrayed in Native Texts*. Translated with Ed Dorn. London: Thames and Hudson, 1979.

Brotherston, Gordon. *Latin American Poetry: Origins and Presence*. Cambridge: Cambridge University Press, 1975.

Browning, John. "Rafael Landívar's *Rusticatio Mexicana*: Natural History and Political Subversion." *Ideologies and Literature* 1, no. 3 (1985): 9–30.

Brumble, H. David. *Classical Myths and Legends in the Middle Ages and Renaissance: A List of Allegorical Meanings*. London: Fitzroy Dearborn, 1998.

Bryan-Wilson, Julia, Adrian Heathfield, and Stephanie Rosenthal. *Ana Mendieta: Traces*. London: Haywood Publishing, 2013.

Buchmann, Stephen. *The Reason for Flowers: Their History, Culture, Biology, and How They Change Our Lives*. New York: Scribner, 2015.

Bull, William. "Nature and Anthropomorphism in *La vorágine*." *Romanic Review* 39 (1948): 307–18.

Cabañas, Kaira M. "Ana Mendieta: 'Pain of Cuba, Body I Am.'" *Woman's Art Journal* 20, no. 1 (1999): 12–17.

Cabrera, Lydia. *El monte*. Miami: Ediciones Universal, 2006.

Carpentier, Alejo. *El acoso*. Barcelona: Editorial Bruguera, 1979.

Carpentier, Alejo. "El adjetivo y sus arrugas." In *El adjetivo y sus arrugas*, 7–9. Buenos Aires: Galerna, 1980.

Carpentier, Alejo. "The Baroque and the Marvelous Real." In *Magical Realism: Theory, History, Community*, edited by Lois Parkinson Zamora and Wendy B. Faris, 89–108. Durham: Duke University Press, 1995.

Carpentier, Alejo. "Lo barroco y lo real maravilloso." In *Obras completas: Ensayos*, 13:167–93. Mexico: Siglo XXI, 1990.

Carpentier, Alejo. *The Chase*. Translated by Alfred Mac Adam. London: André Deutsch, 1990.

Carpentier, Alejo. "The City of Columns." In Zamora and Kaup, *Baroque New Worlds*, 244–58.

Carpentier, Alejo. "La ciudad de las columnas." In *Obras completas: Ensayos*, 13:61–73. Mexico: Siglo XXI, 1990.

Carpentier, Alejo. *La ciudad de las columnas*. Photographs by Paolo Gasparini. Barcelona: Editorial Lumen, 1970.

Carpentier, Alejo. *La ciudad de las columnas*. Photographs by Roberto Martínez Grandal. La Habana: Editorial Letras Cubanas, 1982.

Carpentier, Alejo. *La consagración de la primavera*. Madrid: Alianza, 2004.

Carpentier, Alejo. "De lo real maravilloso americano." In *Obras completas: Ensayos*, 13:100–117. Mexico: Siglo XXI, 1990.

Carpentier, Alejo. *Explosion in a Cathedral*. Translated by John Sturrock. Minneapolis: University of Minnesota Press, 2001.

Carpentier, Alejo. "La Exposición Internacional de París." In *Obras completas, Crónicas 2: arte, literatura, política*, 9:414–19. Mexico: Siglo XXI, 1986.

Carpentier, Alejo. *Guerra del tiempo y otros relatos*. Madrid. Alianza, 2001.

Carpentier, Alejo. *The Kingdom of This World*. Translated by Harriet de Onís. Harmondsworth: Penguin, 1980.

Carpentier, Alejo. *The Lost Steps*. Translated by Harriet de Onís. New York: Noonday Press, 1989.

Carpentier, Alejo. "On the Marvelous Real in America." In *Magical Realism: Theory, History, Community*, edited by Lois Parkinson Zamora and Wendy B. Faris, 75–88. Durham: Duke University Press, 1995.

Carpentier, Alejo. *Los pasos perdidos*. Madrid: Alianza, 1999.

Carpentier, Alejo. "Problemática de la actual novela latinoamericana." In *Obras completas: ensayos*, 13:11–44. Mexico: Siglo XXI, 1990.

Carpentier, Alejo. "Questions concerning the Contemporary Latin American Novel." In Zamora and Kaup, *Baroque New Worlds*, 259–64.

Carpentier, Alejo. *Reasons of State*. Translated by Frances Partridge. London: Victor Gollancz, 1976.

Carpentier, Alejo. *El recurso del método*. Madrid: Alianza, 1998.

Carpentier, Alejo. *El reino de este mundo*. Madrid: Alianza, 2003.

Carpentier, Alejo. *El siglo de las luces*. Madrid, Alianza, 2003.

Carpentier, Alejo. *Tientos y diferencias: Ensayos*. Mexico: UNAM, 1964.

Carpentier, Alejo. "Visión de América." In *Letra y Solfa*, edited by Alexis Márquez Rodríguez, 1:105–34. Buenos Aires: Ediciones Nemont, 1976.

Carpentier, Alejo. *War of Time*. Translated by Frances Partridge. New York: Knopf, 1970.

Carpentier, Alejo, and Joaquín Santana. "Los pasos encontrados." In *Entrevistas: Alejo Carpentier*, edited by Virgilio López Lemus, 185–92. La Habana: Editorial Letras Cubanas, 1985.

Carpentier, Alejo, and Ignacio Solares. "Nunca he utilizado la pluma para herir; sólo creo en la literatura que construye, no en la que destruye." In *Entrevistas: Alejo Carpentier*, edited by Virgilio López Lemus, 227–34. La Habana: Editorial Letras Cubanas, 1985.

Carrasco, Davíd. "Cortés and the Sacred Ceiba: A Maya Axis Mundi." In *The History of New Spain by Bernal Díaz del Castillo*, edited by Davíd Carrasco, 399–404. Albuquerque: University of New Mexico Press, 2008.

Carreño, Antonio. "Of 'Orders' and 'Disorders': Analogy in the Baroque Lyric (from Góngora to Sor Juana)." In *Coded Encounters: Writing, Gender and Ethnicity in Colonial Latin America*, edited by F. J. Cevallos-Candau, N. M. Scott, and N. Suárez-Araúz, 224–35. Amherst: University of Massachusetts Press, 1994.

Carrillo, Jesús. "From Mt. Ventoux to Mt. Masaya: The Rise and Fall of Subjectivity in Early Modern Travel Narrative." In *Voyages and Visions: Towards a Cultural History of Travel*, edited by Jaś Elsner and Joan-Pau Rubiés, 57–73. London: Reaktion, 1999.

Carson, Rachel. *Silent Spring*. London: Penguin, 2000.

Casement, Roger. *Sir Roger Casement's Heart of Darkness: The 1911 Documents*. Edited by Angus Mitchell. Dublin: Irish Manuscripts Commission, 2003.

Castellano, Katey. *The Ecology of British Romantic Conservatism, 1790–1837*. London: Palgrave Macmillan, 2013.

Catallus, Gaius Valerius. *The Student's Catallus*. Edited by Daniel H. Garrison. Abington: Routledge, 2005.

Celorio, Gonzalo. *Ensayo de Contraconquista*. Mexico: Tusquets Editores, 2001.

Chamberlain, Alex F. "On the Words for 'Fear' in Certain Languages. A Study in Linguistic Psychology." *American Journal of Psychology* 10, no. 2 (1899): 302–5.

Chao, Ramón. *Conversaciones con Alejo Carpentier*. Madrid: Alianza, 1998.

Chase, Cynthia. *Decomposing Figures: Rhetorical Readings in the Romantic Tradition*. Baltimore: Johns Hopkins University Press, 1986.

Chateaubriand, François-René. *Atala. René.* Translated by Irving Putter. Berkeley: University of California Press, 1980.

Chateaubriand, François-René. *The Genius of Christianity or the Spirit and Beauty of the Christian Religion.* Translated by Charles I. White. 9th ed. Baltimore: John Murphy, 1871.

Clarke, D. C. "Silva." In *The Princeton Encyclopedia of Poetry and Poetics,* edited by Roland Greene, Stephen Cushman, Clare Cavanagh, Jahan Ramazani and Paul Rouzer, 1306. 4th ed. Princeton, NJ: Princeton University Press, 2013.

Coccia, Emanuele. *The Life of Plants: A Metaphysics of Mixture.* Cambridge: Polity, 2019.

Collins, Marsha S. *The "Soledades," Góngora's Masque of the Imagination.* Columbia: University of Missouri Press, 2002.

Concha, Jaime. *Neruda, 1904–1936.* Santiago: Editorial Universitaria, 1972.

Cook, Roger. *L'Arbre de vie.* Paris: Seuil, 1975.

Cook, Roger. *The Tree of Life: Image of the Cosmos.* London: Thames and Hudson, 1974.

Corominas, Joan. *Diccionario crítico etimológico de la lengua castellana.* 6 vols. Madrid: Gredos, 1954.

Cortázar, Julio. *La vuelta al día en ochenta mundos.* Mexico: Siglo XXI, 1967.

Crosby, Alfred W. *The Columbian Exchange: Biological and Cultural Consequences of 1492.* Westport, CT: Greenwood Press, 1972.

Cruz, Mary. "'Sab,' su texto y su contexto." In Gertrudis Gómez de Avellaneda, *Sab,* prologue and notes by Mary Cruz, 7–123. La Habana: Instituto Cubano del Libro, 1973.

Culler, Jonathan. *The Pursuit of Signs: Semiotics, Literature, Deconstruction.* London: Routledge and Kegan Paul, 1981.

Cussen, Antonio. *Bello and Bolívar: Poetry and Politics in the Spanish American Revolution.* Cambridge: Cambridge University Press, 1992.

Dale, George I. "Parícutin, Jorullo, and Rafael Landívar." *Hispania* 28, no. 4 (1945): 522–25.

Damrosch, David. "The Aesthetics of Conquest: Aztec Poetry before and after Cortés." *Representations* 33 (1991): 101–20. Special issue, "The New World."

Dantín Cereceda, Juan. *La vida de las plantas.* 2nd ed. Madrid: Espasa-Calpe, 1934.

Darvill, Timothy. *The Concise Oxford Dictionary of Archaeology.* Oxford: Oxford University Press, 2002.

Dauksta, Dainis. "From Post to Pillar: The Development and Persistence of an Arboreal Metaphor." In *New Perspectives on People and Forests,* edited by Eva Ritter and Dainis Dauksta, 99–117. Dordrecht: Springer, 2011.

Davies, Catherine. "Introduction." In Gertrudis Gómez de Avellaneda, *Sab,* edited by Catherine Davies, 1–33. Manchester: Manchester University Press, 2001.

Davies, Catherine. "The Gift in Sab." *Afro-Hispanic Review* 22, no. 2 (2003): 46–53.

Davies, Nikolas, and Erkki Jokiniemi. *Dictionary of Architecture and Building Construction.* Amsterdam: Elsevier, 2008.

Dávila Durand, Javier. "Lo que se debe hacer." In *¡Más aplausos para la lluvia! Antología de poesía amazónica reciente,* edited by Jeremy G. Larochelle, 85–86. Iquitos: Tierra Nueva, 2012.

Dawes, Greg. *Verses against the Darkness: Pablo Neruda's Poetry and Politics.* Lewisburg: Bucknell University Press, 2006.

De Costa, René. *The Poetry of Pablo Neruda*. Cambridge, MA: Harvard University Press, 1979.

DeGrave, Analisa. "Ecoliterature and Dystopia: Gardens and Topos in Modern Latin American Poetry." *Confluencia* 22, no. 2 (2007): 89–104.

Deitering, Cynthia. "The Postnatural Novel: Toxic Consciousness in Fiction of the 1980s." In *The Ecocriticism Reader*, edited by Cheryll Glotfelty and Harold Fromm, 196–203. Athens: University of Georgia Press, 1996.

De la Cadena, Marisol. *Earth Beings: Ecologies of Practice across Andean Worlds*. Durham, NC: Duke University Press, 2015.

De la Cadena, Marisol. "Indigenous Cosmopolitics in the Andes: Conceptual Reflections beyond 'Politics.'" *Cultural Anthropology* 25, no. 2 (2010): 334–70.

De la Rosa, Luis. *Memoria sobre el cultivo del maíz en México*. Mexico: Sociedad Literaria, 1846.

De la Sagra, Ramón. *Historia económico-política y estadística de la isla de Cuba*. La Habana: Viudas de Arazoza y Soler, 1831.

Deleuze, Gilles. *The Fold: Leibniz and the Baroque*. Translated by Tom Conley. Minneapolis: University of Minnesota Press, 1992.

DeLoughrey, Elizabeth. "Globalizing the Routes of Breadfruit and Other Bounties." *Journal of Colonialism and Colonial History* 8, no. 3 (2008): n.p.

De Man, Paul. *The Rhetoric of Romanticism*. New York: Columbia University Press, 1984.

Descola, Philippe. *Beyond Nature and Culture*. Translated by Janet Lloyd. Chicago: University of Chicago Press, 2013.

DeVries, Scott M. *A History of Ecology and Environmentalism in Spanish American Literature*. Lewisburg: Bucknell University Press, 2013.

Diccionario de la lengua española. 2 vols. 21st ed. Madrid: Real Academia Española, 1992.

Dolan, Kathryn Cornell. *Beyond the Fruited Plain: Food and Agriculture in U.S. Literature, 1850–1905*. Lincoln: University of Nebraska Press, 2014.

D'Ors, Eugenio. *Lo barroco*. Madrid: Aguilar, 1964.

Douglas, Mary. *Purity and Danger: An Analysis of Concepts of Pollution and Taboo*. London: Pelican, 1970.

Dryden, John. *The Poems of John Dryden*. Edited by Paul Hammond and David Hopkins. Vol. 5. London: Routledge, 2005.

Dugan, Holly. *The Ephemeral History of Perfume: Scent and Sense in Early Modern England*. Baltimore: Johns Hopkins University Press, 2011.

Duporté, Jorge. *La flora de este reino: imágenes de Jorge Duporté*. Havana: Biblioteca Nacional José Martí, 2004.

Duporté, Jorge. *Hacía una cultura de la naturaleza: Barrera de cerdas ardiente. Cincuento dibujos por Jorge Duporté; texto Alejo Carpentier*. Havana: Fondo Cubano de Bienes Culturales; Galería de los Vidrales, 1986.

Durán, Manuel, and Margery Safir. *Earth Tones: The Poetry of Pablo Neruda*. Bloomington: Indiana University Press, 1986.

Durán Luzio, Juan. "Alexander von Humboldt y Andrés Bello: etapas hacia una relación textual." *Escritura* 12, nos. 23–24 (1987): 139–52.

Echenberg, Myron. *Humboldt's Mexico: In the Footsteps of the Illustrious German Scientific Traveller.* Montreal: McGill-Queen's University Press, 2017.

Edwards, Jorge. *Adiós, Poeta.* Barcelona: Tusquets, 1990.

Edwards, Karen L. *Milton and the Natural World: Science and Poetry in Paradise Lost.* Cambridge: Cambridge University Press, 1999.

Eliade, Mircea. *Zalmoxis, the Vanishing God: Comparative Studies in the Religions and Folklore of Dacia and Eastern Europe.* Translated by Willard R. Trask. Chicago: University of Chicago Press, 1972.

Evelyn, John. *Sylva: or, A Discourse of Forest-Trees, and the Propagation of Timber in His Majesties Dominions, &c.* 4th ed. 2 vols. London: R. Scott, R. Chiswell, G. Sawbridge and B. Tooke, 1706.

Faverón Patriau, Gustavo. "Judaísmo y desarraigo en *María* de Jorge Isaacs." *Revista Iberoamericana* 70, no. 207 (April–June 2004): 341–57.

Favret, Mary A. *War at a Distance: Romanticism and the Making of Modern Wartime.* Princeton, NJ: Princeton University Press, 2010.

Feinstein, Adam. *Pablo Neruda: A Passion for Life.* London: Bloomsbury, 2004.

Felstiner, John. *Translating Neruda: The Way to Macchu Picchu.* Stanford: Stanford University Press, 1980.

Fernández de Oviedo y Valdés, Gonzalo. *Historia general y natural de las Indias, islas y tierra-firme del mar océano.* Edited by José Amador de los Rios. 4 vols. Madrid: Real Academia de la Historia, 1851–1854.

Ferrari, Guillermina de. "Las palabras y las cosas: el lenguaje de la revolución en *El siglo de las luces*, de Alejo Carpentier, y *Los palacios distantes*, de Abilio Estévez." In *Nuevas Lecturas de Alejo Carpentier*, edited by Alexis Márquez Rodríguez, 231–58. Caracas: Fondo Editorial de Humanidades y Educación, 2004.

Forns-Broggi, Roberto. *Nudos como estrellas: ABC de la imaginación ecológica en nuestras Américas.* Lima: Nido de Cuervos, 2012.

Foster, Lynn F. *Handbook to Life in the Ancient Maya World.* Oxford: Oxford University Press, 2002.

Franco, Jean. "Image and Experience in *La vorágine*." *Bulletin of Hispanic Studies* 41 (1964): 101–10.

Frankfort, Henri. *Kinship and the Gods: A Study of Ancient Near Eastern Religion as the Integration of Society and Nature.* Chicago: University of Chicago Press, 1978.

Frazer, J. G. *Folk-Lore in the Old Testament.* 3 vols. London: Macmillan, 1919.

Frazer, J. G. *The Golden Bough: A Study in Magic and Religion.* London: Macmillan, 1971.

French, Jennifer L. *Nature, Neo-Colonialism, and the Spanish American Regional Writers.* Hanover, NH: University Press of New England, 2005.

Freud, Sigmund. *The Interpretation of Dreams.* Edited and translated by James Strachey, revised by Angela Richards. The Pelican Freud Library, vol. 4. Harmondsworth: Penguin, 1976.

Gagliano, Monica. "The Flowering of Plant Bioacoustics: How and Why?" *Behavioral Ecology* 24, no. 4 (2013): 800–801.

Gagliano, Monica, Stefano Mancuso, and Daniel Robert. "Towards Understanding Plant Bioacoustics." *Trends in Plant Science* 17, no. 6 (2012): 323–25.

Gagliano, Monica, John C. Ryan, and Patrícia Vieira. "Introduction." In Gagliano, Ryan, and Vieira, *Language of Plants*, vii–xxxiii.

Gagliano, Monica, John C. Ryan, and Patrícia Vieira, eds. *The Language of Plants: Science, Philosophy, Literature*. Minneapolis: University of Minnesota Press, 2017.

Galeano, Juan Carlos. *Amazonia*. Bogotá: Literalia, 2003.

Galeano, Juan Carlos. *Amazonia*. Translated by James Kimbrell and Rebecca Morgan. Iquitos: CETA, 2012.

Galeano, Juan Carlos. *Cuentos amazónicos*. Iquitos: Tierra Nueva, 2007.

Galeano, Juan Carlos. *Folktales of the Amazon*. Translated by Rebecca Morgan and Kenneth Watson. Westport, CT: Libraries Unlimited, 2009.

Galeano, Juan Carlos, and Valliere Richard Auzenne, dir. *The Trees Have a Mother*. Florida State University, 2008.

Gallegos, Rómulo. *Canaima*. 12th ed. Madrid: Espasa-Calpe, 1977.

Gamble, John W. "In the Presence of the Divine: The Use of Hallucinogens in Religious Practice." In *Religion and Alcohol: Sobering Thoughts*, edited by C. K. Robertson, 111–44. New York: Peter Lang, 2004.

García-Goyco, Osvaldo. "The Mapa de Cuauhtinchan No. 2 and the Cosmic Tree in Mesoamerica, the Caribbean and the Amazon-Orinoco Basin." In *Cave, City and Eagle's Nest: An Interpretive Journey through the Mapa de Cuauhtinchan No. 2*, edited by Davíd Carrasco and Scott Sessions, 357–88. Albuquerque: University of New Mexico Press, 2007.

Garfield, Evelyn Picon. *Poder y sexualidad: El discurso de Gertrudis Gómez de Avellaneda*. Amsterdam: Rodopi, 1993.

Geisweidt, Edward J. "Horticulture of the Head: The Vegetable Life of Hair in Early Modern English Thought." *Early Modern Literary Studies* 19, no. 6 (2009): 1–24.

Gerbi, Antonello. *Nature in the New World: From Christopher Columbus to Gonzalo Fernández de Oviedo*. Translated by Jeremy Moyle. Pittsburgh: University of Pittsburgh Press, 1985.

Gibson, Prudence. *The Plant Contract: Art's Return to Vegetal Life*. Leiden: Brill Rodopi, 2018.

Gibson, Prudence, and Baylee Brits, eds. *Covert Plants: Vegetal Consciousness and Agency in an Anthropocentric World*. Santa Barbara: Brainstorm Books, 2018.

Gilmore, John. *The Poetics of Empire: A Study of James Grainger's* The Sugar Cane *(1764)*. London: Athlone Press, 2000.

Glantz, Margo. "De la amorosa inclinación a enredarse en cabellos." In *Obras reunidas 2: Narrativa*, 291–432. Mexico: FCE, 2008.

Glantz, Margo. "La húmeda identidad: *María* de Jorge Isaacs." In *La lengua en la mano*, 84–90. Puebla: Premia, 1983.

Goethe, Johann Wolfgang von. *The Sorrows of Young Werther*. Translated by Michael Hurse. London: Penguin Classics, 1989.

Gomes, Miguel. "Las *silvas americanas* de Andrés Bello: una relectura genológica." *Hispanic Review* 66, no. 2 (1998): 181–96.

Gómez de Avellaneda, Gertrudis. *La hija de las flores*. In *"Baltasar" y "La hija de las flores,"* edited by María Prado Mas, 255–413. Madrid: Publicaciones de la Asociación de Directores de Escena de España, 2000.

Gómez de Avellaneda, Gertrudis. *Obras de La Avellaneda*. 2 vols. Havana: Edición del Centenario, 1914.

Gómez de Avellaneda, Gertrudis. *Sab*. Edited by Catherine Davies. Manchester: Manchester University Press, 2001.

Gómez de Avellaneda, Gertrudis. Sab *and* Autobiography. Translated by Nina M. Scott. Austin: University of Texas Press, 1993.

González, Aníbal. *La novela modernista hispanoamericana*. Madrid: Editorial Gredos, 1987.

González Echevarría, Roberto. *Alejo Carpentier: The Pilgrim at Home*. Ithaca: Cornell University Press, 1977.

González Echevarría, Roberto. *Celestina's Brood: Continuities of the Baroque in Spanish and Latin American Literature*. Durham: Duke University Press, 1993.

González Echevarría, Roberto. "Colonial Lyric." In *The Cambridge History of Latin American Literature*, edited by Roberto González Echevarría and Enrique Pupo-Walker, 1:191–230. Cambridge: Cambridge University Press, 1996.

González Echevarría, Roberto. "La nacionalidad de Alejo Carpentier." *Foro Hispánico* 25 (2004): 69–84.

Gonzenbach, Alexandra. "Bleeding Borders: Abjection in the Works of Ana Mendieta and Gina Pane." *Letras femeninas* 37, no. 1 (2011): 31–46.

Goodman, Jordan. *The Devil and Mr. Casement: One Man's Struggle for Human Rights in South America's Heart of Darkness*. London: Verso, 2009.

Goody, Jack. *The Culture of Flowers*. Cambridge: Cambridge University Press, 1993.

Goya, Francisco. *Paintings, Drawings and Prints*. Selected and edited by Philip Troutman. London: Folio Society, 1971.

Granziera, Patrizia. "Concept of the Garden in Pre-Hispanic Mexico." *Garden History* 29, no. 2 (Winter 2001): 185–213.

Grigson, Geoffrey. *The Englishman's Flora*. London: Phoenix House, 1955.

Guerra, Lucía. "Estrategias femeninas en la elaboración del sujeto romántico en la obra de Gertrudis Gómez de Avellaneda." *Revista Iberoamericana* 51, nos. 132–33 (1985): 707–22.

Gutiérrez González, Gregorio. *Memoria sobre el cultivo del maíz en Antioquia*. Bogotá: Panamericana, 1997.

Hall, Matthew. "Plant Autonomy and Human-Plant Ethics." *Environmental Ethics* 31, no. 2 (2009): 169–81.

Hall, Matthew. *Plants as Persons: A Philosophical Botany*. Albany: SUNY, 2011.

Hall, Michael, and Jörg Witte. *Maderas del sur de Chile: árboles, aplicaciones y procesos*. Santiago: Editorial Universitaria, 1998.

Handley, George. *New World Poetics: Nature and the Adamic Imagination of Neruda, Whitman, and Walcott*. Athens: University of Georgia Press, 2007.

Haraway, Donna J. *Simians, Cyborgs, and Women: The Reinvention of Nature*. London: Free Association Books, 1991.

Haraway, Donna J. *When Species Meet*. Minneapolis: University of Minnesota Press, 2007.

Harss, Luis, and Barbara Dohmann. *Los nuestros*. Buenos Aires: Editorial Sudamericana, 1966.

Hart, Stephen. *A Companion to Spanish-American Literature*. London: Tamesis, 1999.

Harter, Hugh. *Gertrudis Gómez de Avellaneda*. Boston: Twayne, 1981.

Hartman, Joe. "The Ceiba Tree as a Multivocal Signifier: Afro-Cuban Symbolism, Political Performance, and Urban Space in the Cuban Republic." *Hemisphere* 36 (2011): 16–41.

Heffes, Gisela. *Políticas de la destrucción/poéticas de la preservación. Apuntes para una lectura (eco) crítica del medio ambiente en América Latina*. Rosario: Beatriz Viterbo, 2013.

Henríquez Ureña, Pedro. *Ensayos en busca de nuestra expresión*. Buenos Aires: Editorial Raigal, 1952.

Herrera, Hayden. *Frida Kahlo: The Paintings*. London: Bloomsbury, 1991.

Herrera-Sobek, María, ed. *Celebrating Latino Folklore: An Encyclopedia of Cultural Traditions*. 3 vols. Santa Barbara: ABC-CLIO, 2012.

Hersey, George. *The Lost Meaning of Classical Architecture: Speculations on Ornament from Vitruvius to Venturi*. Cambridge, MA: MIT Press, 1988.

Hesiod. Theogony *and* Works and Days. Translated by M. L. West. Oxford: Oxford University Press, 1988.

Higgins, Antony. *Constructing the Criollo Archive: Subjects of Knowledge in the* Bibliotheca Mexicana *and the* Rusticatio Mexicana. West Lafayette: Purdue University Press, 2000.

Hoeg, Jerry. "Andrés Bello's 'Ode to Tropical Agriculture': The Landscape of Independence." In Rivera-Barnes and Hoeg, *Reading and Writing*, 53–66.

Horace. *Carminum Liber I*. Edited by James Gow. Cambridge: Cambridge University Press, 2013.

Howard, Richard A. "Harold William Rickett (1896–1989)." *Taxon* 40, no. 2 (1991): 345–49.

Hughes, John. *The End of Work: Theological Critiques of Capitalism*. Malden: Blackwell, 2007.

Hutchins, Zachary McLeod. *Inventing Eden: Primitivism, Millennialism, and the Making of New England*. New York: Oxford University Press, 2014.

Ibarra, Rogelia Lily. "Gómez de Avellaneda's *Sab*: A Modernizing Project." *Hispania* 94, no. 3 (2011): 385–95.

Impey, Oliver R., and Arthur MacGregor. *The Origins of Museums: The Cabinet of Curiosities in Sixteenth- and Seventeenth-Century Europe*. Oxford: Clarendon Press, 1985.

Irigaray, Luce, and Michael Marder. *Through Vegetal Being: Two Philosophical Perspectives*. New York: Columbia University Press, 2016.

Isaacs, Jorge. *María*. Edited by Donald McGrady. Madrid: Cátedra, 2001.

Jackson, Shirley M. "Fact from Fiction: Another Look at Slavery in Three Spanish-American Novels." In *Blacks in Hispanic Literature*, edited by Miriam DeCosta, 83–89. Port Washington: Kennikat Press, 1977.

Jaksić, Iván. *Andrés Bello: Scholarship and Nation-Building in Nineteenth-Century Latin America*. Cambridge: Cambridge University Press, 2002.

Janick, Jules, and Robert E. Paull. *The Encyclopaedia of Fruit and Nuts*. Wallingford: CABI, 2008.

Janzen, Janet. *Media, Modernity and Dynamic Plants in Early German Culture*. Leiden: Brill Rodopi, 2016.

Jaramillo, Camilo. "Green Hells: Monstrous Vegetations in Twentieth-Century Representations of Amazonia." In Keetley and Tenga, *Plant Horror*, 91–109.

Jazmín, Florencio. *El lenguaje de las flores y el de las frutas*. Barcelona: Manuel Saurí, 1870.

Kaempfer, Álvaro. "Economías de redención: 'La agricultura de la zona tórrida' (1826) de Andrés Bello." *Modern Language Notes* 122, no. 2 (2007): 272–93.

Kane, Adrian Taylor, ed. *The Natural World in Latin American Literatures: Ecocritical Essays on Twentieth Century Writings.* Jefferson, NC: McFarland, 2010.

Karban, Richard. "The Language of Plant Communication (and How It Compares to Animal Communication)." In Gagliano, Ryan, and Vieira, *Language of Plants,* 3–26.

Katz, Robert. *Naked by the Window: The Fatal Marriage of Carl Andre and Ana Mendieta.* New York: Atlantic Press Monthly, 1990.

Kaup, Monika. *Neobaroque in the Americas: Alternative Modernities in Literature, Visual Art, and Film.* Charlottesville: University of Virginia Press, 2012.

Keetley, Dawn. "Introduction: Six Theses on Plant Horror; or, Why Are Plants So Horrifying?" In Keetley and Tenga, *Plant Horror,* 1–30.

Keetley, Dawn, and Angela Tenga, eds. *Plant Horror: Approaches to the Monstrous Vegetal in Fiction and Film.* London: Palgrave Macmillan, 2016.

Kelemen, Pál. *Baroque and Rococo in Latin America.* 2nd ed. 2 vols. New York: Dover, 1967.

Kennedy, William J. "Fradubio." In *The Spenser Encyclopedia,* edited by Albert Charles Hamilton, 318. Toronto: University of Toronto Press, 1990.

Kerson, Arnold L. "The Heroic Mode in Rafael Landívar's *Rusticatio Mexicana.*" *Dieciocho* 13, nos. 1–2 (1990): 149–64.

Kerson, Arnold L. "The Republic of Beavers: An American Utopia." *Utopian Studies* 11, no. 2 (2000): 14–32.

Kiple, Kenneth F. *A Movable Feast: Ten Millennia of Food Globalization.* New York: Cambridge University Press, 2007.

King, Anya H. *Scent from the Garden of Paradise: Musk and the Medieval Islamic World.* Leiden: Brill, 2017.

Kirkpatrick, Susan. *Las Románticas: Woman Writers and Subjectivity in Spain, 1835–1850.* Berkeley: University of California Press, 1989.

Kissam, Edward, and Michael Schmidt, trans. *Flower and Song: Poems of the Aztec Peoples.* London: Anvil Press Poetry, 2009.

Kohn, Eduardo. *How Forests Think: Toward an Anthropology Beyond the Human.* Berkeley: University of California Press, 2013.

Kosiba, Steve. "Cultivating Empire: Inca Intensive Agricultural Strategies." In *The Oxford Handbook of the Incas,* edited by Sonia Alconini and R. Alan Covey, 227–46. New York: Oxford University Press, 2018.

Kristeva, Julia. *The Powers of Horror: An Essay on Abjection.* Translated by Leon S. Roudiez. New York: Columbia University Press, 1982.

Laird, Andrew. *The Epic of America: An Introduction to Rafael Landívar and the Rusticatio Mexicana.* London: Duckworth, 2006.

Laist, Randy, ed. *Plants and Literature: Essays in Critical Plant Studies.* Leiden: Brill Rodopi, 2013.

Landa, Diego de. *Relación de las cosas de Yucatán.* Mexico: Porrúa, 1959.

Landívar, Rafael. "*Rusticatio Mexicana,* the Latin Text and an English Prose Translation by

Graydon W. Regenos." In Andrew Laird, *The Epic of America: An Introduction to Rafael Landívar and the* Rusticatio Mexicana, 119–258. London: Duckworth, 2006.

Larochelle, Jeremy. "Writing under the Shadow of the Chullachaqui: Amazonian Thought and Ecological Discourse in Recent Amazonian Poetry." *Review: Literature and Arts of the Americas* 45, no. 2 (2012): 198–206.

Las Casas, Fray Bartolomé de. *Brevísima relación de la destruición de las Indias.* Edited by José Miguel Martínez Torrejón. 1552. Madrid: Real Academia Española, 2013.

Las Casas, Fray Bartolomé de. *Short Account of the Destruction of the Indies.* Translated by Nigel Griffin. London: Penguin, 1992.

Latour, Bruno. *We Have Never Been Modern.* Translated by Catherine Porter. Cambridge, MA: Harvard University Press, 1993.

León-Portilla, Miguel. *Bernardino de Sahagún: First Anthropologist.* Translated by Mauricio J. Mixco. Norman: University of Oklahoma Press, 2002.

Leving Jacobson, Jenna. "Nation, Violence, Memory: Interrupting the Foundational Discourse in *Sab*." *Hispanic Issues On Line* 18 (2017): 173–91. Special issue on "Gender and the Politics of Literature: Gertrudis Gómez de Avellaneda," edited by María C. Albin, Megan Corbin, and Raúl Marrero-Fente.

Lewis, Simon L., and Mark A. Maslin. "Defining the Anthropocene." *Nature* 519, no. 7542 (2015): 171–80.

Lezama Lima, José. "Baroque Curiosity." In Zamora and Kaup, *Baroque New Worlds*, 212–40.

Lezama Lima, José. "La curiosidad barroca." In *La expresión americana*, edited by Irlemar Chiampi, 79–106. Mexico: Fondo de Cultura Económica, 1993.

Llarull, Gustavo. "The Long and Winding Road of Technology from *María* to *Cien años de soledad* to *Mantra*: An Ecocritical Reading." In Kane, *Natural World in Latin American Literatures*, 89–110.

Locatelli M., and G. De Falco. "The Regulation of Pesticides in Argentina." *Residue Reviews* 44 (1972): 39–64.

López Terrada, María José. "Hérnandez and Spanish Painting in the Seventeenth Century." In *Searching for the Secrets of Nature: The Life and Works of Dr. Francisco Hernández*, edited by Simon Varey, Rafael Chabrán, and Dora B. Weiner, 151–69. Stanford: Stanford University Press, 2000.

Lottman, Maryrica Ortiz. "The Gardens of Teresa de Ávila." In *A New Companion to Hispanic Mysticism*, edited by Hilaire Kallendorf, 323–42. Leiden: Brill, 2010.

Low, Anthony. *The Georgic Revolution.* Princeton, NJ: Princeton University Press, 1985.

Lucie-Smith, Edward. *Flora: Gardens and Plants in Art and Literature.* Köln: Taschen, 2001.

MacKian, Sara. *Everyday Spirituality: Social and Spatial Worlds of Enchantment.* New York: Palgrave Macmillan, 2012.

Mackintosh, Fiona J. "Classical Reference in Silvina Ocampo's Poetry." In *New Readings of Silvina Ocampo*, edited by Patricia Nisbet Klingenberg and Fernanda Zullo-Ruiz, 143–72. Woodbridge: Tamesis, 2016.

Maffie, James. *Aztec Philosophy: Understanding a World in Motion.* Boulder: University Press of Colorado, 2014.

Mahood, Molly M. *The Poet as Botanist*. New York: Cambridge University Press, 2008.

Mallon, Florencia E. "Bearing Witness in Hard Times: Ethnography and *Testimonio* in a Postrevolutionary Age." In *Reclaiming the Political in Latin American History: Essays from the North*, edited by Gilbert M. Joseph, 311–54. Durham: Duke University Press, 2001.

Marder, Michael. *The Philosopher's Plant: An Intellectual Herbarium*. New York: Columbia University Press, 2014.

Marder, Michael. "The Place of Plants: Spatiality, Movement, Growth." *Performance Philosophy* 1 (2015): 185–94.

Marder, Michael. "Plant-Soul: The Elusive Meanings of Vegetable Life." *Environmental Philosophy* 8, no. 1 (2011): 83–99.

Marder, Michael. *Plant-Thinking: A Philosophy of Vegetal Life*. New York: Columbia University Press, 2013.

Marder, Michael. "Vegetal Anti-metaphysics: Learning from Plants." *Continental Philosophy Review* 44 (2011): 469–89.

Márquez Rodríguez, Alexis. *Lo barroco y lo maravilloso-real en la obra de Alejo Carpentier*. Mexico: Siglo XXI, 1982.

Martel, Patricia. "El árbol y la piedra: fórmula poético-ritual en los textos mayas." In *Flor-flora: su uso ritual en Mesoamérica*, edited by Beatriz Albores Zárate, 177–94. Zinacantepec: El Colegio Mexiquense; Gobierno del Estado de México, 2015.

Martí, José. "Nuestra América." In *Ensayos y crónicas*, edited by José Olivio, 157–68. Madrid: Cátedra, 2004.

Martínez Domingo, José María. *Los espacios poéticos de Rubén Darío*. New York: Peter Lang, 1995.

Martínez-Pinzón, Felipe. "La voz de los árboles: fiebre, higiene y poesía en *La vorágine*." *Bulletin of Hispanic Studies* 91 (2014): 163–81.

Mascia, Mark J. "Pablo Neruda and the Construction of Past and Future Utopias in the *Canto general*." *Utopian Studies* 12, no. 2 (2001): 65–81.

Masson de Gómez, Valerie. "Las flores como símbolos eróticos en la obra de Jorge Isaacs." *Thesaurus* 28, no. 1 (1973): 117–27.

Matilla, J. M. *Goya en tiempos de guerra*. Madrid: Museo Nacional del Prado, 2008.

Matus, Pablo L., and Emilio A. Novoa. *Enciclopedia regional del Bío Bío*. Santiago: Pehuén Editores, 2006.

McCook, Stuart. *States of Nature: Science, Agriculture and Environment in the Spanish Caribbean (1760–1940)*. Austin: University of Texas Press, 2001.

McGrady, Donald. "Las fuentes de *María*, de Jorge Isaacs." *Hispanófila* 24 (1965): 43–54.

McGrady, Donald. *Jorge Isaacs*. New York: Twayne, 1972.

McMeekin, Dorothy. "Representations on Pre-Columbian Spindle Whorls of the Floral and Fruit Structure of Economic Plants." *Economic Botany* 46, no. 2 (1992): 171–80.

Meeker, Natania, and Antónia Szabari. "From the Century of the Pods to the Century of the Plants: Plant Horror, Politics, and Vegetal Ontology." *Discourse* 34, no. 1 (2012): 32–58.

Mejía Prado, Diego, Juan Carlos Galeano, and Herman Ruiz Abecasis. "Amazonia: Looking for the Earthly Eden and Finding the Planet's Next Landfill." In Anderson and Bora, *Ecological Crisis*, 257–68.

Mejías-López, Alejandro. "Textualidad y sexualidad en la construcción de la selva: gene-alogías discursivas en *La vorágine* de José Eustasio Rivera." *Modern Language Notes* 121, no. 2, Hispanic Issue (2006): 367–90.

Méndez Rodenas, Adriana. "Picturing Cuba: Romantic Ecology in Gómez de Avellaneda's *Sab* (1841)." *Hispanic Issues On Line* 18 (2017): 153–72. Special issue on "Gender and the Politics of Literature: Gertrudis Gómez de Avellaneda," edited by María C. Albin, Megan Corbin, and Raúl Marrero-Fente.

Mendieta, Ana. *Grass Breathing*. c. 1974. Super 8mm. film, silent, color. 3 min.

Mendieta, Ana, and Judith Wilson. "Ana Mendieta Plants Her Garden." Interview with Ana Mendieta conducted by Judith Wilson for *Village Voice*, May 27, 1980. Judith Wilson Papers, 1966-2010. Archives of American Art, Smithsonian Institution.

Menton, Seymour. "*La vorágine*: Circling the Triangle." *Hispania* 59 (1976): 418–34.

Merchant, Carolyn. *The Death of Nature: Women, Technology and the Scientific Revolution*. New York: HarperCollins, 1983.

Meyer-Minnemann, Klaus. "Poesía de fundación y subjetividad en las 'Silvas americanas' de Andrés Bello." *Iberoamericana* 24, nos. 2–3 (2000): 72–87.

Miller, Shawn William. *An Environmental History of Latin America*. Cambridge: Cambridge University Press, 2007.

Miller, Theresa L. *Plant Kin: A Multispecies Ethnography in Indigenous Brazil*. Austin: University of Texas Press, 2019.

Mintz, Sidney W. *Sweetness and Power: The Place of Sugar in Modern History*. New York: Viking, 1985.

Miranda, Julio E. "Andrés Bello: Poesía, paisaje y política." *Cuadernos Hispanoamericanos* 500 (1992): 153–67.

Monguió, Luis. "Kingdom of This Earth: The Poetry of Pablo Neruda." *Latin American Literary Review* 1, no. 1 (1972): 13–24.

Monzote, Reinaldo Funes. *From Rainforest to Cane Field in Cuba: An Environmental History since 1492*. Translated by Alex Martin. Chapel Hill: University of North Carolina Press, 2008.

Moore, Bryan L. *Ecology and Literature: Ecocentric Personification from Antiquity to the Twenty-First Century*. Basingstoke: Palgrave Macmillan, 2008.

Moore, Jason W. *Capitalism in the Web of Life: Ecology and the Accumulation of Capital*. London: Verso, 2015.

Moraña, Mabel. "Baroque/Neobaroque/Ultrabaroque: Disruptive Readings of Modernity." In *Hispanic Baroques: Reading Cultures in Context*, edited by Nicholas Spadaccini and Luis Martín-Estudillo, 241–82. Nashville: Vanderbilt University Press, 2005.

Morehart, Christopher T. "Ritual Time: The Struggle to Pinpoint the Temporality of Ritual Practice Using Archaeobotanical Data." In *Social Perspectives on Ancient Lives from Paleoethnobotanical Data*, edited by Matthew P. Sayre and Maria C. Bruno, 145–58. Cham: Springer, 2017.

Morgado, Patricia. "'Stone upon Stone': From Pablo Neruda's House in Isla Negra to *The Heights of Macchu Picchu*." *Traditional Dwellings and Settlements Review* 22, no. 2 (2011): 33–48.

Moshenska, Joe. "Screaming Bleeding Trees: Textual Wounding and the Epic Tradition." In *Blood Matters: Studies in European Literature and Thought, 1400–1700*, edited by Bonnie Lander Johnson and Eleanor Decamp, 92–108. Philadelphia: University of Pennsylvania Press, 2018.

Musselwhite, David. "The Colombia of *María*: 'Un país de cafres.'" *Romance Studies* 24, no. 1 (2006): 41–54.

Mutis, Ana María, and Elizabeth Pettinaroli. "Visions of Nature: Colombian Literature and the Environment from the Colonial Period to the Nineteenth Century." In *A History of Colombian Literature*, edited by Raymond Leslie Williams, 406–30. Cambridge: Cambridge University Press, 2016.

Myers, Natasha. "Conversations on Plant Sensing: Notes from the Field." *Nature Culture* 3 (2015): 35–66.

Myers, Natasha. "From the Anthropocene to the Planthroposcene: Designing Gardens for Plant/People Involution." *History and Anthropology* 28, no. 3 (2017): 297–301.

Nealon, Jeffrey. *Plant Theory: Biopower and Vegetable Life*. Stanford: Stanford University Press, 2016.

Neruda, Pablo. *Canto general*. Translated by Jack Schmitt. Introduction by Roberto González Echevarría. Berkeley: University of California Press, 1991.

Neruda, Pablo. *Confieso que he vivido. Memorias*. Edited by Darío Oses. Santiago: Seix Barral, 2017.

Neruda, Pablo. *Memoirs*. Translated by Hardie St. Martin. London: Souvenir Press, 1977.

Neruda, Pablo. *Obras completas*. Vol. 1, *De "Crepusculario" a "Las uvas y el viento," 1923–1954*. Edited by Hernán Loyola. Barcelona: Galaxia Gutenberg, 1999.

Neruda, Pablo. *Obras completas*. Vol. 2, *De "Odas elementales" a "Memorial de Isla Negra," 1954–1964*. Edited by Hernán Loyola. Barcelona: Galaxia Gutenberg, 1999.

Neruda, Pablo. *Obras completas*. Vol. 3, *De "Arte de los pájaros" a "El mar y las campanas," 1966–1973*. Edited by Hernán Loyola. Barcelona: Galaxia Gutenberg, 2000.

Neruda, Pablo. *Obras completas*. Vol. 4, *Nerudiana dispersa I, 1915–1964*. Edited by Hernán Loyola. Barcelona: Galaxia Gutenberg, 2001.

Neruda, Pablo. *Obras completas*. Vol. 5, *Nerudiana dispersa II, 1922–1973*. Edited by Hernán Loyola. Barcelona: Galaxia Gutenberg, 2002.

Neruda, Pablo. *The Poetry of Pablo Neruda*. Edited by Ilan Stavans. New York: Farrar, Straus and Giroux, 2003.

Newman, Henry. *A History of British Ferns and Allied Plants*. London: Jan Van Voorst, 1844.

Niell, Paul. *Urban Space as Heritage in Late Colonial Cuba*. Austin: University of Texas Press, 2015.

Nolan, James. *Poet-Chief: The Native American Poetics of Walt Whitman and Pablo Neruda*. Albuquerque: University of New Mexico Press, 1994.

Ocampo, Silvina. *Los días de la noche*. Buenos Aires: Editorial Sudamericana, 1970.

Ocampo, Silvina. *Silvina Ocampo*. Translated by Jason Weiss. New York: New York Review of Books, 2015.

Ocampo, Silvina, and Aldo Sessa. *Árboles de Buenos Aires*. Buenos Aires: Ediciones Librería de la Ciudad; Galería del Este; Editorial Crea, 1979.

Ofek, Galia. *Representations of Hair in Victorian Literature and Culture*. Abingdon: Routledge, 2016.

Olivares Briones, Edmundo. *Pablo Neruda: Los caminos de América. Tras las huellas del poeta itinerante, 1940–1950*. Santiago: LOM, 2004.

Oliveira, Gustavo, and Susanna Hecht. "Sacred Groves, Sacrifice Zones and Soy Production: Globalization, Intensification and Neo-nature in South America." *Journal of Peasant Studies* 43, no. 2 (2016): 251–85.

Olivera, Otto. "El romanticismo de *La vorágine*." In *La vorágine: Textos críticos*, edited by Montserrat Ordóñez, 259–67. Bogotá: Alianza Editorial Colombiana, 1987.

Ortega y Gasset, José. "Arte de este mundo y del otro." In *La deshumanización del arte y otros ensayos de estética*, 76–104. 11th ed. Madrid: Ediciones de la Revista de Occidente, 1976.

Ortiz, Fernando. *Contrapunteo cubano del tabaco y el azúcar*. Edited by Enrico Mario Santí. Madrid: Cátedra, 2002.

Oses, Darío. "Pablo Neruda bibliófilo y lector: el amor por la vida y el amor por los libros." *Atenea* 489 (2004): 51–62.

Ovid, *Metamorphoses*. Translated by A. D. Melville. Oxford: Oxford University Press, 1992.

Papapetros, Spyros. *On the Animation of the Inorganic: Art, Architecture, and the Extension of Life*. Chicago: University of Chicago Press, 2012.

Pastor, Brígida. *El discurso de Gertrudis Gómez de Avellaneda: identidad femenina y otredad*. Cuadernos de América sin nombre, 6. Alicante: Universidad de Alicante, 2002.

Paulk, Julia C. "Foundational Fictions and Representations of Jewish Identity in Jorge Isaacs' *María*." *Hispanófila* 162 (2011): 43–59.

Paz, Octavio. *Puertas al campo*. 2nd ed. Mexico: Universidad Nacional Autónoma de México, 1967.

Peleg, Yaron. *Orientalism and the Hebrew Imagination*. Ithaca: Cornell University Press, 2005.

Pérez Firmat, Gustavo. "Ese Idioma: Alejo Carpentier's Tongue-Ties." *Symposium: A Quarterly Journal in Modern Literatures* 6, no. 13 (2007): 183–97.

Plaza, Antonio. *Albúm del corazón: poesías completas de Antonio Plaza*. Prologue by Juan de Dios Peza. 9th ed. Buenos Aires: Maucci Hermanos, 1899.

Pogue Harrison, Robert. *Gardens: An Essay on the Human Condition*. Chicago: University of Chicago Press, 2008.

Pollan, Michael. *The Botany of Desire: A Plant's-Eye View of the World*. New York: Random House, 2001.

Puri, Shalini, and Debra A. Castillo. "Introduction: Conjectures on Undisciplined Research." In *Theorizing Fieldwork in the Humanities: Methods, Reflections, and Approaches to the Global South*, edited by Shalini Puri and Debra A. Castillo, 1–26. New York: Palgrave Macmillan, 2016.

Putzeys Álvarez, Guillermo. "Lo vegetal en la *Rusticatio Mexicana*." *Revista Universidad de San Carlos. Estudios Landivarianos* 61 (1963): 35–67.

Raymond, Marcel. *From Baudelaire to Surrealism*. London: Peter Owen, 1957.

Red Universitaria de Ambiente y Salud / Médicos de Pueblos Fumigados. "The Use of Toxic Agrochemicals in Argentina Is Continuously Increasing." http://reduas.com.ar/the-use-of-toxic-agrochemicals-in-argentina-is-continuously-increasing/.

Regier, Alexander. *Fracture and Fragmentation in British Romanticism*. Cambridge: Cambridge University Press, 2010.

Reichel-Dolmatoff, Gerardo. *The Forest Within: The World-View of the Tukano Amazonian Indians*. Totnes: Themis Books, 1996.

Reiss, Frank. *The Word and the Stone: Language and Imagery in Neruda's* Canto general. Oxford: Oxford University Press, 1972.

Reiss, Timothy J. "American Baroque Histories and Geographies." In Zamora and Kaup, *Baroque New Worlds*, 394–414.

Rich, Vivian A. *Cursing the Basil and Other Folklore of the Garden*. Victoria, BC: Horsdal and Schubart, 1998.

Rickett, Harold William. *The Green Earth. An Invitation to Botany*. Lancaster, PA: Jacques Cattell Press, 1943.

Rickett, Harold William. *La tierra es verde: una invitación a la botánica*. Buenos Aires: Editorial Pleamar, 1946.

Rifelj, Carol de Dobay. *Coiffures: Hair in Nineteenth-Century French Literature and Culture*. Newark: University of Delaware Press, 2010.

Rivera, Ángel A. "El lenguaje de las flores y la extraña en *La hija de las flores* de Gertrudis Gómez de Avellaneda." *Latin American Theatre Review* 32, no. 1 (1998): 5–24.

Rivera, José Eustasio. *La vorágine*. Edited by Montserrat Ordóñez. Madrid: Cátedra, 1998.

Rivera, José Eustasio. *The Vortex*. Translated by E. K. James. London: Putnam, 1935.

Rivera-Barnes, Beatriz. "'I Do Not Weep for Camaguey': Gertrudis Gómez de Avellaneda's Nineteenth-Century Cuban Landscape." In Rivera-Barnes and Hoeg, *Reading and Writing*, 67–82.

Rivera-Barnes, Beatriz. "Pablo Neruda's Latin American Landscape: Nations, Economy, Nature." In Rivera-Barnes and Hoeg, *Reading and Writing*, 145–58.

Rivera-Barnes, Beatriz, and Jerry Hoeg. *Reading and Writing the Latin American Landscape*. New York: Palgrave Macmillan, 2009.

Roberts, E. A. *A Comprehensive Etymological Dictionary of the Spanish Language with Families of Words Based on Indo-European Roots*. 2 vols. Bloomington, IN.: Xlibris, 2014.

Rodríguez, Ileana. *House / Garden / Nation: Space, Gender, and Ethnicity in Post-colonial Latin American Literatures by Women*. Translated by Robert Carr and Ileana Rodríguez. Durham: Duke University Press, 1994.

Rodríguez Monegal, Emir. *El viajero inmóvil: introducción a Pablo Neruda*. Buenos Aires: Editorial Losada, 1966.

Rogers, Charlotte. "Carpentier, Collecting, and 'Lo Barroco Americano.'" *Hispania* 94, no. 2 (2011): 240–51.

Rogers, Charlotte. *Jungle Fever: Exploring Madness and Medicine in Twentieth-Century Tropical Narratives*. Nashville: Vanderbilt University Press, 2012.

Rosaldo, Renato. *Culture and Truth: The Remaking of Social Analysis*. Boston: Beacon Press, 1993.

Rosenthal, Debra J. *Race Mixture in Nineteenth-Century U.S. and Spanish American Fictions: Gender, Culture, and Nation Building*. Chapel Hill: University of North Carolina Press, 2004.

Rosenzweig, Rachel. *Worshipping Aphrodite: Art and Cult in Classical Athens*. Ann Arbor: University of Michigan Press, 2004.

Rowlandson, William. *Reading Lezama's* Paradiso. Bern: Peter Lang, 2007.

Rumrrill, Róger. *Reportaje a la Amazonía*. Lima: Ediciones Populares Selva, 1973.

Ruskin, John. *Proserpina: Studies of Wayside Flowers*. 3rd ed. Orpington: George Allen, 1897.

Russell, Andrew, and Elizabeth Rahman, eds. *The Master Plant: Tobacco in Lowland South America*. London: Bloomsbury Academic, 2015.

Ryan, John Charles. *Green Sense: The Aesthetics of Plants, Place and Language*. Oxford: TrueHeart Press, 2012.

Safónov, Vadim. *La tierra en flor*. Translated by Isabel Vicente. Santiago. Ediciones Vida Nueva, 1953.

Sage, Michael M. *Warfare in Ancient Greece: A Sourcebook*. London: Routledge, 1996.

Saint-Aubin, Stéphanie-Félicité du Crest de. *Veladas de la Quinta*. Madrid: La Viuda de Marín, 1791.

Salazar, Rodolfo, Carolina Soihet, and José Miguel Méndez, eds. *Manejo de semillas de 100 especies forestales de América Latina*. Turrialba: CATIE, 2000. http://hdl.handle.net/11554/2959/.

Saldívar, Ramón. "Speculative Realism and the Postrace Aesthetic in Contemporary American Fiction." In *A Companion to American Literary Studies*, edited Caroline F. Levander and Robert S. Levine, 517–31. Oxford: Blackwell, 2015.

Salgado, César Augusto. "Hybridity in New World Baroque Theory." *Journal of American Folklore* 112, no. 445 (1999): 316–31.

Samson, Alexander. "Outdoor Pursuits, Spanish Gardens, the *huerto*, and Lope de Vega's *Novelas a Marcia Leonarda*." In *Locus Amoenus: Gardens and Horticulture in the Renaissance*, edited by Alexander Samson, 124–50. Chichester: Wiley-Blackwell, 2012.

Santí, Enrico Mario. "Introducción." In *Canto general*, edited by Enrico Mario Santí, 13–99. Madrid: Cátedra, 2002.

Sarduy, Severo. "Baroque Cosmology: Kepler." In Zamora and Kaup, *Baroque New Worlds*, 292–315.

Sarduy, Severo. *Barroco*. Buenos Aires: Editorial Sudamericana, 1974.

Sartillot, Claudette. *Herbarium, Verbarium: The Discourse of Flowers*. Lincoln: University of Nebraska Press, 1993.

Scarry, Elaine. "Imagining Flowers: Perceptual Mimesis (Particularly Delphinium)." *Representations* 57 (1997): 90–115.

Schele, Linda, and David Freidel. *A Forest of Kings: The Untold Story of the Ancient Maya*. New York: Morrow, 1990.

Schiebinger, Londa. *Plants and Empire: Colonial Bioprospecting in the Atlantic World*. Cambridge, MA: Harvard University Press, 2007.

Schiebinger, Londa, and Claudia Swan. "Introduction." In *Colonial Botany: Science, Commerce, and Politics in the Early Modern World*, edited by Londa Schiebinger and Claudia Swan, 1–18. Philadelphia: University of Pennsylvania Press, 2007.

Schlau, Stacey. "Strangers in a Strange Land: The Discourse of Alienation in Gómez de Avellaneda's Abolitionist Novel *Sab*." *Hispania* 69, no. 3 (1986): 495–503.

Schweblin, Samanta. *Distancia de rescate*. Barcelona: Penguin Random House, 2015.

Schweblin, Samanta. *Fever Dream*. Translated by Megan McDowell. London: Oneworld, 2017.

Seaton, Beverly. "Considering the Lilies: Ruskin's 'Proserpina' and Other Victorian Flower Books." *Victorian Studies* 28 (1985): 255–82.

Seaton, Beverly. *The Language of Flowers: A History*. Charlottesville: University Press of Virginia, 1995.

Seaton, Beverly. "A Nineteenth-Century Metalanguage: Le Langage de Fleurs." *Semiotica* 57, nos. 1–2 (1985): 73–86.

Servera, José. "Introducción." In Gertrudis Gómez de Avellaneda, *Sab*, edited by José Servera, 9–93. Madrid: Cátedra, 1997.

Shakespeare, William. *Hamlet*. Edited by Harold Jenkins. London: Methuen, 1982.

Shakespeare, William. *A Midsummer Night's Dream*. Edited by Harold F. Brooks. London: Methuen, 1979.

Shakespeare, William. *Romeo and Juliet*. Edited by Brian Gibbons. London: Methuen, 1980.

Sharman, Adam. *Tradition and Modernity in Spanish American Literature: From Darío to Carpentier*. New York: Palgrave Macmillan, 2006.

Shaw, Donald L. *Alejo Carpentier*. Boston: Twayne Publishers, 1985.

Simms, Andrew, and Hannah Reid. *Up in Smoke? Latin America and the Caribbean*. London: New Economics Foundation, 2006. https://neweconomics.org/2006/08/smoke-latin-america-caribbean/.

Simoons, Frederick J. *Plants of Life, Plants of Death*. Madison: University of Wisconsin Press, 1998.

Sims, Lowery Stokes. *Wifredo Lam and the International Avant-Garde, 1923–1982*. Austin: University of Texas Press, 2002.

Skinner, Lee Joan. "The Functions of Landscape in Jorge Isaacs and Soledad Acosta de Samper." *Symposium: A Quarterly Journal in Modern Literatures* 68, no. 1 (2014): 12–24.

Slater, Candace. *Dance of the Dolphin: Transformation and Disenchantment in the Amazonian Imagination*. Chicago: University of Chicago Press, 1994.

Smith, Amanda M. "Mapping the Amazon: Literary Geography after the Rubber Boom." Unpublished manuscript.

Smith, Nigel J. H. *Enchanted Amazon Rain Forest: Stories from a Vanishing World*. Gainesville: University of Florida Press, 1996.

Sommer, Doris. *Foundational Fictions: The National Romances of Latin America*. Berkeley: University of California Press, 1993.

Sontag, Susan, *Illness as Metaphor*. London: Allen Lane, 1979.

Soper, Kate. *What Is Nature? Culture, Politics and the Non-Human*. Oxford: Blackwell, 1995.

Spenser, Edmund. *The Faerie Queene*. Edited by A. C. Hamilton. New York: Longman, 1977.

Staller, John E. *Maize Cobs and Cultures: History of Zea mays L*. New York: Springer, 2010.

Stepan, Nancy Leys. *Picturing Tropical Nature*. London: Reaktion Books, 2001.

Stirling, Jeannette. *Representing Epilepsy: Myth and Matter*. Liverpool: Liverpool University Press, 2010.

Sullivan, Garrett A. Jr. *Sleep, Romance and Human Embodiment: Vitality from Spenser to Milton*. Cambridge: Cambridge University Press, 2012.

Taiz, Lincoln, and Lee Taiz. *Flora Unveiled: The Discovery and Denial of Sex in Plants*. New York: Oxford University Press, 2017.

Taube, Karl Andreas. *The Major Gods of Ancient Yucatan*. Studies in Pre-Columbian Art and Archaeology, 32. Washington: Dumbarton Oaks Research Library and Collection, 1992.

Taussig, Michael. "The Language of Flowers." *Critical Inquiry* 30, no. 1 (2003): 98–131.

Temkin, Owsei. *The Falling Sickness: A History of Epilepsy from the Greeks to the Beginnings of Modern Neurology*. 2nd rev. ed. Baltimore: Johns Hopkins University Press, 1971.

Tewfik, Lamia M. S. Z. "Indian Veneration of Trees and Plants in Selected Caribbean Poems: Potent Plants and Foliaceous Men." *Journal of Caribbean Literatures* 7, no. 2 (2013): 89–97.

Thacker, Christopher. *The History of Gardens*. Berkeley: University of California Press, 1979.

Thieme, John. *Postcolonial Literary Geographies: Out of Place*. London: Palgrave Macmillan, 2016.

Thomas, Vivian, and Nicki Faircloth. *Shakespeare's Plants and Gardens: A Dictionary*. London: Bloomsbury, 2014.

Tomasi, Lucia Tongiorgi. "Gardens of Knowledge and the *République des Gens de Sciences*." In *Baroque Garden Cultures: Emulation, Sublimation, Subversion*, edited by Michael Conan, 85–129. Washington: Dumbarton Oaks Research Library and Collection, 2005.

Tosh, John. *Manliness and Masculinities in Nineteenth-Century Britain: Essays on Gender, Family and Empire*. Harlow: Pearson Education, 2005.

Tsing, Anna Lowenhaupt. *The Mushroom at the End of the World: On the Possibility of Life in Capitalist Ruins*. Princeton, NJ: Princeton University Press, 2015.

Turner, Tom. *Garden History: Philosophy and Design, 2000 BC to 2000 AD*. Abingdon: Spon Press, 2005.

Tusa, Bobs. M. "A Detective Story: The Influence of Mircea Eliade on Alejo Carpentier's *Los pasos perdidos*." *Hispanófila* 88 (1986): 41–65.

Uribe Uribe, Rafael. *Diccionario abreviado de galicismos, provincialismos y correcciones de lenguaje*. Medellín: Fondo Editorial Universidad EAFIT, 2006.

Urrutia, Matilde. *My Life with Pablo Neruda*. Translated by Alexandria Giardino. Stanford: Stanford General Books, 2004.

Uzendoski, Michael. "Foreword." In Juan Carlos Galeano, *Folktales of the Amazon*, translated by Rebecca Morgan and Kenneth Watson, ix–xii. Westport, CT: Libraries Unlimited, 2009.

Vega, Garcilaso de la. *Selected Poems of Garcilaso de la Vega: Bilingual Edition*. Edited and translated by John Dent-Young. Chicago: University of Chicago Press, 2009.

Vial, Sara. *Neruda en Valparaíso*. Valparaíso: Ediciones Universitarias de Valparaíso, 1983.

Vieira, Patrícia. "*Phytographia*: Literature as Plant Writing." In Gagliano, Ryan, and Vieira, *Language of Plants*, 215–33.

Virgil. *Aeneid 7–12; Appendix Vergiliana*. Translated by H. Rushton Fairclough. Rev. ed. Cambridge, MA: Harvard University Press, 2000.

Virgil. *Eclogues, Georgics, Aeneid 1–6*. Translated by H. Rushton Fairclough. Rev. ed. Cambridge, MA: Harvard University Press, 1999.

Viso, Olga. *Unseen Mendieta: The Unpublished Works of Ana Mendieta*. Munich: Prestel, 2008.

Viveiros de Castro, Eduardo. "Cosmological Deixis and Amerindian Perspectivism." *Journal of the Royal Anthropological Institute* 4, no. 3 (1998): 469–88.

Wagley, Charles. *Amazon Town. A Study of Man in the Tropics*. New York: Knopf, 1964.

Wake, Eleanor. "The Maize Theatre: Mexica State Cult and Symbolic Representations of Maize in Prehispanic Religious Ritual." In *Flor-flora: Su uso ritual en Mesoamérica*, edited by Beatriz Albores Zárate, 155–75. Zinacantepec: El Colegio Mexiquense; Gobierno del Estado de México, 2015.

Wakefield, Steve. *Carpentier's Baroque Fiction: Returning Medusa's Gaze*. Woodbridge: Tamesis, 2004.

Wall, Catherine E. "The Visual Dimension of *El siglo de las luces: Goya* and *Explosión en una catedral*." *Revista Canadiense de Estudios Hispánicos* 13, no. 1 (1988): 148–57.

Ward, Bobby J. *A Contemplation upon Flowers: Garden Plants in Myth and Literature*. Portland: Timber Press, 1999.

Ward, Thomas. "Gertrudis Gómez de Avellaneda's *Sab*: A Cuban Novel in a Latin American Context." In *Changing Currents: Transnational Caribbean Literary and Cultural Criticism*, edited by Emily Allen Williams and Melvin Rahming, 93–117. Trenton, NJ: Africa World Press, 2006.

Ward, Thomas. "Nature and Civilization in *Sab* and the Nineteenth-Century Novel in Latin America." *Hispanófila* 126 (1999): 25–40.

Waters, W. "Apostrophe." In *The Princeton Encyclopedia of Poetry and Poetics*, edited by Roland Greene, Stephen Cushman, Clare Cavanagh, Jahan Ramazani, and Paul Rouzer, 61. 4th ed. Princeton, NJ: Princeton University Press, 2013.

Wellek, René. "The Concept of Baroque in Literary Scholarship." In Zamora and Kaup, *Baroque New Worlds*, 95–114.

Westerfelhaus, Robert. "She Speaks to Us, for Us, and of Us: Our Lady of Guadalupe as a Semiotic Site of Struggle and Identity." In *Communicating Ethnic and Cultural Identity*, edited by Mary Fong and Rueyling Chuang, 105–20. Lanham: Rowman and Littlefield, 2004.

Whitehead, Neil L. "The Crises and Transformations of Invaded Societies: The Caribbean (1492–1580)." In *The Cambridge History of the Native Peoples of the Americas*, vol. 3: *South America*, edited by Frank Salomon and Stuart B. Schwartz, part 1, 864–903. Cambridge: Cambridge University Press, 1999.

Williams, Raymond L. "Nature in the Twentieth-Century Latin American Novel (1900–1967) and in *Cien años de soledad* of García Márquez." In Kane, *Natural World in Latin American Literatures*, 66–88.

Wilson, Jason. *A Companion to Pablo Neruda: Evaluating Neruda's Poetry*. Woodbridge: Tamesis, 2008.

Wirt, Elizabeth Washington Gable. *Flora's Dictionary*. Baltimore: Lucas Brothers, 1855.

Wishnia, Kenneth J. A. *Twentieth-Century Ecuadorian Narrative: New Readings in the Context of the Americas*. Lewisburg: Bucknell University Press, 1999.

Wohlleben, Peter. *The Hidden Life of Trees. How They Feel, What They Communicate: Discoveries from a Secret World.* Translated by Jane Billinghurst. London: William Collins, 2017.

Wylie, Lesley. "Anthropomorphism and Arboricide: The Life and Death of Trees in the American Tropics." In Anderson and Bora, *Ecological Crisis*, 45–62.

Wylie, Lesley. *Colombia's Forgotten Frontier: A Literary Geography of the Putumayo.* Liverpool: Liverpool University Press, 2013.

Wylie, Lesley. *Colonial Tropes and Postcolonial Tricks: Rewriting the Tropics in the* Novela de la selva. Liverpool: Liverpool University Press, 2009.

Wylie, Lesley. "Floriography, Sexuality and the Horticulture of Hair in Jorge Isaacs' *María.*" *Bulletin of Spanish Studies* 95, nos. 9–10 (2018): 147–58. Special issure, "'The Lyf So Short, the Craft So Long to Lerne': Studies in Modern Hispanic Literature, History and Culture in Memory of James Whiston," edited by C. Alex Longhurst, Ann L. Mackenzie, and Ceri Byrne, with an introduction by Ann L. Mackenzie and Ciaran Cosgrove.

Wylie, Lesley. "Of the Margins and the Center: Gertrudis Gómez de Avellaneda." *Hispanic Issues On Line* 18 (2017): 297–306. Special issue, "Gender and the Politics of Literature: Gertrudis Gómez de Avellaneda," edited by María C. Albin, Megan Corbin, and Raúl Marrero-Fente.

Wylie, Lesley. "The Politics of Vegetating in Arturo Burga Freitas's *Mal de gente.*" In *Intimate Frontiers: A Literary Geography of the Amazon*, edited by Felipe Martínez-Pinzón and Javier Uriarte, 177–92. Liverpool: Liverpool University Press, 2019.

Yepes, Enrique. "Derroteros de la ecocrítica en tierras americanas." *Latin American Research Review* 49, no. 2 (2014): 243–52.

Yurkievich, Saúl. "Introducción general." In Pablo Neruda, *Obras completas*, Vol. 1, *De "Crepusculario" a "Las uvas y el viento," 1923–1954*, edited by Hernán Loyola, 9–79. Barcelona: Galaxia Gutenberg, 1999.

Zamora, Lois Parkinson. *The Inordinate Eye: New World Baroque and Latin American Fiction.* Chicago: University of Chicago Press, 2006.

Zamora, Lois Parkinson, and Monika Kaup, eds. *Baroque New Worlds: Representation, Transculturation, Counterconquest.* Durham: Duke University Press, 2010.

Zarcone, Thierry. "The Myth of the Mandrake, the 'Plant-Human.'" *Diogenes* 52, no. 3 (2005): 115–29.

INDEX